# Assessing

# Management

# Skills

a guide to competencies
and evaluation techniques

Margaret Dale & Paul Iles

KOGAN
PAGE

First published in 1992
Reprinted 1993

Kogan Page Limited
120 Pentonville Road
London N1 9JN

© Margaret Dale and Paul Iles

**British Library Cataloguing in Publication Data**
A CIP record for this book is available from the British Library.

ISBN 0 7494 0219 9

Typeset by BookEns Ltd, Baldock, Herts
Printed and bound in Great Britain by
Biddles Ltd, Guildford and King's Lynn

# Contents

# | Preface

Assessment is a technique that has found its time. Managerial competencies are being defined and concern is being expressed about the current standard of management performance. The need to upgrade and improve skills is now widely recognised.

Effort has been made to encourage young people to enter into management as a career in its own right. They are being encouraged to look for employment in organisations that are recruiting those with formal qualifications and offer, in addition, training.

The special needs of the experienced manager are now also being recognised. While this group is in need of help, resources and opportunities to upgrade existing levels of skill, previous achievements are not being denigrated. Ways of assessing current levels of performance to accredit prior learning are being developed. The methods are being used to identify an individual's particular training and development requirements so that action can be targeted to areas of need.

This book is aimed at managers who are involved in the assessment process. This involvement may be in the capacity of:

- managers who are commissioning someone else to establish an assessment process – for these people we hope to provide the information to enable them to ask informed questions;

- managers who are instigating and conducting the assessment – for them we hope to provide guidance on how to implement the process;

- managers who are being assessed – we hope to provide an understanding of the process they are going through so they are able to make the most of the experience.

We aim to be practical and so we provide many examples. These have been drawn from our experience and distorted by our memories. We have tried, however, to give an accurate picture, warts and all, as we experienced and remembered the occasions. We have learnt from both positive and negative experiences, and include examples of both to help our readers learn.

We have tried to keep theories to a minimum, using them as base points when needed. References are given, but we have tried to avoid quoting at length. The interested reader is urged to follow up the cited texts if more information is needed. We have included them because we have found them helpful.

We hope you find this text helpful and enjoyable. Assessment can be very threatening and difficult; alternatively it can be exciting and enjoyable. This is totally dependent on how you, the manager, go about it. We wish to help you achieve the latter. Have fun . . .

*Margaret Dale and Paul Iles*
*1992*

# Acknowledgements

Our thanks are due to each other for mutual support, encouragement and friendship, to Jean for passing on the messages and interpreting Paul's handwriting, to RJP for ideas, examples and stimulation and to RA and TI for their support and inspiration.

# 1

# Introduction

## THE CURRENT SCENE

The question of what a manager is has exercised the minds of writers, both academic and practitioner alike, for many years. The seminal work was done by people such as WF Taylor (1911) and Henri Fayol (1949), and much of what has been offered since has been based on their answers. These have ranged from very task-oriented descriptions of what a manager does – examples of this approach include Fayol himself – to more conceptual models of the role of a manager – Mintzberg (1973) and Stewart (1976)are perhaps the best-known writers. More recently, as occupational psychology has increased its impact on the theories of organisations, these have encompassed the personality of managers. Belbin's (1981) use of psychometric tests to identify team role skills has been an interesting development of this approach.

The latest development, drawing from these previous attempts at defining the complex role a manager is expected to perform, has focused on the identification of managerial skills. This is partially due to the efforts of the Management Charter Initiative. Work was done on both their and the Training Agency's behalf, initially, to develop a profile of a competent manager. Originally this followed the approach adopted by Boyatzis (1982) and the American Management Association, which had aimed to differentiate between an average manager and one whose performance was regarded as being superior. Other methods were explored but very quickly the approach changed to establishing ways of certifying and chartering managerial competence.

This was partially in response to the changes that were taking place in thinking in the education and training world. The creation of the National Council of Vocational Qualifications (NCVQ) has resulted in competency statements being prepared or planned for all occupations, management being no exception. Organisations were also developing their thinking. Some notable examples (Cadbury Schwepps, Rank Xerox, Thorn EMI) began to use profiles and competencies to aid the selection and development of their managers.

There had been a general acknowledgement, which culminated in the

Handy (1987) and Constable/McCormick Reports (1987), that British managers were not as skilled as their major competitors in the world market. This was attributed to management education, training and development programmes being less effective, and not the commitment by employers being less. To be judged truly effective, training and management development needs to be focused towards the requirements of the job as well as the development of the individuals. At the time it was perceived that the activities that were being provided were doing neither.

As the recession took hold performance had to be increased and improved as survival became the name of the game. Other ways of developing the skills needed to improve organisational efficiency and effectiveness were sought. Since then much energy and effort has had to be expended on the specification of managerial skills.

Competency statements have been produced for certificate and diploma qualifications. These are written as outputs and statements of action, but they are not definitions of skills. What is still missing is guidance on 'how to know one when you see one'. We hope to contribute to the filling of this gap by producing a manual that will help the practitioner assess managerial skills at work.

We aim to offer practising managers practical guidance on how the assessment of staff within their organisations can be improved. This book is aimed at personnel people and line managers, and intends to draw on theory without being theoretical. We recognise that for improvements to happen to the assessment process in practice the ideas of how to do so need to be readily applicable.

Naturally, people make judgements about others all the time. There is a useful body of research about this and other parts of the process that can be drawn from to help to understand how these assessments are made. This will be used and augmented by examples of what happens in reality. We use our own and others' experiences to show both good and poor practice.

## ASSESSMENT TECHNIQUES

How assessment is carried out in organisations can have considerable impact on the individuals involved and the organisation itself. Many of the theories are concerned with the way assessments are made outside work in social settings. While this is important to people's lives, we wish to focus on the at-work aspects. We believe that improvements can be made to the process which will affect the way in which people perceive themselves, others and their organisations which will have valuable spin-offs into the rest of their lives. The research, examples and case studies will demonstrate the techniques (and comment on their correct use) which are commonly used to assess managerial performance.

The use of these techniques has increased rapidly, partly because of the influence of the NCVQ and Management Charter Initiative. Some of the rapid growth in their popularity has meant that good practice is not always followed. The area that we think is probably most neglected is the provision of feedback and action aimed at helping the individual to improve their actual performance. Sometimes it seems that once the organisation has its information, then that is the end of the process. This should not be the case. All the stages of the process that we will describe are vital if part of the aim of assessing people is to help them develop their skills and contribution to their organisation's future.

It has also been recognised that people learn better if they are given quality feedback. They are able to change and adapt their behaviour more easily if they know what is expected of them, and know what it is they have to do to improve. We believe that those responsible for carrying out the assessments of others and providing the feedback should have an understanding of what it is they are doing. We also think that those going through the assessment process can benefit from knowing what is happening to them. Therefore, information and training in the skills needed to participate in either role is another essential feature of the process.

We will describe some of the techniques available, concentrating especially on the assessment centre approach and its use in its various forms. The first use of this technique is thought to have occurred as an aid to the selection of military 'managers' during the Second World War. Since then its use has been extended to the selection of managerial and other staff in quasi and non-military organisations in America and Britain, and for the identification of development needs. This use can be applied for career planning purposes, manager and management development, and as a contributory part of an organisational development intervention.

It is a closely defined technique and much research has been done to demonstrate its validity in comparison to other techniques. In America, its design and use is closely monitored by the Task Force on the Development of Assessment Centre Standards. Regular congresses are held and guidance and codes of conduct are issued. This vigilance has grown up in response to the importance given to the issues of fairness and equality of opportunity. The technique's use has increased rapidly in Britain during the last five years, but this has not been accompanied by the same degree of scrutiny and concern about the ethics of its application.

Basically an assessment centre is a process during which a participant's current and potential level of performance is assessed against a set of pre-determined behavioural criteria during the completion of a series of varied, job-related activities. This assessment is made by several trained observers who later pool their observations and provide feedback based on their overall conclusions.

We mention other techniques that are being used to help gather information from which judgements can be made. We will offer some guidance on the selection and validity of these techniques in the context of particular uses. We will also explain how they can be used to reduce the errors and biases to which humans are prone.

Some will be already familiar and well documented elsewhere. We wish, though, to comment on both their correct and perhaps not so correct application. The cases we cite will include examples of both good and bad practice. We think it is important to include the latter as the impact that assessment can have on the individual is often considerable. Examples of negative impact can lead to resignation, illness, sabotage, absenteeism, illness, alienation, poor working relationships, bad industrial relations etc. Positive impact, on the other hand, can lead to increased satisfaction, growth, increased product-ivity (quantity and quality), development of the individuals, the work and the organisation.

Performance-related pay is currently receiving attention. This may par-tially be due to employers' response to the growth of consumerism in the economy and the reaffirmation of money being a motivator. Personnel prac-titioners know this is not the only factor that influences individuals' attitudes to their work. Remembering Herzberg (1968), we know that if the money is wrong, pay can demotivate, but to encourage and stimulate individuals to work more and harder – and for this effort to be sustained – feedback on achievement and challenge are required.

It has also stimulated interest in the assessment of performance against targets in ways which are measurable and can be seen to be fair. Selection decisions are being made increasingly on the basis of evidence of actual per-formance. We will provide examples of how this is being achieved and how the techniques can contribute.

An awareness of the impact of the use of these techniques is beginning to emerge. The decline in the labour market and perceived skills shortages has switched power from the employer to the employee. (The Management Charter Initiative's efforts among students demonstrated their bargaining power.) We will describe the effect the techniques may have on the participants, and attempt to draw some conclusions that can be used to avoid some of the unintentional consequences.

We appreciate that those we are aiming at are busy people who do not want detailed or theoretical descriptions of irrelevant abstractions or concepts. We will concentrate on techniques and how they can be adapted for use in the different situations in which assessment is made. As many of these can be used in different ways for different purposes, we pepper the text with examples, case studies, areas for thought and readings.

The bibliography, in addition to giving references to quoted texts, also contains suggestions for further reading. In some cases it may be more appropriate for an idea to be followed with its originator's own text, rather than us summarising their work.

Chapter 2 is concerned with how the techniques can be used. Whether it is for selection, appraisal, reward or discipline, the process depends on the gathering and presentation of information, the weighing of the different component pieces of data and the making of the judgement. The technique used should be chosen to facilitate the stages and help the decision-maker(s) make the assessment. No technique can do the latter – this is a managerial responsibility that cannot be delegated or avoided. The selection of the best technique needs to take account of each technique's comparative strengths and weaknesses.

Most organisations are based on some hierarchical division of responsibility. Their managers are required and have the power to make assessment. We wish, through this book, to help this to happen in a way that can be beneficial to everyone involved, including the organisation itself. We will not offer any magic answers. A technique can only be as good as the way in which it is used. Sadly, all too often the wrong approach is used at the wrong time in the wrong place, by and for the wrong people. This discredits the approach rather than the application. Evidence of this can be seen through the history of management as an organisational function. It is up to you, the manager, to determine that. You need to consider the impact that the choice and implementation of any technique will have.

It is also the manager's responsibility to develop the organisation. We include, therefore, the wider ways in which some of the techniques of assessment can be used to achieve improvements to overall performance. The technique chosen, as well as the way in which it is applied, makes a mark on the culture of the organisation and says something about its uniqueness.

We appreciate that many of the references we give and the research we quote is American. We are saddened by the absence of comparable British sources and we may be criticised for having included these American sources, but decided to take the risk. These sources, we believe, cross the cultural divide that exists with our common language and we have only included those that we think will help to understand what is happening during the process of assessment.

On the other hand, we are very aware that knowledge about the approaches used on the Continent is limited. As greater contact is made with European organisations it becomes more important that a better appreciation is gained of the techniques used across Europe. Some, because of the cultural differences, may seem strange or have apparently been discredited in Britain. We will look briefly at some of the more common and attempt to re-examine them in a fresh light. After all, we can all learn something from each other.

We trust that you will find this book useful. Assessment can be positive, but all too often its method of presentation and the ways in which the techniques are applied makes it a process to be feared. We aim to help change this by giving you as the assessor or the assessee practical guidance from which to develop the approach and make use of it in your own organisation.

Please let us know what you think, *we* appreciate assessment and constructive feedback too!

# 2

# Why do we assess?

The question of why assessment takes place needs to be examined from two aspects. First, we will look generally at why people assess each other. Is it really necessary for us to interpret and assess how we behave towards each other and make judgements rather than take what we see and experience at face value? If the answer to this question is yes, we must understand why these assessments are made and how the process happens.

Once these assessments have been made, they are used as a basis for decisions. Such decisions may be trivial. Alternatively, they can change the lives of those being assessed. To explain why assessments are made at this level we will use the work that has been produced to describe the processes of perception. These theories will be used to illustrate what happens in practice. Using them to look at personal assessments, we will then move on to look at the other aspects of the question – namely why people are assessed during the course of their work in organisations.

Organisations, large and small, set up elaborate systems to formalise the processes of perception and assessment. They invest in the design and establishment of the systems, and then take the risk of failure during the implementation phase. These systems have to be maintained and revised. For this to be a useful management tool rather than being merely an administrative procedure, there has to be some pay-off and good reasons for formality. We will endeavour to address these points in a way that will help you understand more of the process and decide for yourselves whether to use systematic assessment.

## HOW PEOPLE ASSESS EACH OTHER

We assess each other all the time, summing each other up continuously so that we can predict how we are likely to behave. This helps us to prepare our reaction in response to others' behaviour. We draw data from a number of sources to do this.

We use our senses to gather information from appearance, speech and behaviour. Other available information, such as what is known about the other person from previous experience or reports from others, is added.

This is done to make sense of the world in which we live and the people that inhabit it. The textbooks of social psychology contain useful, fuller explanations of how this information is gathered, collated and used to assess others. These theories are usually described as person perception theories. References for additional reading are given in the bibliography; however, since this process is central to the processes used to make these assessments, we feel that a brief outline is merited here. We strongly urge the interested reader to refer to the authoritative texts for a more complete understanding.

## Personal construct theory

A useful explanation is provided by George Kelly (1955), an American psychologist, who developed a theory to explain how an individual makes interpretations about the world and why these are needed. This he called his personal construct theory and said that people try to explain their world by creating a series of templates through which to view it. These templates or constructs are formed from the individual's personality, education and experiences. The education an individual receives comes from a number of influences other than formal tuition. These include messages taken from influential others, social group norms and family attitudes. The media are also influential in the formation of people's opinions. Experience comes from exposure to new situations and people. Some people learn from these; others learn how to be immune to their influence. Nevertheless, some impact is made which remains in the individual's conscious or subconscious memory and is added on to the template. This forms a pattern of constructs which is unique to the individual, hence the name personal construct theory.

Once established the constructs are laid over reality. They are used to explain, interpret and predict and to make sense of events, one's own behaviour and that of others. Kelly also suggests that constructs are used to reduce anxiety about the uncertainties and unknowns. This helps people in their efforts to cope with their world, but serves to reinforce their own construct theories. This can blind us to reality and lead to inappropriate behaviour in response to situations or people.

---

### Example 2.1

Imagine meeting again an old school friend you have not seen for 20 years. A typical opening conservation might be 'Oh you haven't changed a bit'! It is very easy to plan the meeting based on the old knowledge of the other and then to be surprised to find a totally different meeting to that which you were expecting.

---

We all change as a result of the passage of time. Experience brings new lessons which introduce new ideas and confirm existing ones. Even though we may strive to reinforce our constructs, we add to our own theory. We learn things about other people, develop our insights and reinforce our prejudices.

---

### Example 2.2

For example, imagine that you once bought a second-hand bicycle from a man with red hair. During the course of the transaction you found him to be a pleasant, likeable sort of man. You went away believing you had bought a good bike from someone with whom you got on well. After two weeks of riding you have a puncture. At the bike shop the mechanic tells you that the bike's frame is bent and the bike is not very safe to ride. This all comes as an unpleasant surprise and leads to a sizeable bill. This experience might lead you to believe that pleasant people with red hair should not be trusted.

---

Most of the time the assessments we make of each other are made on superficial information and are of little consequence. Our interactions with strangers tend to be short-lived and superficial. Decisions made on the basis of these assessments are unlikely to lead to earth-shattering events. They may have unpredictable consequences, but usually this is in conjunction with other events.

Our social and family assessments are of more importance. Socially, however, we tend to join with people who have similar beliefs, interests and background. Our social habits are developed over time and are based on learning what kinds of activity we like and do not like. We also learn what types of people's company we most enjoy. We find out what to look for to find the people who are likely to share interests and have similar views. Thus, we make judgements on where to go and who to mix with and then test out our decisions. If we do not like the results, we are able to take alternative action if it matters that much.

---

### Example 2.3

Imagine you decide to join the local Sunday league football team. After two matches you begin to realise that the goalkeeper's after-game behaviour leaves more than something to be desired. You are able to decide whether to tolerate it because of the convenience of the ground or whether to find another team that will let you play for them.

Family groups are somewhat more difficult. We are unable to choose our relations, but most of the time we are able to choose whether or not to be in their company. These decisions may lead to conflict and some find that their inability to relate well to their family is a source of deep distress. There is a great expectation in our society that 'blood is thicker than water' and that families should be close-knit, warm and caring units. This is rarely true but our ability to act on our assessment and exercise choice is limited.

In most cases, however, we draw inferences about others when we first meet them. These inferences come from what we know about them, how they behave and how the resulting perceptions fit into our existing belief system and personal construct theory. From these we make our decisions and act accordingly.

It is now generally accepted that, during a first meeting, pieces of data are exchanged. This data is provided from a range of sources, is gathered via the senses and used to form opinions about others. Some of the data is based on fact (what can be tested and repeated), some is based on interpretation of fact, some is fabricated and some distorted. The means of data gathering can be flawed – your hearing may be faulty or your sight less than perfect. The medium of transmission can easily be subject to interference – your speech may be impeded or slurred. This obviously influences the quality of the data available for processing.

Kelly suggested that the initial and often impressionistic data is compared to our existing construct theories. From the conclusions drawn, judgements/predictions are made about other people and overall impressions formed about them. The impression is used to determine the reply to the opening gambit, the behaviour in response to the hand offered for shaking and the smile returned for the opening smile. This is when the pre-judgements are used to influence subsequent events.

Our personal construct theory contains ideas and attitudes which, if fixed, can lead to assumptions being made about people, their role in life, their subsequent behaviour and their attitudes and opinions. These ideas and attitudes will have been developed over time from personal experience and exposure to people and situations, and from the reports of others. Constructs are formed about the characteristics of others and are given meanings.

---

*Example 2.4*

Imagine that the head mistress of your first school wore her hair in a bun. She retired to be replaced by another woman, who also had a bun. Your favourite storybook described a teacher as having 'her hair piled on top of her head like a cottage loaf'. It would not be surprising for you to grow up thinking that all women with such a hairstyle were also school teachers.

---

## Stereotypes

These characteristics are clustered together to form stereotypes. A stereotype refers to an individual who can be said to represent a group. Assumptions and pre-judgements are made using one group of characteristics as indicators of others.

---

*Example 2.5*

Another example of this is when young men with very short haircuts are labelled as skinheads or punks. Skinheads go about in gangs; gangs go to football matches; gangs that go to football matches get drunk; drunks at football matches break windows. The assumption formed from these constructs would predict that the young man walking down the pavement on a Saturday lunchtime near a football ground will be drunk and will have broken a window by tea-time.

Some of the pieces of data used to form assumptions and build constructs are given more weight than others. These are called the central traits. They have a profound effect on the impression being formed, especially when they are confirmed by other pieces of information.

---

Information is gathered from cues, and inferences are drawn from them. These cues include the behaviour of the person being assessed, their choice of clothes and mode of self-presentation, their physical appearance, non-verbal behaviour, the things they say and the way in which they communicate. Despite the general warning and research that confirms how misleading first impressions can be, they are frequently used to make what sometimes can be very important judgements about others.

---

*Example 2.6*

A young man is due for an interview for the post of office junior. He is 19 and from his CV you see that he is sitting his A-level examinations at the local college, he works part-time for a local firm in the evenings and at a local pub at weekends. Darren walks into your office. He is wearing a fashionable, shiny black suit with the sleeves rolled up. His hair is gelled and curly and, when he moves his head, you note that its length has been disguised by a pony tail. He has a gold earring in his left ear and a large signet ring on his left hand. He walks up to you with his hand outstretched, smiles and says, 'Hi, I'm Darren, pleased to meet you'.

- What do you think he will do and say next?
- Would you give him the job?

---

These first impressions are used to draw inferences about the assessee's personality traints and characteristics. They are not given equal value; they are averaged and weighted according to their desirability. Therefore, if you worked in an advertising agency and wanted outgoing, lively young people in your office, you may well give Darren a job. But if you were the office manager of a very traditional, old-fashioned law firm, you might not.

This example demonstrates how these traits are used to confirm prejudices about stereotypes and how misleading and superficial impressions can be.

---

*Example 2.7*

If you are looking for someone who is outgoing and forward looking, it would not be surprising if you were to seek someone who wears fashionable – maybe avant garde – clothing and behaves in an exaggerated way.

---

In the example given above we stereotype the law firm as being old fashioned and therefore not too willing to take risks. The danger of stereotyping is, that in the effort to confirm our existing pre-judgements, we miss very important pieces of data and as a consequence make decisions that are simply wrong. Thus, the ideal candidate for the job is rejected because the initial impression formed complies with a negative stereotype, regardless of whether the individual complies to type.

It also seems that these pieces of data are joined with others available (and those sometimes merely imagined) to draw conclusions about another person's personality and the degree of control they have or have not over events. Sometimes the cause of events is attributed to individual actions rather than to judging the individual to be a witness or an inactive participant in the situation. It is often assumed that people have more control over events than is really the case. This assumption gives individuals more assumed power over their own destiny and fails to recognise that they might have been a 'victim of circumstances' or just in the wrong place at the wrong time.

## Schema

The assessor, as we know from Kelly, already has a set of constructs. Another name for this network of ideas, experiences and knowledge about the behaviour of other people is schema. Like constructs, a schema is a difficult concept to explain simply. (For a fuller, more accurate definition, the reader is referred to the texts given in the bibliography.) A schema may be described briefly as one person's attitude about particular aspects of others' behaviour and characteristics or a situation.

---

### Example 2.8

Imagine you used to work with an unusually large number of people who wrote with their left hands. All but one had handwriting that was very difficult to read. It would not be surprising to find that you had developed a schema that leads you to predict that the next person you meet who is left handed would also have writing that is hard to read.

---

Schema go deeper than just behaviour and can lead an assessor to make predictions about another's personality. Well-known examples include people with close-set eyes being labelled as shifty. Weak handshakes may be taken as being indicative of a weak character. Once these schema have been formed in an individual's mind it is very difficult to change them.

How one person behaves towards another is more important than their private attitudes. Efforts to change thinking can result in the reinforcement of previously held views, rather than the desired reframing of the participants' constructs and schema. Even when evidence is provided to demonstrate that these views are factually incorrect, holders find it hard to believe that their views are incorrect.

To make sense of this chaotic world in which we live and the unpredictability of other people, we develop and strive to maintain intact an implicit theory of personalities. If this is constantly challenged and in need of change, we would all become insecure. We need some 'faith in human beings'. Some try to keep their theories up to date by revising their constructs as new, discounting information is received, but others reject the new data and stick to their existing views.

---

*Example 2.9*

How often have you heard someone say 'I gave her the benefit of the doubt. But she let me down. I know she was provoked but she should not have done that. I knew I should have trusted my first impression. People with red hair always lose their tempers too quickly'?

---

In addition to finding it hard to accept disconfirming evidence, an active search can be made for confirming evidence. 'Give a dog a bad name . . .'

Confirming one's schema or constructs is very important as a way of re-affirming one's own value. This process is sometimes known as a self-serving bias, and sometimes can be the source of arrogance and fixed thinking. Alternatively, unless some reaffirmation takes place, people would be riddled with irresolution and doubt. One way of dealing with this tendency and source of bias when assessing others is to be as aware as possible of one's own schema.

## Script theory

Other biases creep into perception and assessment of other people. It is expected that people behave in certain ways in certain situations. It is also expected that members of the same peer group have reached a consensus on behaviour, norms which get passed on. These are sometimes called 'scripts'. If the predicted behaviour is not followed, this too leads to inferences being drawn. These are thought to be the source of some forms of indirect discrimination.

Indirect discrimination may be unwitting as often predictions are culturally bound and the person making the assessments may not be aware of other patterns of behaviour. Behaviour at an interview is an example. Someone who has never been interviewed cannot be expected to know all the norms or finer points of interview etiquette. Their lack of knowledge of the process need not have any direct bearing on their ability to perform the job. It may mean that they do not know how to behave in this sort of situation and therefore have no way of knowing what will be expected of them. The way in which they behave may be regarded as being inappropriate and therefore a bad impression is created.

Conclusions drawn about an individual are affected by how recently the information was gathered and what was collected first. The first person to be interviewed and the last interviewee stand a better chance of being remembered than those seen in the middle of the day. Something outstanding – a big nose, a bright dress, a loud voice – also aids the recall of the assessor. How salient someone's behaviour is in relation to the assessor's implicit personality theory influences their assessment.

Script theory, as described by Abelson (1981), suggests that a script is to help us predict what is likely to happen in a given situation or when meeting another person. Like the script of a play, a sequence of events is plotted and lines given to the actors. These scripts again serve to reduce uncertainty and help us prepare.

Scripts are developed, again, from education and experience, and are refined over time. We all know that going into a situation of which we have no previous experience is stressful. Our script helps us to get ready for the event. We rehearse our lines and plan our actions in readiness for what we expect will happen. We may have contingency plans for different occurrences that may or may not result – a bit like planning the moves of a game of chess. When we approach new situations or people of whom we have no prior experience and our advance information is scant, what we worry about is not knowing rather than the occurrence itself. What is thought to be terrible before the event is often dealt with easily, once its reality is apparent. Meeting someone for the first time, especially someone famous, can be awe-inspiring. But it is not uncommon to hear people say of, for example, the Queen Mother, after shaking her hand, 'Oh she was just like you or me'. However, if the person or event do not turn out to be what was expected, dissonnance can result and the individual thrown into disarray.

If you are expecting one thing to happen or certain people to be present you will have prepared yourself to behave in particular sets of ways. If these are not present as you expected, it would not be unreasonable for your conduct to be a little inappropriate or apparently confused.

Thus, the whole process of making assessments of other people is fraught with dangers. The techniques we go on to describe are ways of minimising the impact of the biases and erroneous judgements. They have been designed to take into account the biases and attributions that are known to exist in the process of perception formation. However, they cannot remove them. The best we can say here is that human beings are flawed and they need to be aware of their frailty and the limitations of their own processes of assessment when judging others.

## WHY ORGANISATIONS NEED TO ASSESS PEOPLE

Having looked at why individuals assess each other and having thought about some of the ways in which this occurs, we are able to consider how this process is transferred to large and formal organisations. There are many good texts on group dynamics which address similar issues raised about assessment, feedback and the development of relationships in smaller and informal groups. The interested reader is referred to the bibliography which includes suitable texts. Here we will confine ourselves to the world of organisations which enter into formal relationships with their members. The power structures in such organisations are different, as will be explained, and these have an impact on the assessment process. However, some of the dynamics, as one would expect, are common to other group situations, so we will briefly consider some of these here. The formation, growth and development phase of any group are all similar, so this will be our starting point.

First, we must answer the question of what we mean by a formal organisation. We will then move on to discuss how assessment contributes to, and becomes a necessary and normal part of, its evolution. This is to give you some idea of how assessment processes become in-built features of an organisation's structure and culture both in the formal, procedural sense and as part of the implicit contract between employer and employee.

The consequences of assessment decisions can have quite profound implications for the people involved and the groupings to which they belong. These assessments extend to discussions regarding membership, its continuation, exclusion of members and the successful or unsuccessful achievement of the shared tasks. The formal and informal procedures of the organisation and decisions made as a result of the conclusions can affect people's earnings, their happiness in and out of work, and their future working lives. While this can be true to a degree in small and informal groups, those making the assessment in the world of work need to be aware of the power they hold.

Therefore, the perception of others cannot (and is not) left to natural processes. Later on in the text we will describe the techniques that are available. We include easy, everyday approaches, as well as more sophisticated ones. Some form or mechanism is needed to deal with the errors and biases which are known to creep into assessments and the conclusions that are drawn from them. Many different ways of assessing people have been developed as organisations become more complex and sophisticated. But before looking in detail at the different techniques, especially assessment centres, we will explore the overall dynamics of organisations and the influence they can have on the assessment process.

It is important to grasp a basic understanding of these dynamics before looking at more specific aspects of assessments. Management should consider its own power, authority and the influence it has over the process and techniques.

## WHAT IS AN ORGANISATION?

Many definitions are available and many theoretical statements exist to describe the complexities and variations that exist among the different types of organisation. Simply, an organisation can be described as a group of individuals who have been drawn together for the achievement of a commonly agreed task or purpose. Modern organisations range from publicly funded corporations and governmental bodies, multinational, multiowned businesses, conglomerates, franchised groups, stock holder and/or family controlled companies, voluntary and charity bodies, associations of one kind or another, down to partnerships and sole traders. We cannot hope to discuss the assessment practices used by this very disparate range of organisations. The special dynamics of partnerships and sole traders takes them outside the scope of this book. However, all of these organisations have one thing in common – they had a beginning.

An organisation usually would have originated from the efforts of an individual or a small group of people. Even the very largest, well-established institutions had their roots as someone's bright idea. The modern Navy began under Henry VIII and local government may have had its beginnings in the largess of the local gentry and parish priests. Their modern-day complexity has been as a result of evolution and growth. Evolution is the process that results from an organism's reaction and response to the changes that are taking place around it in its natural environment. Organisations, though, are different. Evolution does not occur biologically. Developments occur, usually, as a result of some form of decision. This decision may be a conscious, rational one taken after full consideration of the relevant factors, likely outcomes and risks involved. It may be an intuitive, instinctive decision seeming to be almost evolutionary in its nature. Alternatively, a non-decision could be made – that is a conscious decision to do nothing or an avoidance of making any decision at all. Regardless of the type of decision made, it will result in some form of action being taken either by the decision-makers themselves or others instructed to respond in certain ways.

## The Evolution

At the beginning of an organisation's life, it is likely that the decision-makers are the founders or individuals with a high degree of vested interest. As they strive for survival and success in their chosen venture, it is typical to find that three phenomena occur:

- the organisation establishes its own identity;

- the culture of the organisation becomes laid down;

- the organisation changes and grows.

More will be said about organisational culture later, for its nature and the modes of behaviour that emanate from it have considerable impact on how the organisation's members are assessed, by whom and the criteria that are used to make judgements.

The evolution of the organisation can be traumatic for those involved. This need not be a negative experience; rather it can be very enriching and rewarding. Even in these cases some pain is experienced. Nevertheless change, even of a gradual nature, means that aspects of the organisation, that may have previously been valued, have to be altered. These changes can vary in severity – from a non-fatal shock to the system from outside (such as the loss of a major client), to an internally taken decision to make minor adjustments to operating procedures. The former tends, historically, to be less common, but in our present turbulent world, many more organisations seem to be experiencing what amounts to radical and fundamental pressure for change. The latter should not be regarded as the soft option. In some ways the effects of internal decisions can be much more far-reaching and lasting.

---

*Example 2.10*

The effects of computerisation provide a useful example. The decision to transfer an operation from a manual system on to a computer has far-reaching effects. Initially intended to make procedures less time-consuming and efficient, the mechanisation of a system is only now a small part of the decision to introduce a computerised system. The knock-on effects can be felt in all areas of an organisation's operations.

---

Regardless of its manifestation, the success of either form of change depends totally on the efforts (or lack of them) of the people in the organisation and those joining it at the time. It is usual for an organisation to move from being a sole operation, through perhaps a partnership, to being larger than what is normally regarded as a small group. For our purposes here we will take a small group to be one with around eight members. Most business organisations are larger than this and get there through gradual expansion, usually as a result of the work of the original member/s.

These founding individual/s – as one would expect – have some vested interest in the organisation's survival. They will have spent heavily in terms of money, energy and emotion to get the organisation set up and running. They will therefore have a sense of ownership about the organisation and its uniqueness. It could be expected that they would be very clear about their shared and several goals. These will have been worked at, fought over and debated during the founding stages of the organisation. Even a sole trader will have questioned, 'what am I doing, where am I going?' They will know each other well as a consequence of their shared experiences and common interest. They will have had times of elation and stress, and will have their areas of conflict and disagreement. These experiences become part of the organisation's culture. Examples can be found in some organisations' mythology and can be seen to set the standards for achievement and behaviour.

## Maturity

Once a business extends beyond a partnership it, by definition, becomes a group, and seems to go through several stages on its way to maturity. Tuchman (1965) has given us a useful model to use to look at the growth and development processes of groups. This model shows that several phases need to be passed through before a group can operate effectively. These phases are usually labelled as follows.

- *Forming* – The initial coming together of the group. Membership is agreed and an individual's place is established as a valid part of the group. It is possible that this will be changed later, but during the initial stages the group's identity is established in the minds of its members and can be recognised by those outside.

- *Storming* – The early conflicts. The group members begin to establish their positions with each other. It is at this stage that roles are clarified as plays are made for leadership and the different individuals work out their place in the group. Goals are established through the deployment of various processes. Some formal, deliberate techniques may be used or the goals could be discussed and debated as part of normal group conversations.

- *Norming* – Parameters and standards of behaviour for group members are set. It is possible that, at this stage, some of the original members decide to leave the group or they may be rejected by other group members. These norms tend to come to characterise the group and their combination makes the group different from others of a similar kind.

- *Conforming* – The group processes come to embody these norms. Pressure is thus placed on its members to adhere to those standards and to remain within their parameters. Ways of dealing with dissent and rebellion are incorporated in better established groups. In others, the conforming stage can result again in termination of membership or isolation of individuals. Formation of cliques or in-groups can also be seen at this stage. The influences of the group's power structure can be seen and the group as a distinct entity becomes recognisable.

- *Performing* – If a group passes successfully through these phases it can be judged as being ready to operate and work towards the achievement of its shared task. A mature group can be regarded as one that has reached this stage of development, but it is needless to say that not all groups get there. Another scenario is that they get there but the patterns of behaviour and the values that have been established are not positive and so the chances of success are reduced.

Passage through these phases establishes the organisation's culture and lays down the unique way in which it functions. Thus, its existence is established as a free-standing organisation; perhaps with its own legal identity and, certainly, a life and existence of its own. Each organisation is distinct as it is a product of the individuals who have contributed to its development and growth. An organisation is complex and interwoven with history, mythology and idiosyncrasy, which all increases as the organisation ages. Even in organisations that are comprised of branches, such as retail chainstores, each separate unit will have its own distinguishing features that set it apart from the rest, despite any control the centre may wish to exercise. It is these and other features, hopefully related to the organisation's operational needs, that underpin the way in which its existing and new members are perceived.

## HOW DOES GROWTH HAPPEN?

It is very rare that an organisation, at some time in its existence, does not expand. Changes in the organisation's environment will require some form of response to be made. This may be expansion, diversification or retraction.

Recent years have seen a lot of the latter and many organisations – especially young ones – do not survive. We have seen from the failure rates that newly established businesses suffer from a variety of dysfunctions that may be fatal. But once an organisation has become established, a phase of expansion is not unusual.

It is rare for growth to happen by accident or for this sort of change to occur as a result of a non-decision. Some decisions are taken and plans formed to determine the direction of expansion and means of growth. The quality of the planning and decision-making may be suspect, but nevertheless will have occurred in some form. In the better organisations this planning is a normal activity. Strategic plans are developed, refined, implemented and reviewed regularly, and can be adapted if the circumstances warrant it. The danger of planning is that the plans themselves become the ends and, as such, become inflexible. But even if the planning is *ad hoc*, some form of thought is normally given to the different ways in which the organisation could expand.

These increases in size, production or range of activity normally require extra people to become involved in the organisation. They are needed to cope with the increased volume or to bring in skills and attributes not available within the organisation at the time. The traditional ways of acquiring these people are to buy in the skills using contractual arrangements or to acquire the organisation's own bank of skills. This can be done through the training of existing people or the recruitment of those who already have (or have the potential to develop) those skills.

The founding members, it will be remembered, are usually well known to each other. We have seen that they will have some experiences in common and will have acquired a set of shared values. It is also likely that they share, or at least have some understanding of, each others' assumptions and attitudes about various subjects. It is this group that will make the initial decisions about the ways in which their organisation is to change, and whether they should grow by finding and including others. Decisions will also need to be made regarding the new people's level of involvement. This can vary – from an equal degree of ownership (for example involving other people to the same extent as the founders, with the same degree of investment) to that of employee with no tangible or formal stakehold in the organisation.

Later we will discuss the assessment techniques available to help decide which people to include in the organisation and how these can best be used. In some ways these assessments need to be distinguished from the assessments of individuals made once they are a part of the organisation. This may only be because there is no historic evidence about the individual assessee's past performance that the assessor can use, knowing it to be accurate.

## THE ORGANISATION'S CULTURE

Once individuals are included in the organisation they become part of its evolution and influence and are affected by its culture. This term was first used by Roger Harrison (1972) to illustrate four different sorts of organisation and was later used by Charles Handy (1978) in his *Gods of Management*. The term has now become part of everyday management jargon, but it is questionable whether its true meaning is properly understood. Schein (1984) gives a useful description of the concept.

Like a nation's culture, an organisation's culture is a complex set of rituals and beliefs that are part of its fabric, and give it its identity. The most obvious manifestations are the common patterns of behaviour displayed by its members. Simple examples include the way in which people address each other – by title and last name or by first names, how work space is personalised, how much effort is expended on work. Behaviour displays the values of the individual, or in this case, the organisation, and is influenced by the assumptions people make about what is and is not acceptable. It also shows what people think they can get away with as they test the boundaries. Because these are assumptions it is assumed that 'everybody knows'. Systems are not recorded in staff instruction manuals, but form an important part of organisational life.

---

*Example 2.11*

One organisation's normal practice is to file the yellow copy of memos and letters in the central filing system, but unless new staff are told this it would be easy for them to assume that it is for individual files.

Or, everyone knows the chair in the corner of the canteen is Ted's and that he takes an instant dislike to any one who dares to use it.

Or, an acceptance that the way to get on is to join the football pools syndicate.

---

Underpinning both behaviour patterns and common assumptions is a set of shared values. These values will have been developed by the founding members and those joining subsequently. They will have been worked out, either explicitly or implicitly. Some will be unquestionable; others will be adapted to suit circumstances.

Examples could include the emphasis on the importance of formality, the prohibition of 'girlie' calendars around the workplace, the standards of performance expected. A new member learns these values as part of the inclusion process. Some organisations formalise this into an induction programme, but many of the implicit factors are discovered by the new person asking a colleague, 'What is it really like to work here?'.

Learning the value system is important as compliance can influence the individual's future success and the way in which performance is assessed. The inclusion process is an important phase of an individual's life in the organisation. While an organisation is able to change its mind about its recruitment decision with few consequences other than increased cost, the individual could have left another job and made a major commitment. The first few months are times of stress as the new employee tries to learn the job and understand the culture.

## Socialisation

The quality of induction is known to affect the subsequent job performance and length of tenure, but research has so far concentrated on formally organised programmes. The less formal aspects of the early months in a job have not received the same attention. Parallels can be made with the dynamics of social groups. This phase is called socialisation or education. A child growing up in a family learns what can and cannot be done, where and when. William Wordsworth in *Intimations of Immortality* (1807) described this development as:

> 'The little Actor cons another part'
> Filling from time to time his 'humorous stage'
> With all the Persons, down to palsied Age,
> That Life brings with her in her equipage;
> As if his whole vocation
> Were endless imitation.

In a group social pressure is applied, reflecting the storming and norming phases of its own growth. Rebellious members are disciplined, renegades rejected and mavericks either neutralised or accepted as eccentric. These processes happen normally and, in social groups, are usually unplanned and probably subconscious. But in formal organisations some more explicit process is used. If the organisation is expanding rapidly and including large numbers of new individuals, some way is needed to ensure that they do not alter the existing norms and standards that the organisation's owners are not prepared to change. Assessment methods are used to help find individuals who fit into acceptable patterns of behaviour and provide them with feedback to assist them to learn how to conduct themselves.

Nevertheless, bringing people in from 'outside' the organisation inevitably means that new and different ideas are brought in, and in some cases this is the very reason for their recruitment. There may be very good reasons why an organisation needs to change its culture so profoundly. One known factor in an organisation's failure to be fully effective is a phenomenon called Groupthink developed by Janis (1972). This is seen when a group or organisation becomes content with its own performance and its desire for agreement overrides the achievement of its task. The features of Groupthink include:

- illusions of invulnerability;

- tendency to moralise;

- feelings of unanimity;

- pressure to conform;

- dismissal of opposing ideas.

One way of dealing with this phenomenon is to bring in an individual or individuals who are able, through the strength of their power base or personal qualities, to influence and effect radical change to the organisation's culture.

## Cultural change

In some organisations this is used as a powerful signal of cultural change. For example, a bank appoints a new chief executive from a marketing background rather than banking, or a health authority appoints unit managers from private industry. Each appointment will send clear messages to the other employees about the general direction the organisation is wishing to take. How to accommodate these differences being brought in and how to incorporate their richness into the organisation's culture creates challenges.

However, if this is the aim it is important to ensure that the people from the different environments are not assessed using inappropriate criteria as their different behaviours and assumptions emerge during selection assessment. Failure to appreciate differences and to learn how to incorporate them can lead to some of the other known factors of dysfunction and create other profound problems for the organisation to deal with.

Examples of these dysfunctions include:

- tribalism and parochialism;

- intolerance and rejection of difference;

- fear and defensiveness;

- condemnation and scapegoating of others;

- adoration and idolisation;

- attack and discrimination.

These and other dysfunctions are all negative results of assessments of people who are viewed as being outsiders and different from the 'normal' sort of person who conforms to the desired stereotype of what is accepted in the organisation. If the wish is to appoint diffferent sorts of people, the organisation will need to take on some of these issues and find ways of addressing them.

The opposite is to appoint new employees who conform to the make-up of the existing staff profile. This is safe(ish) as there is previous evidence of performance. However, if selection on this basis is tolerated and remains unchallenged, the organisation's managers will probably indulge in recruiting new members in their own image. Maybe this type of appointment was successful in the past, but in times of rapid and unprecedented change, there is no guarantee that it will be the case in the future.

More attention will be paid to the impact of these issues surrounding appointment assessments later in the book. It is worth noting, though, that as organisations decide to increase their membership, the founding member(s) should be aware of the dangers of excessive strengths in some areas at the expense of under-representation in others. Some degree of differentiation seems to be beneficial, but this must be balanced against creating an organisation whose members have no common ground. Not an easy balance to achieve, but some of the techniques we will be describing have been designed to aid in the assessment of similarity and difference, and to help managers decide how best this balance can be achieved.

## Recruitment and replacement

The decision to recruit more people can happen in several different ways, and occasionally can be as a result of chance. Both the organisation and the individuals deciding whether to join or not make some form of assessment. The decision made by the parties results in a legally binding agreement that contains explicit and implicit conditions. Both parties must determine what these are and whether they are acceptable. How the assessment is made can help or detract from the decisions made. It can tell the individual a lot about how the organisation conducts itself and something about its value systems, as well as providing information about the individual for the organisation.

It is natural for an organisation to need additional people at some time in its development, and it is also normal that people will leave it. Leaving may be as a result of a decision made by the individual, such as a new job, a different way of life, a career break/change, termination by the employer, retirement or death. The gap left by the individual's departure either remains or is filled by others in one way or another. This again requires search and assessment of whether the new person is right for the organisation and the organisation is right for the person.

Replacement is not always achieved by bringing in new people. Even when the person is simply replacing a departed colleague, some assessment of suitability for the post is made. Many tools and techniques are available to assist the process of increasing and/or replacing staff. Some are the subject of codes of practice which have legislative and professional backing. These codes will be referenced later, but deserve acknowledgement here as they provide a framework for good practice. Despite their existence, they can only assist the process through the provision of an operational framework. They do not prescribe how the techniques are used in practice, nor do they lay down how the final decision should be made. The final decision on who to appoint to a particular job is made by people and therefore it is always subject to the cognitive and affective processes that determine the way in which perceptions of other people are made. Even if the most sophisticated process were to be used, the decision whether or not to accept the outcome still remains to be made by managers.

## SUMMARY

In this chapter we have looked at the following:

- How people make judgements of each other and how this process is transferred into the world of work. The major difference is that, at work, many of the processes have been formalised. One reason for using these processes is to reduce the errors and biases that are known to exist in the way assessments are made. These are partially products of the need to make sense of the world so that employees are able to prepare for meetings with people and events, and are equipped to make appropriate responses.

- The processes of assessment and making judgements about others also help to preserve a group's identity. The group's belief systems, values and behaviour patterns are reinforced and preserved through the inclusion of new members who are similar, and who are then socialised into the culture of the organisation. This process is extended into the formal systems used by organisations as employment methods and practices.

- The techniques that have been developed to assist recruitment and selection are also used, with others, to assess people already in employment. They help the decision-makers decide who to appoint and provide information to the outsiders to help them decide whether they want to join the organisation.

- Assessments made during the course of employment provide information on levels of performance, predictions of further potential and development needs. They also provide information for the individual – both on how well or otherwise they are actually performing and how they are perceived by the organisation. (These may be different.)

- Feedback is part of the socialisation process as information is provided to the individual on the sort of behaviour expected and the standards that are to be achieved. The methods used for assessment and the provision of feedback send very clear messages about the culture of the organisation.

Assessors should by now have acquired an insight into the processes of perception, organisational growth and culture. We have looked at these aspects before examining the techniques in order to help you put them into a broader context. Before deciding which is the best for your own particular circumstances and culture, we think these factors should be taken into account. We will now consider the occasions on which assessment takes place and will then look in detail at how different techniques can contribute to improving the effectiveness of the assessment.

# 3

# When assessment takes place

## ASSESSING EMPLOYEES' 'FIT'

In the previous chapter we looked at theories of perception – the processes that take place between people when they meet and make assessments of each other. In it, we also looked at the nature of organisations, how they grow and what happens as they expand by taking in new members. This was to provide some insights as a basis from which to examine the different opportunities that are available for assessments to be made as part of an individual's employment. It is usually taken as read that an organisation, as part of the implicit contract of employment, has the right to assess an employee's performance. The culture of an organisation and the decisions taken by its managers about the sort of organisation they want determine the types of assessment made and the techniques used to carry them out. Whether formal or informal, assessments will be made of individual employees, their performance and their 'fit' in the organisation.

At the same time, these individuals will be assessing their own performance and their perceptions of their fit. Much of this will be happening continuously, but assessments will also be made, formally, at fixed times and on certain occasions. These assessments will be outlined below. Most attention has been given to assessment of individuals at the time of organisational expansion. The recruitment and selection of new members takes much time and energy, and is very important, as it is the time when many of the ground rules, cultural elements and organisational expectations are communicated to new members. First impressions are known to have an impact on the length of employees' tenure, affinity to the organisation and longer-term productivity. Reflecting the importance of getting these processes right, a number of specialist books have been written recently analysing the recruitment and selection process from a number of different perspectives. The texts on personnel management recommended in the general bibliography will give more general outlines.

Once an individual has joined the organisation, assessment occurs in many different ways and at various times during their stay in the organisation. There are many alternative ways of making these assessments and some of them will be well known, having been given differing degrees of attention in the literature. Some have texts devoted entirely to them, while others barely get a mention. Some of the less well known are limited in their use which tends to be confined to specialist areas or large organisations that can afford their costs and need their degree of sophistication.

Some of the techniques may be applied overtly and will be accompanied by procedures and systems. These will have been developed over time and have become part of the organisation's normal way of working. Their introduction will have been made with the knowledge of the assessee – even if it was with compliant agreement. Other techniques are less formal or obvious – and some are even covert. In these cases it may be that the assessee will not know that assessments are being made. Reference requests are examples of these. In these cases, it is unusual for the assessee to be able to make any contribution to or influence the outcome of the assessment. These assessments raise issues which the organisation and assessors concerned need to address as they impact on organisational culture and the way in which individuals are treated.

## Feedback

It is accepted that the kind of feedback given to individuals about their performance has a direct effect on the subsequent level of that performance. The literature on motivation stresses that, to increase the will to work and do more, in terms of quantity and quality, individuals need to know, in fairly specific detail, what is expected of them, the areas in which improvement is needed and in which their performance has been acceptable or better. It contributes directly to individuals' job satisfaction (Hackman and Oldham's (1975) meaningful outcomes), and is now believed to affect individuals' ability to cope with pressure and uncertainty, almost essential qualities in the present degree of turbulence being experienced in many organisations.

Feedback is helpful, also, in the acceptance and understanding of roles. Role ambiguity, especially during times of change and uncertainty, can result in people working towards different, perhaps conflicting, goals. This can lead to tension within teams and between individuals, stress and a loss of productivity.

These and other opportunities for assessment will be outlined in this chapter. We will also look at the information that is produced as a result of these assessments. The value of this information, and its 'accuracy' and relevance, need to be considered in the light of our understanding of the perception processes and the inherent bias they, inevitably, contain. These opportunities need to be related to the organisation's culture and to the appropriateness of using a particular mode of assessment.

## Timeliness

Consideration needs to be given to the timeliness of the approach and the circumstances and context in which you, as a manager, and your organisation find yourselves. You may wish to make use of an opportunity but the degree of uncertainty in the organisation's world makes being able to follow up the assessment in the way you would wish seem unlikely. It may be better, in these circumstances, to leave well alone until the situation is clearer.

# RECRUITMENT AND SELECTION

Most of the discussion in Chapter 2 focused on the recruitment of new members of staff during a phase of expansion. For most organisations this type of growth is comparatively rare. About two-thirds of recruitment activities are undertaken to replace an existing member of staff who has left the organisation. The remaining third is for jobs that are newly created.

For the purposes of this book, we are separating recruitment from selection. While the processes are linked, different factors and considerations come into play. Here, we define recruitment as being the activities undertaken to attract an appropriate range of candidates for the vacancies in question, while selection is the assessment of their suitability and the process of making the decision to offer employment.

## Recruitment

In recent years there has been a recruiter's market. The economic recession and high levels of unemployment have meant that there has been no shortage of applicants for jobs. The opportunity for advances to be made in recruitment and selection practices have been taken. Employers have found it difficult to distinguish between candidates all presenting themselves with the desired qualifications and experience. Ways of identifying and assessing other criteria were sought.

This pattern is now changing. Recruitment in some areas of employment is becoming more difficult as skills become short and more in demand. The decline in the birthrate and the knock-on effect of a decline in numbers of school leavers has also led recruiters to examine their methods and approaches. Attention is shifting from selecting the very best candidate to encouraging them to apply. Thus, the focus has moved from straight selection, even though this is still important, to a more equal process which aims to present the employer in the best possible light. This can be achieved through the use of good and imaginative employment practices which demonstrate concern for the potential employee in addition to providing the information needed for the assessment of skills and for selection decisions.

For the purposes of recruitment and selection, the assessment of skills is made from two angles as follows:

1. the assessment of the skills needed to perform the job in question to the desired standard;

2. the assessment of the possessors of those skills.

This second assessment is aimed at judging whether assessees will be able to perform the job to the standard required, whether they will fit into the organisation and be able to work with the people already in employment. The possessors of the skills also assess whether the organisation will suit them, provide the opportunity for them to practise their skills and to obtain whatever it is they are seeking from a job and an employer.

All too often most attention is given to the assessment of the individual applying for the post. We think that, generally, not nearly enough attention is given to the assessment of the skills being sought. This should be done in a way that is helpful for all involved. The definition of those skills should be made at the beginning of the recruitment process and should be the result of job analysis and the preparation of a job description. Techniques to help the analysis and production of job descriptions will be described in Chapter 4. If these are not prepared, it means that subsequent assessment will be carried out using criteria that is not necessarily related directly to the job in question. Without job-related criteria, the subsequent assessment becomes more susceptible than it needs to be to the biases of perception outlined above. Simple methods of defining these criteria are discussed and examples given later.

We think helpful criteria are those specified in terms of behaviour. Personality factors obviously have a major influence on how an individual applies their skills. They also impact on the person – organisation fit. But the final assessment should be of what an individual is able to do and whether it is anticipated that they will be capable of applying their skills in the context of the employing organisation. Specifying and writing specifications of behaviour is not commonly carried out. The introduction of statements of competency as a result of the NCVQ's (National Council for Vocational Qualifications) work has increased the use of output descriptions, but these tend to be generally related to occupations rather than to specific jobs. Nevertheless, they can guide and help managers prepare their own specifications.

In some situations, it is appropriate that personality factors are assessed. If certain attributes are being sought which are directly related to the job in question, some means of identifying them is needed. The methods used to assess personality vary considerably in their validity and they need to be used with caution and skill. Their selection should therefore be undertaken carefully, and efforts need to be made to ensure that they are used correctly, according to the designer's intent. Often the results obtained are given more credibility than that intended. This is due as much to the form in which they are presented as the actual contents. Personality assessments, as with all other techniques, are only capable of assessing what they purport to assess. The use of the data also needs careful consideration and control. Again, it should only be used for the purpose for which it is obtained.

Behavioural criteria can be designed fairly easily for a particular job. Defining what a post-holder is required to do and the standard to be reached can be done by asking, 'How would I know one if I saw one, what would they be doing?' Providing the answer, of course, is more time-consuming and mind-stretching. More will be said about both this approach and approaches to personality assessments later.

*Table3.1* A seven-point plan

| Criteria | Applicant 1 | 2 | 3, etc |
|---|---|---|---|
| Education | | | |
| Experience and attainments | | | |
| Knowledge and skills | | | |
| Physical attributes | | | |
| Special attributes | | | |
| Interests (relevant to job) | | | |
| Disposition (relevant to job) | | | |

## Personnel specification

The principle, however, of clearly specifying what is being sought should underpin the recruitment and selection process. Once the job description has been prepared, it should be possible to consider the make-up of the ideal candidate. This is known as a personnel specification. From this specification a search strategy can be determined. Various different approaches to the preparation of a personnel specification can be found. Rodgers's (1951) seven-point plan is useful in our experience, and has been adapted to form a matrix in which the applicants can be compared uniformly (see Table 3.1).

Many different ways of attracting candidates are possible, but as this book is not about personnel practice, the reader is referred to the standard text books cited in the bibliography. The choice of recruitment method, though, says something about the organisation in addition to providing information about the job and the sort of person being sought.

## Application procedures

The way in which interested people are asked to submit their application also says things about the organisational culture. More importantly it provides the vehicle for the information on which the first assessment of applicants will be made. A structured, provided application form limits the applicant's scope for presenting information in their own way and dictates the contents to some extent. The request for a letter provides very little guidance on the sort of information and amount of detail required by the organisation. But it gives the applicant the scope and freedom for self-expression. A CV falls somewhere between the two. While governed by convention, it does give the applicant some flexibility and choice.

A structured application form helps the assessor compare like with like, but can be restrictive. Letters and CVs may mean that needed information is not offered, but the way they are presented and what is omitted can say a lot in themselves. But will the inferences drawn be relevant to the job? The method of application should help the applicants present themselves in the ways they choose. At the same time it should provide the vehicle for gathering the information needed to assess initially the applicant's potential ability to perform that task. Again, we consider that more thought could be given to this part of the process.

Surprisingly, there is little reported research on shortlisting. In theory applications should be compared to the job description and personnel specification using tools such as the one shown above in Table 3.1. What happens in practice, in our experience, seems to vary considerably between the systematic examination of all applications to a 'three heaps' approach. The manager has three piles – interview, reserve and reject. The application is allocated to a pile according to a number of different criteria. These have been known to include factors such as the colour of ink used, the amount of additional information supplied, schools attended, etc!

The lack of reported research, in a way, is alarming as this is a critical stage in the recruitment process, determining whether the applicants are given or denied the chance to demonstrate their abilities personally. The application provides the information, but it is also a barrier to effective communication. It may facilitate attributional errors, and allows for inter-pretation biases and misrepresentation. But without this medium, how else could organisations deal with large numbers of individuals expressing an interest in working for them?

## Selection

An increasing number of techniques are being used to assist in the selection of staff. As mentioned above, levels of unemployment have created an employer's market. As a result, the process is frequently portrayed as being one way. The employer assesses potential employees against whatever criteria are thought fit, using whatever methods, techniques or devices the employer chooses. However, in reality, this is not the case. While the employer does have the power to do the above, the final decision is not one-sided. The employer decides which candidate will be offered the job in question, but it is the applicant who decides whether or not to accept the job. The final decision will be made as a result of the candidates' own experience of the organisation's behaviour and the impression it creates, as assessed by them against their own criteria.

We will describe later the different techniques that can be used for selection purposes. Some of them can also be used for the diagnosis of training and development needs. The assessment centre technique is particularly useful for both. Whichever technique is used, it should be based on job-related crite-ria, identified through such methods as job analysis. There are conditions that need to be complied with during the technique's design and implemen-tation. This, however, is different for the different applications. Selection tech-niques, generally, produce information that is 'owned' by the employer and is only partially disclosed, if at all. The relationship between the assessor and the assessee tends to be distant and the information is used to aid decision-making and should have short shelf-life. The use of assessment for diagnosis of need has different considerations and so requires different conditions to be applied.

## INITIAL FEEDBACK

Once employees have started work in an organisation, they begin to receive feedback. This is sent from different people with varying degrees of power and influence in the organisation, using various channels and probably conveying different messages.

The new starters will rightfully expect to receive feedback about how well or otherwise they are performing in their new job. How this feedback is given depends on the organisation's practices and culture. Some organisations still use probationary periods and initial reports, even though they no longer have the same importance under employment protection legislation as they once did. Other organisations link the assessment to their appraisal and performance review schemes. Some organisations allow feedback to seep down through the grapevine and let the individuals draw their own conclusions. Some do nothing at all.

---

*Example 3.1*

A library assistant was recruited. She was very lively, outgoing and, at the same time, very quick to pick up the component parts of the job. She was personable and seemed to be an ideal choice to complement the existing staff. They too were enthusiastic and energetic. A good appointment, by all initial measures, and seemingly very acceptable to her new colleagues. But, after three months, when her supervisor was approached to make the initial report, he said that he was going to give her an unfavourable assessment. This was surprising, as her performance had seemed to be more than adequate. After further questioning, it emerged that the rest of the staff were not talking to her and had rejected her from their group. This called for further investigation. The reason for her exclusion, it eventually transpired, lay in the fact that she did not know the rules about storing personal belongings – shoes and bags – behind the counters. She had repeatedly violated these rules and had not picked up the hidden messages. She could not understand what she had done wrong and was becoming increasingly unhappy at work. Once the full situation had been opened up, it did not take the supervisor long to sort it out to the satisfaction of everyone involved. The organisation very nearly lost an employee who eventually proved that indeed she did have the high potential that was anticipated at the time of her appointment.

---

In addition to receiving feedback about the performance of the task, individuals will receive some messages about their fit into the organisational society and their particular work group. The case given in Example 3.1 illustrates the importance of both and how assessments of one can affect the other.

The way in which feedback is given ultimately depends on the style and approach of the assessor; it is also influenced by the culture. Some managers and organisations put people down and keep them firmly in their place as underlings. Others create a climate of growth, risk-taking and encouragement. The nature of the organisation is conveyed via these feedback messages as the new member finds the boundaries of acceptable behaviour, begins to understand the assumptions that are made about other people, the ways and measures of success and begins to find out what is important. All too frequently, however, these very important messages are wrapped up in covert hints rather than being communicated clearly.

The criteria for assessing how well an individual is fitting into an organisation can be equally well hidden. To ensure that the individuals understand how well they are performing and what they need to do to improve and be successful in the organisation, they require, and deserve, these messages to be conveyed in ways which are unambiguous and constructive. It is the responsibility of the manager to provide this feedback. If the organisation's culture does not include this, the manager has the ability to choose whether to accept it or change the culture . . .

Performance of the task, usually, is more open to systematic assessment than social acceptability. If the organisation has used the recruitment procedures outlined above, documents will have been prepared and thinking will have been done. These can be the subject of agreement and used to inform new employees about what will be expected of them, and to plan their initial training. They will also form the base from which measures of success can be developed. The latter seem to be increasing in importance as more organisations introduce performance-related pay schemes.

The information gathered during the selection process can be used to good effect during the initial settling-in stage. It is rare that the perfect performer is recruited. Usually there are some areas of doubt in the selector's mind and some perceived weaknesses. If new appointees are told about these, in a way that does not add to their stress or undermine their self-confidence, this information can be the starting place of a development plan or training programme.

There is no doubt that new employees need feedback both about their achievement in the job and their inclusion in the organisation's and work group's society. Quality feedback, given in a way that is constructive and positive, helps the individual to achieve, and then go on to achieve more. It also contributes to self-esteem – a factor often ignored and usually low just after starting a new job. Effective performance demands a degree of self-confidence and reasonably high self-esteem. The giving of feedback can serve to enhance or destroy self-image. If the feedback, albeit about poor performance, is given based on fair assessments on known criteria with some indication of what can and is expected to be done, the individual knows what they need do and exactly where they stand.

If the feedback, which may be accurate, is given in a negative, demoralising, carping, judgemental way, the individual may easily decide that they are failing. If they decide to leave the organisation, at the very least, more time and money will have to be expended in finding a replacement. Alternatively, the employee may decide to stay as a switched-off underachiever. Neither of these alternatives are very satisfactory for anyone concerned.

## PERFORMANCE REVIEWS

Individual levels of performance are the subject of continuous review during the time spent within an organisation. This will be done, as with initial feedback, by different people using different measures to convey different kinds of messages. Assessments will be made regarding the performance of the job, the individual's potential to achieve more or less, and continuing acceptability and fit with the organisation.

Increasingly, organisations are striving to find ways of making assessment of performance more tangible. Some techniques are well known and have been in common usage for many years. Many of these grew from Taylor's theory of scientific management and work study techniques (1911). Piece rates, measured day rates and bonus schemes are all products of payment by results which require some form of performance measurement. But as the shift in employment has moved from manual, skill-based work to clerical, service and managerial jobs, it has proved more difficult to find quantifiable measures. The traditional payment by results schemes have declined in popularity in all but a few sectors. For example, sales is an occupation that remains well suited to this form of payment and assessment system.

More recently payment by results and performance-related pay schemes are being used by organisations as a way of rewarding achievement and motivating managers to increase their performance. (Its appropriateness can be debated elsewhere.) The payments are made on the basis of measurable outputs assessed by the paymaster. These methods raise two questions:

- What are the measurable outputs?

- How is the assessment to be made?

We are focusing here on managerial skills and will continue to do so for the remainder of the book but much of what we will be saying can be applied to other occupational skill areas. Managerial skills, we find, are the most fascinating as they are difficult to express as they are closely related to interpersonal effectiveness just as much as task performance. Their very nature, in their broadest sense, has recently been the subject of open debate. Work has been done for some years on their specification, but since the publication of the Handy (1987) and Constable McCormick reports, there has been growing interest in describing these skills precisely.

This interest has resulted in the development of competency statements written in a form in line with the requirements of the NCVQ. These competencies are expressed as outputs of behaviour. The previous attempts to produce descriptions of the managerial role have focused on activities (eg Fayol, (1949), leadership responsibilities (eg Tannenbaum and Schmidt 1973) or role (eg Stewart, 1976 and Mintzberg, 1973).

Most management education has been concerned with the tasks a manager is required to perform. In contrast training has emphasised the skills, especially those concerned with interpersonal relationships. The latest developments have been aimed at bringing the two together. The works of McClelland (1965) and Boyatzis (1982) have demonstrated ways of defining a superior performing manager. Organisations can use this thinking to develop their own profile of a competent manager and generate criteria for their own assessment of managerial performance and skill.

These can be used as a basis for selection, feedback, performance evaluation and development. The example shown in Figure 7.1 on page 182 is one we have used for several years and can be applied to many different organisations.

Assessment of individuals' continued fit into the organisation's society will also be made on a continuing basis. The effect of cliques and in/out groups on the effectiveness of an organisation and on the power structures can be dramatic. The process of assessment informs the decisions and opinions of those with that power and ability to determine the membership of the controlling group. The criteria for these judgements is, by their very nature, subjective, often implicit and may be unexplainable. Yet they can affect the success or failure of an extremely able and competent individual. How these implicit and interpersonal assessments are made is not the subject of this book, despite the fact that the processes are very interesting in themselves.

The interested reader is referred to the texts on group dynamics and behaviour given in the bibliography.

## PROMOTION

The way work is organised in Britain means, generally, that if someone wants to 'get on' and advance in their career, they have to go into management. Until recently this career path began following a period of initial training in a craft, trade, technical or professional role. After a few years of operational experience, junior management/supervisory responsibilities were acquired and a foot was established on the ladder of success. Very little training was given to help the individual assume the new role. It is reputed that promotion was made on the basis of Buggins's turn (ie longevity in the company), neutralising troublemakers, or the last out of the tea hut.

This is now changing. It was initiated by people like Michael Edwardes at British Leyland who began the debate about professional managers. Could a manager of a car production line manage a hotel to equally good effect? The British Institute of Management and organisations such as the Foundation for Management Education had made efforts to increase and improve the standing and standards of management education. However, take-up on education and training programmes was limited as the need for skills and knowledge was not widely accepted.

The debate on the professional role and standing lessened as organisations fought to survive during the recession. The Handy and Constable/McCormick Reports (see above) and the Management Charter Initiative have started it up again in Britain. These developments complement the work of organisations which have recognised that the responsibility for loss of production and effectiveness cannot be laid at the door of the workers and their trade unions. The lack of managerial skills and abilities is now seen as a contributing factor to poor organisational performance.

### Management skills

Graduate management schemes, fast tracks, first degrees in management studies and a proliferation of post-experience management training and education courses are all indicative of this realisation and changed thinking. Newish initiatives are being taken which are aimed at creating a cadre of professional managers. But it involves more than the application of a set of managerial principles and techniques. Effective performance of the role requires skills that can be acquired, developed and practised. Many of these skills concern working with others, and the establishment and maintenance of effective relationships and process.

The ways in which management skills are assessed and potential identified therefore become even more critical. The risk of making bad appointments is now too great. Slimmed down organisations needing to achieve high levels of performance cannot afford to support passengers. Techniques for appointment and promotion are now being employed that are known to have greater validity in predicting future success than some of the traditional methods. We will discuss the effectiveness of these various techniques later, but it must be said that even the best gives only a 50 per cent chance of getting the promotion decision right. The ultimate responsibility still rests with the person that makes the decision.

The assessment of 'success' is even more difficult if the candidates have never performed a managerial role. It is easier when an individual has some sort of record of achievement to show on a CV. But when individuals are applying for their first managerial job, how can a realistic assessment be made of their potential? Is it reasonable to expect someone to perform a complex, demanding and stressful role without any experience and, more than likely, any preparatory training? The steps being taken to improve management education, training and development will provide people with the opportunity of gaining an understanding of the role and a chance to acquire some of the skills before assuming its responsibilities. Similarly, some of the techniques available for the assessment of performance and potential for selection purposes, provide an insight into the job and can contribute to the diagnosis of training and development needs.

## TRAINING AND DEVELOPMENT

Even though training and development are so closely interlinked, they provide distinct opportunities for assessment of performance.

Training can be defined as being linked to the present and, possibly, a future job. The skills needed are known and the required level of performance can be established. Some of the well-known techniques of assessment, such as observation, work trials and achievement records, are frequently used. Training takes place in a stable environment, the skills and knowledge required for effective performance of the job are not subject to fluctuation and their need is predictable and continuing. Examples of this include interviewing, work scheduling and budgeting.

Development, on the other hand, is a longer-term process. The acquisition of pre-determined skills is a lesser concern. The main focus is on the release and realisation of potential through growth and challenge. Learning is obtained from facing and dealing with the unknown. The relevancy and direct applicability of the skills and knowledge is of lesser importance than their acquisition. Development can be seen as being an investment for a longer-term improvement in performance, for the individual and the organisation. Training, however, is more concerned with shorter-term improvements.

The amount invested in any form of training and development, in Britain, is known to be very low. Most managers have less than one day's training per year. Efforts are being made to change the attitudes of organisations and to encourage them to invest more, but this takes time. Work is also needed to improve the ways in which the stimulated demand can be satisfied.

The marketing of training and development as a means of improving organisational effectiveness has concentrated on the performance of the individual, especially the aspiring or newly-appointed manager. Two groups seem, so far, to have been badly neglected. The existing, experienced manager needs additional help. This group of individuals has special requirements which need to be approached in a sensitive way. Often these managers hold the keys to the organisation's culture and can have a major influence over group attitudes. Their training and development needs should be assessed in a way that in itself is credible, does not denigrate their existing knowledge and skill level, and respects their status and position in the organisation.

The other group is the management team as a collective entity. Group development was in vogue in the 1960s and 1970s, but seems to have lost favour as the focus has switched to individual performance. Organisation development is now popularly seen to be concerned primarily with interpersonal relationships. Its contribution to role clarity and goal setting seems to receive less attention. Meanwhile, management development is generally taken as referring to manager development. It is important to distinguish between the two, as the former can also refer to the processes in which the manager is engaged. Consequently, if an organisation wishes to improve its performance, it needs to find ways of training and developing the groups that manage the organisation collectively. This requires the acquisition and improvement of both task and process skills. We will discuss both this and organisational development at greater length later in the book. Here we will concentrate on the opportunities to assess the individual in readiness for training and development.

## Training

Most training activity is regarded as being course-based. Learning occurs as a result of participating in some form of event or programme. Several ways of getting involved exist.

- 'It is your turn.'

- 'You have worked hard – you deserve a day out.'

- 'That looks interesting, go and see what it is all about.'

- 'Old Joe could do with a shake up. Let's send him on a course.'

- 'Freda may learn something about management from this, she needs some new ideas.'

- 'Have you thought about different ways of tackling the task? Could some training help you think it through? You can do this job better if you learnt how to . . .'

The latter two are the ideal. Systematic training should be carried out, based on the assessment of need in relation to the job in hand and the current level of performance. The satisfaction of the identified need can be achieved through the creation of learning opportunities or the provision of some sort of activity appropriately chosen or designed. This assessment requires judgement to be made against some measures of performance and success. These measures can be developed using similar systematic analysis techniques to those that are used for other forms of assessment. The process of identifying training needs is described by Boydell (1990). The interested reader is also referred to Kennedy and Reid (1986) and Harrison (1988).

Even though the technique should already be well known by personnel professionals, we suspect that it is not used in reality. Most people get sent on courses and participate in training events for other reasons. This means that the chance of the training being applicable and relevant to the person, the job and the organisation is reduced. This results in a waste of the investment of the time, effort and money, and damage to the credibility of training as a valid contributor to organisational and individual effectiveness. Systematic identification of need through the use of valid assessment techniques and the design of appropriate means of satisfying those needs is the best way of avoiding this.

## Development

Development has been defined as being concerned more with the future and the unknown, in contrast to the here and now focus of training. Helping individuals to work out how their skills can be enhanced need not be incompatible with the achievement of organisational objectives or future survival. In fact they can, and should, be complementary. However assessing potential is not as simple as assessing an individual's performance against a pre-defined set of skills. More scope needs to be allowed for change, unpredictable occurrences and, above all, personal preference and characteristics.

---

### Example 3.2

A very clear example was seen in one of the assessment centres that was run for the purposes of diagnosing individual development needs. A young housing management officer came out of the assessment with an interesting profile. Her planning, organising and decision-making abilities were very high, but her interpersonal skills (delegating, leadership etc) were woefully weak. The assessors concluded that she was not management material. During the feedback session it emerged that she had been questioning her own career choice. In discussion she concluded that she really wanted to develop her research skills and move into a job that did not involve organising other people so much.

---

Career development need not be exclusively aimed at management development. There are very few general managers; most have functional responsibilities which require some specialist knowledge and skills. Most managers are advised to remove themselves from the detail of carrying out the function, but sometimes it is appropriate that these skills be developed further. The term 'career development' will be used here to refer to the acquisition and development of skills and knowledge that are used in functional specialisms.

At one time it was thought that professional/technical knowledge took seven years to fall to half of its original value. The increasing rate of change, and the spread of information technology, must have considerably reduced this. Nevertheless it can be assumed that some of the principles remain constant. But can one rely on that; and how can one tell which bits of an individual's knowledge or skills areas have changed and which have not? Clearly some form of assessment is needed and some bench-marks with which to compare are required.

We have found among all professions traces of arrogrance and a reluctance to specify criteria for assessing 'professional' skills. Neither are there techniques for doing so being used. Another barrier is to gaining agreement on competency across organisations' boundaries. Many organisations use the updating and development of specialist knowledge and skills as a way of gaining competitive advantage. So exchange and sharing could prove to be difficult. Also deciding that one's managers are out of date requires an organisation to admit that its overall performance needs to be improved. This is another difficult assessment to make and admit.

The economic recession and high levels of unemployment have meant that some people, the ranks of the long-term unemployed, will have skills that have not been used for some years. A similar situation exists for others, for example those leaving the armed forces after serving their full term, those who have suffered from long-term illness or have had career breaks. Other examples include those who have suffered from some form of disability that requires them to change occupation. The lack of practice and the need to transfer skills from one type of organisation to another could lead an assessor to believe that the skills have been lost or have never existed. It is possible to create a way of assessing those skills that allows an individual the opportunity to show what they are able to do. Some of the work that is being done on the accreditation of prior learning and expereince is pointing to ways of doing this.

Above, we distinguished between manager development and management development. The former is taken to refer to the growth and enhancement of the skills and knowledge of the individual manager. We also said that we are taking development to relate to the needs of the future. Development should be part of the everyday reality of the effective manager. We live in a constantly changing world and tomorrow can present untold opportunities for learning. Specific opportunities for development present themselves on occasions such as promotion or organisational change.

The chance is constantly there for the manager to be assessed, and for their present skill level to be compared to the skills predicted as being needed to deal with the new situation. These skills could also deal with managing the changes themselves. For example, rapid change requires managers to learn how to create and share a vision of the future. They need to be able to share that vision and convince their staff and colleagues to travel into the uncertain world with them. They need to learn how to deal with the stresses this imposes upon them and others, and how to develop their staff's abilities to do the same. They have to acquire the skill of dealing with ambiguity, while making enough sense of the uncertainty to be able to plan strategically.

To develop one's own and others' ability to deal with these challenges requires some stepping back and reflective assessment, based on some usefully defined criteria.

Management development is used to refer to the development of management processes and the collective skills of those involved in their operation. We guess that attention will move from the individual back to the management team. Belbin (1981) demonstrated effectively that a team is more productive than an individual alone. Neither is it possible for one individual to acquire, and excel in, all the skills required for effective management. It is a complex process that requires multi-faceted input. A team can hope to cover most of the areas while one person, inevitably, would have blind spots and weaknesses. Some of the techniques available for assessing individual performance can be applied equally well to groups. While the opportunities for their assessment, again, can occur daily, the main stimuli for attention are usually as a result of threat or change. It takes some courage for a management group to step outside its day-to-day activity and undertake some form of self-exploration. Commonly this is done using some external specialist help. The development of the management processes based on useful assessment can have benefits for other aspects of the organisation's operations.

Examples are:

- the personnel practices used for career development and promotion can be improved if the managers acquire new skills;

- the way used for work allocation can be altered as a result of these new skills being used;

- the communication channels and skills employed can have a direct influence on how the workforce receives the news of these changes;

- the organisational planning process can become more participative if managers build teams to draw up their plans;

- productivity could be improved through the skilled introduction and operation of management techniques such as quality circles (ie groups of workers set up to recommend ways in which productivity and quality may be improved).

All these initiatives require the acquisition of skills by the individual managers and changes to the management processes used by the organisation. In consequence it is highly likely that the organisation's culture will alter, and its ability to learn, change and adapt are likely to be enhanced. A learning, developing organisation can become a reality.

# PUNISHMENT

As we have already done with training and development, punishment is divided into two. Penalty will be the term used to refer to the negative aspects of the process; the punitive approaches used by many organisations to reinforce required behaviour patterns and, in some cases, as an attempt to impose desired value systems. Discipline will be used to refer to the corrective and remedial processes that can be used to help an individual change their behaviour and improve on sub-standard performance.

Punishment can be used overtly, with the measures of performance and the standards required being common knowledge within the organisation, among all employees. In other cases it is covert. This use can take two forms. In some cases people generally know the standards and measures, and can recognise that punishment is being applied. In other circumstances the standards and measures are unknown to all save those who are making the assessment. The measures being used to exact punishment need not be recognisable as such. For example training can sometimes be used to punish an employee. The allocation of particularly onerous tasks or a location in an undesirable part of the organisation are other forms of indirect punishment existing in organisations.

## Group pressure

We discussed earlier the influence of group processes and dynamics. Group pressure is a well-known way of controlling an individual's behaviour. This pressure can be applied extremely subtly; sometimes unknowingly even among those applying it. Members may know the criteria they are using and are able to articulate their perception of what is happening. It may be that their behaviour is a product of the organisation's culture and that the pressure imposed on a rebel is regarded as normal. The individual will then be seen as being 'beyond the pale', or as assuming irrational attitudes or as making unreasonable demands. In these cases, it is possible that precise criteria cannot be defined and that these exist only in the perceptions of those with the power to make the assessment and to determine group membership. It need not be the manager who makes these assessments.

## Penalty

The most common form of penalty in organisations is the application of some formal disciplinary procedure. Codes of practice and advice on how to conduct these procedures fairly can be found in the standard texts on personnel practice. The Advisory and Conciliation and Arbitration Service Code of Practice (1977) is strongly recommended for anyone wanting to know more about the procedures to be followed to ensure that both the legal requirements pertaining to wrongful and unfair discipline and dismissal are met.

All advice stresses the need for the reasons for the disciplinary action to be clearly communicated to the employee. It requires the criteria used for the assessment of standards of performance to be made explicit. Also the mode of assessment should be explained. The laws regarding unfair and wrongful dismissal are aimed at protecting employees from the misapplication of systems, bad practice and the use of disciplinary measures for other or no good reason. To make sure that good practice is used, an agreed procedure should be established and widely communicated. This procedure should include indications of the required standards and limits of behaviour that will be used to assess, the measures that will be applied during the assessments, who will be conducting the process and the likely outcomes. The procedure should also include guidance on how the individual being assessed will be informed of areas in need of change and improvement, what support and training may be provided to help the changes happen, and the time-scale in which these should occur and reassessment take place.

Covert penalties are, obviously, not the subject of explicit guidance. Yet there is no point in pretending that this form of punishment does not occur. It can be said that most of the formal disciplinary procedures relate to the performance of the task, while informal penalties concern process and social behaviour. It is not just what someone does; it is also the how. We talked above about the pressures that exist within groups. Similar pressure exists between groups. It is also found between those with power and those who are subjected to that power.

---

*Example 3.3*

A typical example of inter-group penalties is the administration department that is the subject of unjust jokes and is excluded from the organisation's social activities. It may have absolutely nothing to do with the individuals employed in the department, but result from a past unsuccessful power struggle by a former departmental head. The penalties are not connected to the work produced by the department nor the conduct of the staff; the measures of assessment being used remain unclear. But nevertheless the individuals receiving the 'treatment' would know they were being penalised.

---

Examples of power-based assessments are the individual excluded from the clique, the recipient of the section's practical jokes, or the person who takes the blame every time something goes wrong. These patterns of behaviour may be condoned by the organisation. But they can set up incorrect attributions. For example, in Example 3.3, if an individual from the administration department applies for promotion, it is likely that their department's reputation will be used to assess their achievements (or lack of them) and to predict their ability to perform the new job to the standard required. It is possible to attempt to ignore this halo effect and make ill-informed judgements about the individual's likely ability to perform in a different set of circumstances with different people.

## Disciplinary procedures

The word discipline comes directly from 'disciple'. This word is defined as being a 'branch of instruction or learning; mental and moral training, adversity as effecting this; systems of rules for conduct; behaviour according to established rules'. The first part of the definition is very different from the second given by the *Concise Oxford Dictionary* – 'order maintained; control exericsed over'. Yet often it is the second meaning that is used in an organisational context.

We want to distinguish between these two aspects. It is very important that those making assessments recognise that they are able to approach poor performance from the two very different meanings. If the aim is to help, rather than force an individual to improve or change their behaviour, very different forms of assessment are needed.

- It must be obvious that assessment of behaviour is taking place. Many of the better appraisal schemes facilitate this approach.

- The criteria being used need to be clearly defined, understood and agreed.

- The action to be taken needs to be specified with an indication of time-scale, responsibilities and method of review.

We will discuss below in greater depth ways of learning and changing behaviour through feedback and planned action for training and development. In the ideal world, disciplinary procedures should follow the same principles as those we are advocating for assessment in general. These should be used before the application of any formal corrective procedures, which should be seen as the last resort. In the better organisational procedures, reference is made to these less formalised procedures, with formal disciplinary measures being taken when all other approaches have failed to produce any change or improvement in performance.

The stages in discipline can be seen as follows:

- agree that assessment is taking place;

- agree the criteria to be used;

- identify behaviour that is not to the required standard;

- specify areas in which change or improvement is required;

- define what action is needed to change or improve behaviour;

- plan how the action is to be implemented;

- agree how change or improvement is to be monitored and reassessed.

These principles can be applied to both task-related and process-related behaviours. To achieve the latter, however, requires the manager to think carefully about the dynamics of the particular work group and the relevant features of the organisation's culture. It also requires that assessors are clear in their own thinking about the way in which they perceive others and the criteria they are applying. Questions need to be answered about whether these criteria conform to those of the organisation, whether they are being applied equally and equitably to all members of staff and whether they are valid (ie are they really related to organisational effectiveness) or are they products of historically grounded, but no longer appropriate standards?

## Non-punishment

As with the allocation or denial of rewards, made on the basis of implicit or covert criteria, the decision not to subject an individual to disciplinary or punitive action may be taken. The reasons for making these decisions can be based on rational, longer-term grounds.

---

*Example 3.4*

The case of Jim springs to mind. Jim is brilliant, an inventive genius. However, he is totally incapable of complying with the organisation's rules. His time-keeping is random, his ability to exceed his budget huge, his administration *ad hoc* and his personal hygiene somewhat lacking. All attempts to get him to comply with both procedures and accepted standards of behaviour had failed dismally. Nevertheless, everyone agreed that he should be tolerated – without him the company would not be able to stay ahead of its field in product development. He was irreplaceable.

---

In other situations the reasons may not be so clear or acceptable. Take the service manager in Example 3.5

---

### Example 3.5

He ran the department badly for some time. Standards dropped, followed by a loss of clients. Staff became disaffected and demotivated. One by one, they found other jobs. Eventually the manager was replaced by another brought in from elsewhere in the organisation. The newcomer was faced with an almost impossible task as the old manager had not been subjected to any formal punishment for his obvious failure. Instead he was demoted, within the department, but was allowed to maintain all the trappings of his previous status – car, telephone allowance and salary. No explanation was offered to the remaining staff and the reasons for this course of action were not apparent. They were left to draw their own conclusions. The end result, unsurprisingly, was a greater loss of morale and a very difficult situation for the new manager to recover. What criteria were used for assessing the original manager's performance? Would the same measures and standards be applied to others? How great a trade-off was needed between the cost of keeping the individual in the organisation and the cost of losing him? What was the real cost of the non-decision?

---

There is a proper place for punishment in organisations. However, discipline can and needs to be regarded differently to formal penal (disciplinary) measures. While both are aimed at effecting some change in behaviour, one takes a corrective stance; the other is more consensual. Both need some agreement from the individual concerned for the action to be effective. The former, however, tends to acquire that agreement through compliance rather than the commitment which can be gained with the latter. We recognise that there is a place for both in organisations. Two reasons can be given. First, for an organisation to survive and prosper, it requires some standards and ways of enforcing those norms. Secondly, work is based on a legal contract. Some way of remedying breaches of that contract's explicit or implicit terms needs to exist.

## REPORTS

There are many ways in which reports of one person are made to another. It is not uncommon for the subject of conversation between two people to be concerned with a third party. Even at work, comments are made about an individual's behaviour and judgements based upon them. As we have seen above, this information is stored and used in the formation of perceptions, and can be the subject of error, bias and distortion. If a manager is not careful, it is possible to believe the reports of others in preference to gathering one's own data from its primary source – the other person in question.

References supplied and used in recruitment and selection provide an ideal example. It is usual for an applicant for a job to be asked to supply the name of someone who is willing and able to give a reference or testimonial. This is the third party's assessment of the subject's ability to perform the job for which they are applying. References have long been seen as suspect. Libel laws have tended to make the writers of such documents wary of telling the truth – whatever that may be. A lot can be said between the lines and by inference. Good references can be written for staff the organisation wants to lose and bad ones given to those it wants to keep.

There is a place for asking a previous employer to confirm certain matters, but wise managers should ask whether someone else's opinion of the applicant's potential performance carries more weight than their own assessment. If reliable forms of assessment and data gathering are used by the organisation in its selection procedure, references need only be used for confirmation. A bad reference can ignore the effects the situation had on an individual's performance and a good reference can actually say nothing about the person concerned. It should also be remembered that, as part of the perception processes, an individual searches to confirm their own constructs and implicit personality theories, rejecting discounting evidence. It is easy, therefore, to interpret someone else's words in the desired way.

In saying this we must acknowledge that the custom of asking for and supplying references is widespread and traditional. Most managers will find themselves required at some point to write a reference for a member of their staff. This will mean that some form of assessment needs to take place. Some organisations supply information about the job in question. This can make the task easier, but it still requires the manager to make judgements in the context of another (unknown) organisation.

Other reports are requested by external organisations, and in very large organisations, other sections. These can range from the very confidential (some domestic situations require contact to be made with an individual's employer), to requests confirming employment details. We will not dwell too long on these as the same principles regarding the writing of references apply.

# HUMAN RESOURCE AUDIT

Most of the opportunities for assessment we have discussed so far are aimed at the assessment of the individual. The only other we have mentioned is the assessment of a management team's performance. Other opportunities do exist to assess the performance of groups and the whole organisation. For the want of a better phrase, we have decided to use the term 'human resource audit' to describe these.

Any occasion that requires an organisation to take stock of its overall strengths and weaknesses can fall into this category. Such cases could include expansion either through diversification or an increase in capacity. An organisation will look to what is needed to achieve the objective and decide whether additional staff or skills are required. Before that decision can be made, however, an organisation should look at what it already has, though this does not always occur. Most people have talents they are not applying to their current job, have the potential to apply their existing talents more effectively or to develop and/or acquire them, given the opportunity. An organisation ignores its existing staff at its peril. Rejecting or failing to acknowledge the skills of its existing workforce at a time of growth can lead to a drop in morale and disaffection at the very time the organisation wants and needs the full commitment of staff.

Retraction, although the opposite situation, presents similar decisions. What core skills does the organisation need and want to retain? If the reduction in capacity is to be achieved through redundancy, how are these judgements to be made? What criteria will be used for selecting which jobs are to be shed, which individuals need to be retained and who should go? In both cases the organisation is also able to choose which skills are central to its operation and which are peripheral.

Some writers, for example Clutterbuck (1985), suggest that a spider's web will be the shape of employment in the future. Key skills will be obtained and retained through contracted employment, as now. Transient skills or skills required from time to time will be obtained on a contractual arrangement. Temporary, part-time or contracted staff will increase in number. If this is to be the case, organisations will need to improve their abilities to define and assess which skills fall into which category. It will also be necessary to make more precise judgements of an individual's ability to perform those skills to the standards required by that employer. Decisions will be needed regarding the renewal of contracts and the rewards offered in return for labour. The move to knowledge-based work rather than manual skills also challenges traditional methods of assessment. The need for quality, rather than quantity, also stretches the commonly used methods.

To be truly strategic, an organisation needs to develop a vision of where it is going, and to have shared and tangible goals to be achieved along the road to organisational success. From this vision plans of action can be drawn up which should contain a provision for contingencies and a full assessment of the organisation's strengths and weaknesses. An assessment should be made of all the resources available for deployment. Taking stock of its financial assets, its physical resources and gaps can be done using quantative methods. The auditing of intangible resources is more difficult; goodwill and reputation are difficult to price. Some brand names have a figure attached to their worth, but this tends to be restricted to a very few household names.

Human resources are even more difficult to cost. The audit needs to include both existing skills and potential – and the employee's contribution as a unique individual to the organisation's strengths and weaknesses. Organisational achievement is never the product of one individual's efforts. The effect of teams has been known since the days of the Roman Empire. Synergy is the product of each person's contribution, moulded by humanity. To use this asset strategically needs careful thought, planning and assessment. But it can be done. The techniques of assessment given later in this book can be applied both to groups and to a whole organisation. The main requirement for success is for the need for a systematic, strategic audit of the human resource to be recognised and clear criteria to be established. Then it is possible to assess the skills currently available and the gaps that exist between them and those needed, using well-known and acceptable techniques. When this has been done plans can be made for acquiring those skills needed as a result of a lack of skills or for shedding those no longer needed.

## Access and control of information

It is not possible to finish this chapter on the opportunities for assessing skills without including some consideration of the human factors involved. It is very easy to discuss skills as if they exist in abstraction. Skills are the product of people's talents, attributes and efforts. They can be very personal and the source of individual satisfaction and pride. The assessment of skills, therefore, cannot be divorced from the assessment of the person. We have already made some comments about the assessment of personality; this is not the same as judging a person. Personality factors are inherent and, it is accepted, they are difficult to change. People's behaviour and the way in which they apply their skills can be subject to individual choice. The use of skills can also be the source of feelings of self-worth and value. Any assessment process should take account of these feelings, other emotions and self-efficacy. We will discuss these in greater depth later, but it is appropriate to pass comment here about the power structures, the strength of the process and the value of the emergent information.

## Ownership

Who owns information about one person's performance? We have already said that this information is sensitive and that the assessment process needs to be handled with care and consideration. The individual being assessed, at the very least, is likely to be interested in the outcome and probably the criteria against which their performance is being assessed. The question, though, about entitlement to that information is one which each organisation needs to answer for itself, taking into account its existing and its desired culture, and the different reasons for conducting the assessment.

It can be argued, convincingly, that the assessments made for recruitment and selection are the property of the employing organisation. Certainly when it is an employers' market, candidates are 'processed' – assessed, selected or rejected as if they were any other commodity. Opportunities for receiving the results of the assessment are usually confined to internal candidates, if they were offered at all.

Also, the introduction of more systematic techniques, such as personality testing and assessment centres, requires candidates to supply more information about themselves than at the traditional interview. As a consequence, there is a rightful expectation that some information regarding outcome and performance will be given back. Therefore, this information cannot be regarded as the sole property of the organisation; the individual also has some legitimate claim on it and the right to feedback.

Assessments done as part of one's employment are different as the relationship is ongoing. The selection process may be the only time an individual comes into contact with a part of the organisation or assessor. Assessments made for promotion, performance review, training and development needs, or punishment purposes are part of the continuing relationship between employer/manager/employee. The power relationships are different from those in the selection process and the working relationship is a product of the personalities involved and the organisation's culture. Different levels of ownership of the information generated by assessment will be appropriate to different organisations and/or sections within them. In some situations it is right that the organisation retains control and ownership over the assessment results, especially in the case of formal disciplinary cases.

But if assessment is to contribute to the development and improvement of performance, both the criteria and results of assessment should be known to the individual concerned. Some of the techniques we mention cannot hope to be effective, or even work at all, without the willing participation of the employees involved. For a thorough job analysis to be compiled, the person who knows the job best (ie, the person doing it) needs to contribute. Similarly, if appraisal is to be open and honest, individuals need to know what they are required to achieve, how well or otherwise they have succeeded, and what they need to be doing differently either to improve or achieve more. They also need to know that their contribution is valued and needed. Without knowledge of the criteria and the assessment, the individual is shooting at stars. In some cases, especially if they are being used as an aid to management development, assessment centres can benefit from having the participants involved in the definition of the criteria and the development of the scenarios used for the activities.

## Power

The nature of the employment contract implies a power relationship between the person employed and the person who represents the employer. The latter are now usually managers, who are also employees but have some authority as a result of their structural position. This gives a basis for a power relationship to exist, no matter how egalitarian the organisation tries to be. There is no escape from the legal nature of the contract.

Sometimes the structural authority confers expert authority as well, whether this is deserved or not. Thus, it may be assumed that the manager knows best. While this may be fictitious, it is nevertheless important in considering the comparative values of opinion during assessment. If it assumed that assessors have greater, better judgement in one area, this can be transferred to another. Thus, their assessment of an individual has to be right. When this assumption is coupled with the sort of organisation that keeps the criteria secret, a large amount of power is given to the manager making the assessments. The negative aspect of this is that such an uneven distribution of power between the assessor and the assessee can lead to the assessment being viewed with some degree of trepidation, even fear. Despite statements to the contrary, overcoming this perception among assessees, especially during the introduction of a new technique, requires hard work on behalf of those with the power.

## Access

Linked to power and ownership is the question of who has the right to see the outcome of assessments. If individuals have rights of access to their personal files, it follows that they also have the right to see the results of any assessment. It is likely also that other people have rights to see and use information contained in personal files and records. Obviously this extends to personnel staff, who should operate under a strict code of confidentiality as a matter of course. But there are occasions when both senior and other managers may need to see the files.

Files of this nature tend to contain a variety of information, ranging from factual detail, which can be totally uncontroversial to very personal matters which may or may not relate directly to the individual's present employment. (An example could be a request for unpaid leave of absence to deal with a now resolved domestic crisis.) How much of this type of information should be available and how far should its availability extend? It is up to each organisation to resolve these questions in their own context.

## Use

In relation to assessment data, however, another question is raised regarding the use of assessment information obtained for one purpose being used for another. For example, should the record of an appraisal discussion be available when promotion or payment issues are being considered? And if it is being used, should the individual concerned know about it? Again, it is the culture and nature of the organisation in question that will resolve these issues. Consideration needs to be given to the integrity of the assessor and the validity of any assurances that have been given to the assessees. If they have been told that the results of personality tests will be destroyed and find that they have been used to influence the results of the merit payments for the year, those individuals are unlikely to trust the assessor who gave the undertaking or the organisation in the future. Such actions will also have a negative effect on the general level of morale. Staff tell each other about these betrayals.

*Example 3.6*

We know of one organisation that was extremely punitive in the way in which staff were treated. As part of an attempt to influence the culture a series of career development workshops were offered to its junior managers. The only way in which the managers would agree to participate in the centres was as a result of cast-iron guarantees being given that the outcomes of the assessments would not be disclosed to anyone that had not been directly involved in the running of the centre. The individuals were promised that, if they so wished, they would be able to witness the shredding of the paperwork. This is an extreme but real example of the perceived value of such information and the fear of penalty that can exist in organisations.

It is also possible that information collected by one process contains some bias as a result of the technique used. A technique can only assess what it is designed to assess. It is possible that later judgements are made about aspects of someone's performance that were not covered by the mode of assessment. It need not be evidence of a skill that is lacking in the individual (see below). It is also possible for the information to be interpreted in a way that was not intended.

*Example 3.7*

An example of the former would be a criterion, say delegation, that was not among the key criteria used for a particular manager skill assessment centre. It was generally assumed that a skilled manager is able to delegate effectively. The omission of comment on this area in the feedback report could be taken by a manager who was not involved to mean that the individual had not demonstrated these skills and therefore is an ineffective manager.

Misinterpretation can result from using the same terms to mean different things. We all know what we mean by good communication skills – don't we? Value judgements also mean that criteria are given different weighting by different people at different times. People skills could be important at times of rapid change, while at times of stability it may be administrative skills that are needed. Assessments that are made during the first phase of an organisation's life would inevitably place emphasis on the former at the expense of the latter.

The way in which aspects perceived by different people are prone to the attribution of bias and errors was mentioned early on when we discussed the processes of perception. These should be thought of in this context as well as during the assessment process itself.

## *Longevity*

We have referred to different emphases being placed on assessment information at different times. Additionally, the age of an assessment needs to be taken into account in its subsequent usage. Even if care is taken to ensure that the information is used consistently for one purpose alone and that access is controlled, the assessor using old information should take account of the fact that people change with time. If a main use of assessment is to aid development it is only reasonable to expect that development may have taken place. As a result it is hoped that the person concerned will have effected some change and/or improvement to their performance.

Old information should therefore be used for what it is – historic information grounded in a point of time. The criteria used for the assessment should also be referred to and the two seen in the context of the time at which the assessment was made.

## SUMMARY

In this chapter we have looked at the following.

- Some of the occasions when assessments can and do get made about individuals at work. We cannot hope to be exclusive and cover every occasion. Undoubtedly you will know of others from your own experience of being assessed, making assessments of others or listening to tales of others' experiences.

- While describing the opportunities, we have given some indications of good and bad practice. We have all come across incidents when a good technique has been badly applied. This can do damage to the technique's validity, to the individual being assessed, to the assessor's credibility and reputation and to the organisation. Sometimes, it is better not to start at all than to do it badly.

- Mainly assessments are made about individuals and their separate performance in a job and potential abilities in future jobs. We discussed briefly the assessment of a management team and the contribution this can make to the development of the organisation. This will be covered in greater depth later in the book.

- Guidance on the use and storage of information generated by assessment. While these factors need to be considered in relation to the organisation's other practices, there are certain points that need to be taken into account which affect the subsequent value of the assessment information.

- The ownership and power relations that are implicit in assessment have been discussed. These will be mentioned later at greater length when we consider the impact the assessment process can have on the individuals involved.

Next, we will describe the various techniques for conducting assessments. Our main concern is the use and design of assessment centres so this technique will be described in detail. We will also discuss other issues which, in addition to having a place in assessment in their own right, can be used as component parts of assessment centres.

Regardless of which technique is used there are some general principles that need to be incorporated into the design and use of assessment methods. These and the principles applying to the specific technique under consideration will be discussed.

# 4

# What should be assessed?

## JOB ANALYSIS

Job analysis is not only central to effective personnel selection, but to a variety of other purposes; including training, job evaluation, personnel appraisal, job design, human resource planning, and health and safety policies. It involves collecting and analysing information about a job, and is the crucial first stage in the whole staffing process (Example 4.1). Much of the impetus behind recent developments in job analysis has come from America, as the courts there have tended to regard selection procedures based on a rigorous job analysis as necessary to reduce bias against women and minority groups.

The information collected in a job analysis provides the basis for the job description which includes the context in which the job is performed and its associated tasks, responsibilities and duties. Job analysis methodologies can be quite complex and may be divided into task-oriented and worker-oriented analyses.

Task-oriented analyses generate a list of required activities, or tasks, derived from observations and interviews with job holders and supervisors. This list is often made into a questionnaire and given to a larger sample of job holders, who rate the tasks listed in terms of their importance and frequency. This list of tasks can then be used to generate job samples for selection procedures.

Unfortunately, task-oriented job analyses tend to be cast in terms specific to a particular job and do not say very much about the skills or characteristics an employee needs to possess to do the job adequately. Worker-oriented job analyses focus much more directly on the skills or behaviour required to perform the job. Instead of describing a manager's work, for example, in terms of recruiting and selecting staff and chairing meetings, a worker-oriented job analysis will describe it in such terms as the need for oral communication, interpersonal and analytical skills.

One of the aims of conducting a job analysis and producing a job description is to specify the skills and characteristics needed to do the job (the personnel specification). Producing a statement of work tasks is insufficient. Moving from the job description to the personnel specification is often left to intuition or guesswork, unless this link is made more rigorously. Some more worker-oriented job analyses do try to bridge this gap between job description and personnel specification more systematically. We will look in particular at two such techniques, the critical incidents technique and the repertory grid technique. Smith and Robertson (1986) or Pearn and Kandola (1988) provide more detail about job analysis techniques.

## Techniques of job analysis

### Observation

Employees are observed as they perform the job, and information is collected and analysed about the tasks performed. A good example of this method is Mintzberg's (1973) study of managerial work, involving the shadowing of a small number of executives. Observation is clearly time-consuming and costly to carry out.

### Interviews

Present job holders and their supervisors are interviewed in order to ascertain the main purposes of the job, the activities it involves and the relationships it entails. Interviewing can, however, be time-consuming to organise and carry out, though it may be undertaken with groups.

### Diaries

Job holders are asked to keep a detailed log of their activities over a period of time. The method is most suitable for more complex jobs involving analytical rather than manual skills, and it should be noted that not all diary-keepers will make their entries accurately. Some may exaggerate the time spent on 'important' tasks, and diaries are often difficult and time-consuming to analyse and interpret. One classic example of a diary study of managerial work is that of Stewart (1967).

### Questionnaires

In this method employees answer a set of questions about the tasks they perform, their frequency and their importance.

Producing questionnaires can be tedious, involving much preparation, field trials to ensure that no important activity is omitted, and large samples. Questionnaires also close down the options available as they limit the questions asked. A number of general-purpose scales have been developed, however, which can be used with many jobs. These include some American scales, such as McCormick's position analysis questionnaire.

This is perhaps the most widely used questionnaire, containing 187 items split into 6 categories. It can be completed by the job holder, the job holder's boss or a job analyst, and a set of weightings can enable an estimation of the skills needed. This allows links to be made to the personnel specification. It is not very appropriate for managerial jobs, where the related professional and managerial position questionnaire (PMPQ) is more relevant. We will discuss later job analyses conducted in the health service and also a brewery which both used this questionnaire, alongside repertory grid and critical incident techniques.

Recent British developments in job analysis include the job components inventory which was developed at the Sheffield University Social and Applied Psychology Unit by Michael Banks and others. This involves around 400 items covering 7 sections: tools and equipment; physical and conceptual requirements; mathematical skills; communication skills; decision-making and responsibility; job conditions; and perceived job characteristics. It has been extensively used in youth training, and is particularly useful for skilled, semi-skilled and unskilled work. It is less useful for managerial jobs.

A case study of the use of British job analysis methods for personnel selection in a brewery is given in Example 4.1, below. It includes another job analysis technique, the critical incident method, which will be discussed in greater detail later.

---

*Example 4.1*

A large British brewery wished to recruit new employees to new higher-speed filling lines. The brewery wanted the new job analysed and relevant job-related criteria identified so that person specifications for each job or group of jobs could be drafted. The analysts used observation and interviews with experienced workers, the job components inventory and the position analysis questionnaire. They also used critical incident interviews with supervisors to gain more information on the skills required in the more complex jobs. Supervisors were asked for descriptions of real job behaviour which they had observed and which they felt was more effective and less effective. For each group a person specification was developed identifying the critical skills and abilities required.

For each of the 22 skills identified, an interview checklist was developed providing guidelines on the types of interview questions to ask and how to interpret responses, as well as which aptitude tests to use. The resulting selection procedure seemed to appoint better quality staff needing less training time, and to be fair to ethnic minorities in terms of proportion hired.

*Source*: Pearn and Kandola (1989)

## Critical incident technique

This technique (Flanagan, 1954) requires observers who see people frequently doing the job such as supervisors, clients, peers or subordinates. Observers are asked to describe incidents of effective and ineffective behaviour over the past year; that is, occasions when job holders did something well, and occasions when job holders did something badly. A typical format might be as follows:

> I am analysing the job of (secretary, supervisor, manager etc) to identify what makes the difference between an effective and an ineffective performer. By effective performance I mean behaviour you have seen over the last 6–12 months which you might wish all employees to perform under similar circumstances. By ineffective performance I mean behaviour which if it occurred repeatedly would cause you to doubt the competence of the individual. Please do not give any names.

For each incident, the analyst will ask questions like these.

- What were the circumstances or background?

- What exactly did the employee do that was effective or ineffective? For example, exactly how did he or she show initiative?

- How is this incident an example of effective or ineffective behaviour?

An interviewee might be asked to report up to ten effective or ineffective incidents in changing situations. The critical incident technique has the advantage that it focuses on those aspects of a job that are crucial to success, and allows behavioural incidents to be grouped into more general dimensions. It also allows performance dimensions to be operationalised in relation to performance appraisal systems, and the dimensions can also be directly related to the skills and qualities required by the personnel specification.

## Repertory grid technique

This technique, derived from Kelly's personal construct theory (Kelly, 1958), is also useful in highlighting those behaviours associated with effective performance. For example, effective, less effective and average job holders might be compared and contrasted in terms of how they do their job, with discussions followed by such questions as, 'Can you tell me exactly what that means?' and 'What would I see someone actually doing?'. For example, the effective manager of a management development unit might have business awareness, the ability to sell ideas, the ability to pull resources together, the ability to come up with new initiatives, the ability to integrate with other groups, the ability to work well with the team and the ability to encourage others. A less effective one might show less business awareness, and while technically excellent might spend time out of the office and away from the team.

The advantage of the repertory grid technique is that it can elicit the skills needed to do the job from knowledgeable observers, with no constraints placed on the answers given, unlike questionnaires. The information obtained may be expressed in terms of a grid or matrix with skills down the side and tasks along the top. This information can be computer analysed for trends and the jobs represented graphically.

## Strategic job analysis

Conventional job analysis tends to assume that the job is a stable collection of tasks, and that the specification of the tasks to be performed and the knowledge, skills and abilities required for performance are for a job that currently exists. However, given technological change, strategic redirection and internationalisation, this is unlikely to be the case. To take such trends into account, it will be necessary to identify what skills will be required of jobs in the future. Information about the future may be collected in a workshop where participants identify the kinds of issues in the job, the organisation and the wider environment that might affect the way the job will go in the future. Such issues might be demographic changes, changes in the labour market, computerisation of the job, equal opportunity legislation, the impact of the Single European Market, better training, the predicted state of the economy, possible mergers and acquisitions, or a move from a quantity to a quality strategy. A brainstorming session, for example, might generate various future issues that could affect a managerial job. These might include:

- computerisation;

- changes in work group size;

- more women and black workers;

- changes in location;

- changes in markets;

- increased Europeanisation and internationalisation;

- changes in work quantity;

- changes in product range;

- introduction of new selection and training programmes;

- changes in skills, expectations or attitudes of employees;

- changes in corporate culture (eg from production to marketing);

- mergers and takeovers;

- changes in levels of responsibility.

It may then be possible to rate the target job in the future in terms of task importance or time spent. This allows the tasks and knowledge, skills and abilities developed for the present job to be re-rated in the light of these changes. Comparison of present and future ratings can allow an assessment of the degree to which these changes are significant. Such a procedure may be useful also for jobs that do not yet exist, such as in new facilities to produce new goods or services.

Such procedures may be costly, involving a considerable investment of time, skill and energy, and perhaps requiring external specialists. They may seem useful only for large organisations. But any job analysis should include a consideration of future trends.

Example 4.2 shows how jobs within the personal financial services sector, especially those of branch managers, have been changing and the new skills involved.

---

*Example 4.2*

The UK financial services sector has been experiencing unprecedented change, challenge and uncertainty in the 1980s and 1990s. Many of the traditional divisions between companies in this sector have broken down, under the pressure of 'Big Bang' of 1986, deregulation, the rapid development of information technology, the internationalisation of trading, greater international competition, the growth of institutional investors, and greater sophistication among consumers. Managers in this sector now need new skills, and competition for talented people has increased. Some of the challenges and changes faced by companies in this sector include:

- increased competition;
- less differentiation between products and companies;
- less standardisation of products;
- expanding product ranges;
- shorter product life-cycles;
- rapid changes in product ranges;

- greater product innovation;
- mergers and acquisitions;
- ventures into non-traditional areas;
- greater flexibility;
- greater customer awareness and sophistication;
- greater customer focus;
- greater emphasis on efficiency and quality;
- greater emphasis on team working and problem solving.

*The personal finance sector*
In particular, retail banks, building societies and insurance companies have competed fiercely for personal deposits, investment lending and money transmission services. There have been severe pressures on extensive and expensive branch networks to change their role, especially with developments in new technology. Some smaller organisations have sought 'niche' markets, with larger organisations trying to compete across a wide range of products and markets. All of this has contributed to a shift in the role of the branch manager from that of lender and administrator to that of marketeer, seller and entrepreneur of a wider range of products and services. Many branches have aimed at becoming 'one-stop' financial services organisations, offering such services as money transmission, lending, mortgages, personal insurance, savings and investment services, and estate agency, not always successfully. Branch layout and opening hours have changed to a 'retail shopping' format, with an emphasis on approachability, user-friendliness and flexibility of response.

All of these changes in mission, culture and values have led to significant programmes of organisational design, recruitment and selection, performance appraisal, cultural change, and management and organisation development. Organisations have needed to develop new skills and abilities against a background of fierce competition for talent, salary escalation, the problematic retention of key people, the integration of diverse skills, and the growth in importance of human resources management (HRM) policy and practice.

*Managerial skills and competencies*
Managerial jobs have become increasingly outward looking, market-focused, and team-oriented, with greater room for discretion. The needs to manage professionals and technical specialists, and to engage in strategic planning, have also increased. These changes have required managers who:

- are flexible and adaptable;
- tolerate ambiguity;
- show commercial awareness;
- demonstrate 'helicopter vision';
- show an ability to learn;
- are decisive and resilient;

- have good communication skills;
- possess good interpersonal skills;
- demonstrate good marketing and selling skills;
- have a broad vision.

Though the traditional criteria of technical competence and professionalism remain important in promotion, they only do so in conjunction with commercial and managerial skills. What kinds of skills will be required in future jobs, and the development of specific future job profiles and key post criteria have become increasingly important. This has required the effective identification of the skills and qualities needed to meet current and future needs, and a more comprehensive inventory of the skills, abilities and aspirations of current employees. In the past, success has often been based on technical competence, single career paths, upward progression, job experience, and job rotation and generic skills, with succession planning based on 'what has been needed'. Future potential has been based on an informal identification of future potential, often not clearly distinguished from the appraisal of current job performance, rather than on a profile of future skills needed.

More recently, companies have begun to develop more sophisticated assessment techniques and a greater linkage between performance appraisal, staff development and business strategy. Some organisations have recognised the need for a 'tiered' recruitment strategy and 'tiered' career paths, in contrast to the former assumption that every entry job gave access to a single career path to the top, at least for males. Some companies now recruit into specific basic jobs rather than careers, though with some possibilities for transfer and with different career paths for different businesses and different product life cycles. This has involved:

- early identification of potential, performance, skills, aspirations and development needs;
- early identification of career paths;
- tiering recruits as corporate resources;
- corporate management of careers;
- definition of job requirements in terms of future skills requirements;
- jobs profiled in terms of skills and behaviour;
- more sophisticated assessment techniques;
- continuous assessment tied closely to job profiles and business needs at business unit and corporate levels.

In later cases we will examine in some detail some organisations in this sector which have attempted to respond to these challenges.

*Source* M Higgs (1988) *Management Development Strategy in the Financial Sector*

## The personnel specification

One of the reasons for conducting a job analysis is to derive a personnel specification. Often, however, what is being sought in a candidate for a post is defined very imprecisely. It is usually a combination of abilities, aptitudes, skills, qualities, personality traits, interests, motivations, styles and competences, with little clear distinction between these terms. It may be that all have their place, but each needs to be specified and each is best assessed by a different technique. We will primarily be concerned with the measurement of skills or competences, especially managerial skills and competences. These are, we feel, best assessed by certain techniques, such as biodata, work samples, interviews and assessment centres. We will be focusing on these and will be giving them extended treatment. However, we need to comment on other personal attributes or qualities that might be measured or assessed, to complement the assessment of skills and competences, and help contribute to a whole picture of the person. Such attributes often call for specific measurement techniques, in particular, the use of psychometric tests.

## COGNITIVE ABILITY AND PSYCHOMETRIC TESTS

'Psychometric' literally refers to 'mental measurement', and psychometric tests attempt to make objectives standardised measures of behaviour. They are often divided into tests of general intelligence, tests of specific aptitudes and tests of personality, but tests purporting to measure other qualities or attributes also exist.

Most of the valid and reliable psychometric tests are available only to suitably qualified, trained personnel, in order to ensure that tests are used appropriately. Given the proliferation of occupational tests in recent years, it is best to consult a chartered psychologist, the British Psychological Society and the National Foundation for Educational Research before using such tests. From January 1991, the British Psychological Society are offering a new Certificate of Competence in Occupational Testing, which will only be available to those whose competence has been affirmed by suitably qualified chartered psychologists, and such people can have their names entered on a Register of Competence in Occupational Testing. Standards of competence cover such areas as relevant underpinning knowledge, task skills, task management skills, contingency management skills, contextual skills and instrumental skills. A set of training modules, based on the requirements of this Certificate of Competence, has been developed (Bartram 1991).

Measures of cognitive or mental abilities are increasingly used to provide data for decisions about selection, placement, training and development. This is not the place to enter into debates about the nature of intelligence, the relative contributions of heredity and environment, or the best way to measure mental abilities in the workplace. However, most, if not all, jobs often involve considerable amounts of information processing, analysis and logical deduction, and therefore mental abilities contribute greatly to successful job performance.

Most research conducted over several decades has shown that cognitive ability tests are among the best predictors of job performance that we have. Computerised testing may increase the importance and use of occupational testing. However, at present, the major measures of cognitive ability used in organisational environments in Britain in the 1990s would seem to be the following.

## General ability tests

One of the most popular tests in British industry of general intelligence is Heim's AH4 test, a relatively short test presenting verbal, numerical, perceptual and spatial problems. For application to populations of above average ability, the AH5 and AH6 are also useful. Many other tests of global ability and of specific mental abilities are also available, such as tests of mechanical or spatial abilities.

## Tests of critical reasoning

An American test of critical reasoning is the Watson-Glazer critical thinking appraisal; two related British tests are the Saville and Holdsworth verbal critical reasoning ability test and their numerical critical reasoning ability test. All three tests were devised to assess the ability to assimilate information, analyse content, identify assumptions and make logical inferences, such as whether any conclusions drawn in fact apply. All three are suitable for managers, but the British tests not only provide relevant UK norms for various types of managers, but also include items drawn from managerial environments.

## Specific aptitudes and aptitude tests

There are a variety of tests which measure aptitudes for specific occupations, especially clerical occupations. These often combine numerical and verbal ability tests and tests of spelling, vocabulary and comprehension. More specific tests have been developed for word processors and for computer jobs.

## Interests and values

There are several tests of personal values and of occupational interests that are of particular help in the careers counselling, vocational guidance and career development area, such as the Strong vocational interest blank (or the Strong-Campbell interest inventory) or the Kuder preference record and the Rothwell-Miller interest blank. Saville and Holdsworth, in Britain, have also introduced general occupational interest inventories, advanced occupational interest inventories and managerial interest inventories.

Most reviews have concluded that though such tests are very useful in a career development context, they are rather poor predictors of job success.

## Motives

Personnel specifications often include lists of motives and motivations, and motivation clearly has an influence on job success. Research by McClelland in particular has shown that people differ in their needs for affiliation, power and achievement, and that such motives are linked to different specific occupations. Such motives may be measured by self-report inventories or by projective tests, where versions of the thematic apperception test or picture story exercise are often used. In these, subjects are usually shown rather vague pictures and asked to say what is happening, what has happened and what will happen in the future. The subject's responses are then content-analysed to discern the main motives exhibited.

Recent American research has shown that 'managerial motivation' consisting of the 'leadership motive pattern' – low need for affiliation, high need for power, moderate need for achievement, high inhibition of activity – seems to be associated with managerial success in large corporations, but not necessarily with success in technical or professional settings. High need for achievement, rather than a high need to influence others, seems to be associated with entrepreneurial success.

## Personality traits

Personnel specifications typically contain many lists of personal traits like assertiveness, self-confidence, decisiveness, enthusiasm or stability, realism or independence. Recruiters and those involved in making staffing decisions have often tried to assess these at interview. A variety of psychometric tests, often derived from clinical settings, have been developed to try and assess personality traits more objectively. Many people remain suspicious of the claims of personality testers, and many psychologists feel that they underplay the contributions made by situations to behaviour. However, their usage in British industry for selection, promotion and career development has been growing. The rekindling of interest in personality tests has in part been sparked by the development of tests specifically designed to enable assessments to be made among the adult working population with much higher 'face validity' and acceptability than many clinical tests. It is probably the case that the major two personality tests used for selection in Britain are the following.

## Cattell's 16 personality factors (16PF)

This test identifies 16 personality factors and generates a personality profile which needs to be carefully interpreted. It was originally based on American general/clinical research, but norms for a variety of British work contexts now exist.

## Saville and Holdsworths' occupational personality questionnaire (OPQ)

This is a recently developed British test with a greater work orientation, available in a number of formats and generating a personal profile very suitable for organisational decision-making. Computerised versions are available and data on preferred team roles and leadership styles can also be provided.

Both these tests are of great value in personal feedback and development contexts, but should not be over-used in personnel selection situations. They can be a valuable supplement to data gathered at interview or in assessment centres. They may often be used to compare personal profiles against the profiles of people already in the job or target position and rated as successful in that position. There is then the temptation to reject candidates whose personality profiles do not match those of existing incumbents. This may lead to racial or gender bias, given the likelihood that senior positions will already be held by white men, and this approach assumes that the styles or personalities that led to success in the past will lead to success in the future. Given that many organisations have changed in many ways in the face of changing environmental demands, it is likely that they will require different kinds of people in the future.

## Cognitive or managerial styles

Another increasingly popular area is in the assessment of cognitive, leadership, interpersonal, team or managerial styles of behaviour, rather than levels of performance. The implication here is that, unlike the situation with abilities, there are different ways of doing things. These different ways are not necessarily better or worse, effective or ineffective, but involve different preferences. Different organisational cultures and value systems may favour different styles of behaviour. Areas of interest include the following.

## Creativity styles

A relatively new measure here is the Kirton adaptation inventory, a measure of tendency to innovate and break boundaries or adapt within existing boundaries. Innovators may lack discipline but generate original solutions; adaptors prefer order and prefer developing and implementing others' ideas. Both styles are seen as necessary and equally important, but individuals, having different preferred styles, work best in different phases of a project and in different environments. The inventory does not seem suitable for selection purposes, but may be useful for team-building, development, counselling and stress management purposes.

## Team roles – Belbin's team role preferences

This was developed in Britain from an analysis of successful teams and of the preferred team roles adopted by team members. Though sometimes used to select individuals to existing teams, it is mainly used in team-building, and in management and organisational development. It is also possible to identify the Belbin team roles from an analysis of individuals' OPQ scores.

## Interpersonal styles – FIRO B and F

These tests are concerned with preferred styles of interacting with others, and with people's behaviour and their feelings about their behaviour. Individual needs for inclusion, control and affection are identified, and the tests seem most useful for team-building and personal development.

## Myers-Briggs type inventory (MBTI)

The Myers-Briggs type inventory (MBTI), though American in origin, is very popular in British practice to identify ways in which people assess and respond to their environment, based on early work by Carl Jung. The dimensions identified are: extraversion versus introversion; sensation versus intuition (preference for acting on data or on hunches); thinking versus feeling (rationality versus emotion in making judgements); and judgment versus perception (judgemental attitudes as against generalised awareness). Managers often tend towards an extraversion, sensation, thinking, judgemental profile, while research scientists and technical specialists may tend towards an introversion, intuition, thinking, perception one.

Promoting the best research scientist or technical specialist to research and development manager or head of unit is clearly not necessarily the most effective strategy. Different managerial levels, contexts and functions may require different ways of processing information, and different teams may require different styles. The MBTI seems clearly useful for counselling, feedback and team development, if not for selection. There is some evidence that many women managers adopt a different style to male managers, one that is more 'visionary' or less 'traditional', according to research at Cranfield by Vinnicombe.

## Learning styles

Other inventories have attempted to assess how people learn best, such as the learning-style inventories of Kolb (1974) and Honey and Mumford (1986).

## MEASURING SKILLS: WORK SAMPLES AND ASSESSMENT CENTRES

In order that skills may be assessed, applicants are required to do something that we can observe and evaluate. We are concerned here with behaviour that can be learned over a relatively short period of time and directed towards achieving a goal or task. Applicant skills can often be assessed by means of work samples, where applicants are required to perform a sample of the job in question. Work sample tests are among the best predictors of job performance that we have, and have high face validity in that candidates tend to regard them more highly than paper and pencil tests. They tend to see them as fairer and more accurate than many other tests. In addition, they seem to be less discriminatory against minority groups, and have a variety of other advantages. They can provide candidates with a 'taste' of the job in question and allow them to make a more realistic assessment of their suitability for the job, and they can generate useful developmental information.

In the professional and managerial area, work samples might include in-tray exercises, oral presentations, leaderless group discussions, management games and one-to-one role-played interviews. These are often the constituent elements of an assessment centre, which is perhaps the most comprehensive method yet derived to assess rigorously managerial skills and potential. We consider that assessment centres are among the best ways we have of assessing managerial and professional skills at work, and will discuss them in some detail.

The criteria assessed at an assessment centre are often termed dimensions or competences. Since there has been increasing interest in assessing and developing competences, we need to examine this area more fully.

## Assessing competences

The term 'competence' or 'competency' has become very fashionable both in Britain and America in recent years, especially in the managerial area. In part this has been due to the activities of the Management Charter Initiative (MCI), the Training Agency, and the National Council for Vocational Qualifications (NCVQ) in Britain.

American approaches to managerial competence have been primarily designed to discover what makes for excellence or superior performance in managers. They have tended to use variants of the critical incident or assessment centre method, and have tended to see 'competence' as an 'underlying characteristic causally related to superior performance' (Boyatzis, 1982). The competences generated have been primarily behavioural, specifying the skills or qualities that a person will use to do a job. They have also often been generic, trying to describe as succinctly as possible the behaviours that all high performers may display, though in different proportions according to level or function or context.

These American approaches, in particular those of Boyatzis (1982) and Schroder (1989), have influenced British practice in many companies. Such practice is often linked to the use of assessment centres or development centres. Example 4.3 describes these approaches, and Example 4.4 their use in Manchester Airport and the National Westminster Bank.

However, the British approach championed by the Management Charter Initiative is much more linked to job performance in specific functions, and is much more geared to certification and accreditation. Here, occupational competence is defined as the ability to perform the activities within an occupation to the standards expected in employment. These standards are expressed as elements of competence plus performance criteria and range statements. The element of competence identifies a required function which the competent individual should be capable of carrying out. The performance criteria identify what acceptable performance in the function might be, while the range statements indicate the contexts in which the standards are to be met.

*Example 4.3*

*McBer/Boyatzis approach*

This originated in the desire by the American Management Association to discover what generic characteristics made for superior managerial performance. These were identified through:

- behavioural event interviews (a critical incident technique);
- picture story exercise;
- learning styles inventory.

A competency was defined as 'underlying, characteristic of a manager causally related to superior performance on the job' and the competency model was validated empirically against job performance.

The model identifies 18 generic competencies, clustered into 4 groups:

1 *Goal and action management*

—efficiency orientation
—proactivity
—impact
—diagnostic use of concepts;

2 *Directing subordinates*

—use of unilateral power
—developing others
—spontaneity;

3 *HRM*

—self-assessment
—self-control
—stamina and adaptability
—perceptual objectivity
—positive regard
—managing group process
—use of socialised power;

4 *Leadership*

—self-confidence
—conceptualisation
—logical thought
—oral presentations.

It has been used at Manchester Airport (Jackson, 1989), involving 15 of the McBer competencies and generating a profile which defined the core competencies required for superior performance by the top 23 senior managers. Job holders were assessed against the competencies in a development centre, with the development of a personal profile, feedback and personal improvement plans involving a self-development guide, in-house training and business education.

The competencies derived were:

critical reasoning
strategic visioning        what needs to be done
business know how

achievement drive
proactivity
confidence        getting the job done
control
flexibility
concern for effectiveness
direction

motivation
interpersonal skills
concern for impact
persuasion        taking people with you
influence

(Jackson, 1989)

The American conceptualisation of competences permits major roles for the assessment of competence through assessment centres, simulations and criterion-referenced interviewing, as well as in the workplace. The British approach, however, tends to lay the greatest stress on workplace assessment, and work-based portfolios or journals, followed by such methods as:

● work-based projects;

● analytical projects;

● simulations;

● oral and written questions;

● multiple choice tests;

● self-assessment.

The British approaches seem much more closely tied to specific qualifications, to accreditation and to certification. They are also closely associated with the accreditation of prior learning.

*Example 4.4*

*Schroder's approach*

This approach originally involved examining the factors which made for high performing teams in experimental simulations, later broadened to assessment centre simulations with managers. This identifies 11 'high performance competencies':

information search
concept formation
conceptual flexibility
interpersonal search
managing interaction
developmental orientation
impact
self-confidence
presentation
proactive orientation
achievement orientation

It has been used in National Westminster Bank (Cockerill, 1989) to link behavioural assessment to unit performance, build teams and cope with dynamic/complex environments. Assessments are made on the job and in assessment centres and development consists of using strengths, compensating for weaknesses, and developing one or two limitations into strengths.

## FAIR TREATMENT AND EQUAL OPPORTUNITIES

Whatever is being assessed, and however assessment is being made, it is important to ensure that people are being treated fairly and that unfair discrimination is not occurring. It is important to do this for various reasons, including:

- moral, political and ethical values concerning justice and fairness;

- avoidance of contraventions of anti-discrimination legislation;

- the utility to organisations of ensuring that the best person for the job is appointed, that personnel decisions are taken only on job-relevant grounds, and that all potential and actual staff have equal opportunity fully to utilise their talents.

It is important that assessors are aware of the relevant legislation making unfair discrimination illegal, such as the Sex Discrimination Act 1975 (as amended), the Race Relations Act 1976 and the Disabled Person (Employment) Acts of 1944 and 1958 in Britain. This legislation recognises two forms of discrimination, namely direct and indirect. Direct discrimination occurs when a person is treated less favourably than others on the grounds of their sex, race or marital status (eg 'Our clients won't want a black salesperson'; 'Women with children are unreliable'). Indirect discrimination occurs when a certain group of employees are unable to comply with a requirement which may not be essential to the job anyway.

Both the Sex Discrimination and the Race Relations Acts allow employers also to take 'positive action' to overcome the effects of past discrimination, such as the training and encouragement of black people or women where few or none have been in the job in question in the preceding 12 months. 'Positive discrimination' in the sense of discrimination at the point of selection is, however, illegal. In some situations such discrimination is not unlawful, where a person's sex or race is regarded as a 'genuine occupational qualification' for the job. One example is the employee who provides individuals with personal services which can be most effectively given by a member of a particular race or sex.

It is important, whatever is being assessed and whatever assessment method is selected, to use criteria that are job-related and methods that can accurately assess those criteria. This applies as much to the methods of assessing skills that we are going on to discuss as to psychometric tests. It is also important that assessors and selectors are thoroughly trained in recruitment and selection, and a variety of organisations exist which can do this (Iles and Auluck, 1991).

## SUMMARY

In this chapter we have looked at the following.

- Job analysis is central to a whole range of personnel decisions, including selection. It provides the basis for the job description and the personnel specification. It can be carried out in various ways, but two particularly useful techniques are the critical incidents technique and the repertory grid technique. It needs to take into account the skills required in the future.

- The kinds of criteria specified in a personnel specification are often ambiguous – they include abilities, aptitudes, interests, motives, traits, styles, skills and competences. Each of these criteria is most appropriately assessed by a different technique; for skills and competences particularly useful techniques include the assessment centre and the work sample. Abilities and traits can be assessed by psychometric tests.

- American and British approaches to competences differ. The American approach identifies behaviour assessed through assessment centres, work samples and interviews, and British approaches identify functions which need to be performed to specific standards assessed primarily through workplace observation or work-based portfolios.

- Assessors need to be aware of the relevant anti-discrimination legislation and thoroughly trained.

# 5

# How should assessment be made?

## CLASSIFYING ASSESSMENT METHODS

A variety of assessment methods now exists, and it is possible to classify them in various ways. One way is to classify them according to whether the data obtained about candidates are derived from their past work or non-work behaviour, their present performance in tests, exercises and interviews, or their future intentions of how they will behave if selected or promoted.

We are primarily concerned with the assessment of skills and competences rather than interests, traits, abilities or motives. For this purpose, the following are particularly useful:

- application forms;

- life-history approaches (eg accomplishment records, assessment of prior learning, biodata);

- interviews (eg criteria referenced, patterned behaviour description situational);

- assessment centres, work samples.

In order to choose which assessment method to use in which situation, we need to have some evaluative standards against which to compare the different methods available.

The major criteria by which assessment methods have traditionally been judged have been the psychometric ones of reliability and validity. By reliability we mean the extent to which scores on a measure are free from random error – a concept somewhat similar to that of consistency. If a measure is reliable, then something is being measured with consistency. This is important, but what we also want to know is whether what is being measured is actually what our measuring instrument claims it is measuring – that is, the validity of the measuring instrument. There are many technical discussions of validity, but generally three types of validity are recognised.

- *Content validity*   The extent to which a measure adequately samples all aspects relevant to job success. For instance is a work sample actually representative of the job?

- *Criterion-related validity*   In particular, predictive validity, the extent to which a measure can predict how well a candidate will score on some criteria such as a measure of job performance at some future assessment.

- *Construct validity*   The extent to which the test scores relate to other measures purportedly of the same trait, quality or construct.

For personnel practitioners, the most important consideration is perhaps criterion-related predictive validity – to what extent do candidates' scores on a test, exercise or interview predict future job success as measured by criteria such as output or rated performance?

Another standard by which assessment methods can be evaluated is their potential for bias against specific groups, such as women, racial and ethnic minorities, or groups defined in terms of age. One way of looking at this is through the adverse impact of a method, that is, the degree to which it rejects a disproportionate number of applicants from  that group, or screens out group members unfairly.

If we look at the various procedures available, we can rank them according to their predictive validity and potential for bias. There are some methods which perform poorly on both criteria, such as references or unstructured interviews. Other techniques perform moderately well on both criteria, such as biodata, personality inventories and structured interviews. Tests of cognitive ability seem to display relatively high validity alongside relatively high potential for bias. There is some evidence that women tend to think in different ways to men. Some methods such as work sample tests and assessment centres seem to perform well on both criteria. These two methods seem to display high predictive validity and appear to be generally fair to both minorities and women.

However, there are other standards which should be employed. One is the utility of the measure, or the monetary value of selection and the monetary benefits a selection procedure might confer. Another is the acceptability or impact of the procedure on participants, which is an issue we will explore at some length. On both criteria, it appears that work samples and assessment centres come out very well, despite their apparently high initial set-up costs.

It appears that some British companies, and even more French and German ones, use graphology or the analysis of handwriting, to assess candidates. Despite the claims of graphologists, there is little independent evidence for the predictive validity of graphology in personnel assessment. Despite this, it appears that handwriting is commonly assessed in an informal way to shortlist candidates as evidenced by the way they fill in application forms. A recent comparison of French and British selection practices by Shackleton and Newell (1991) showed that British companies were a little more likely to use assessment centres and cognitive tests, and a lot more likely to use references. French companies in contrast were much more likely to use graphology.

Another useful technique in a variety of contexts is self-assessment. This is likely to be of most relevance to development, training and counselling, rather than to selection. Self-assessment can play a significant role in enabling applicants to make a better choice of organisation, and it can play a major role in assessment centre techniques, especially in 'development centres'. Peer assessment, requiring as it does the existence of a group of individuals who know each other, is also less useful for selection than for promotion or team placement. Again, a major exception exists with assessment centres, where groups of candidates may rate each others' performances on specific exercises and give each other an overall rating. Peer assessments typically have high validity. We will discuss how both self-assessment and peer assessment can be used for both selection and development purposes in using assessment and development centres later. Peers are more likely to exhibit greater empathy, to understand more clearly group dynamics, and to observe more open and candid behaviour than superiors.

## USING APPLICATION FORMS

Application forms are often used by organisations for a variety of personnel purposes, but one major use is for shortlisting candidates for interviews or other assessment procedures. They are often badly designed for this purpose, however. Candidates need to be assessed at this stage, as at all other stages, against the criteria derived from the personnel specification. However, many recruiters do not do this, but use unrelated criteria such as age, sex, ethnicity, address, how much or how neatly the person writes, and whether or not the applicant types the form. Organisations need to design application forms which allow the gathering of information relevant to the criteria drawn from the personnel specification, so that they can assess candidate skills and potential more accurately. The exact format used will vary according to the kind of organisation involved and the kind of job for which applications are invited.

## Case study - Natco

We will now consider the case of a large organisation recruiting management trainees for managerial positions.

This organisation may have used a targeted job analysis to discover that management trainees needed to display evidence of the following criteria:

- general high academic ability;

- leadership and influencing skills;

- organising skills;

- written communication skills;

- career motivation;

- achievement motivation.

It will need to design its application form so as to allow candidates to display evidence of these criteria, and provide its recruiters with a set of guidelines to enable them to make accurate assessments. Example 5.1 shows what a possible application form might look like, while Example 5.2 shows guidelines that might be provided to recruiters. It is possible to use these guidelines to pre-select candidates by giving them an overall score.

For other kinds of jobs, other kinds of information and questions may be appropriate (eg word-processing or secretarial qualifications). The application form can be used to guide an interview schedule and identify areas for further probing.

In a financial services organisation we studied (which we shall call Natco) management trainee candidates were assessed on a five-point scale at first interview on the following criteria:

- personal impact and communications skills (appearance, confidence, enthusiasm, alertness, fluency, self-presentation);

- people skills (leadership, team skills, influencing skills, relationship skills);

- intellectual skills (learning ability, application of intelligence, logic, flexibility, practicality);

- task and organising skills (organising, following through, prioritising, achieving);

- adaptability (toughness, resilience, adaptability);

- motivation and commitment (ambition, competitiveness, value, compatibility, career assessment, motivation, professional commitment).

At second interview, they were assessed on the following dimensions:

- personal impact;

- communication skills;

- leadership and team skills;

- relationships with others;

- intellectual ability;

- practical judgement;

- task and organising skills;

- adaptability;

- motivation and commitment;

- attitudes and values.

In addition, candidates took a personality inventory, the Saville and Holdsworth occupational personality questionnaire (OPQ), and their scores on its various dimensions were aligned with the dimensions above to generate a total dimensional score. An overall score was also computed.

It may be desirable to weight criteria in terms of their importance to the job. For example, the job analysis might show that communication skills are so important that candidates' scores on this dimension need to be doubled, so that they make twice the contribution to the overall score compared to other dimensions.

It is important to note that participation in extra curricular activities is in part related to cultural differences and in part to opportunities to participate. Many female candidates and black candidates, for example, may not have had the opportunity to participate in debating societies, sports, teams, clubs or uniformed youth organisations. Using such participation as evidence of leadership, sociability, organising or influencing skills may therefore be problematic. This is one reason why we feel that the use of biodata, or objectively scored biographical information about an individual, presents severe problems. We feel that it is important to distinguish between life history information which is under an individual's control, such as work achievements, from information which is not.

The following examples show extracts from application forms and guidelines for recruiters in pre-selection.

*Example 5.1*

*Personal details*

> name
> address
> telephone number
> date of birth
> work permit
> previous applications to organisation

*Education*

> secondary schools, with years
> GCSE/GCE/O level passes or equivalent, with grades and years
> A level/equivalent passes, with grades and years

It might be appropriate here to ask questions on such areas as:

- likes/dislikes at school;
- academic strengths and weaknesses;
- reasons for subject choice.

*Higher education*

> college, university, polytechnic, with dates
> qualification, status, class with dates
> academic reference
> results
> options chosen with reasons
> extramural activities, eg first aid

*Work history*

> employment, with responsibilities, duties
> vacation employment, with responsibilities, duties
> placements, with responsibility, duties
> post-college employment, with responsibilities, duties
> present salary if employed
> reasons for changes
> activities if unemployed
> courses taken

*Activities, achievements and skills*

> school achievements – clubs, societies, teams, voluntary work
> out of school achievements – leisure, projects, community, voluntary and
>     other achievements
> college achievements – positions, responsibilities, achievements

other interests, activities and skills
foreign language skills and qualifications
other skills and qualifications

*Career choice*

reasons for career choice
reasons for considering this organisation
other careers considered
self-assessment of relevant strengths and weaknesses, motivations, interests, values in relation to the career considered

*Further information*

further details candidate wishes to add (with space provided)

*Equal opportunity monitoring*

ethnic origin and other data required to monitor the effectiveness of the organisation's equal opportunity policy, eg gender, disabilities, special needs

---

*Example 5.2*

Mobility – yes/no
Work permit needed – yes/no
Previous application – yes/no
Academic ability – rated on scale, evidenced by O, A, GCSE, degree results
Leadership and influencing skills – rated on scale, evidenced by leadership, influencing roles
Organising skills – rated on scale, evidenced by organising of projects, clubs, societies etc in school, college, work
Written communication skills – rated on scale, as evidenced by application
Career motivation – rated on scale, as evidenced by application form
Achievement motivation – rated on scale, as evidenced by career reasons given
Total score
Observations of recruiter – eg key points highlighted, areas to probe
Decision – eg select/reject/hold pending.

## THE USE OF BIODATA

Faced with considerable excess of applicants over vacancies, organisations may try to raise the levels of existing criteria or find more criteria by which to distinguish between applicants. As we have seen, recruiters might use personal background items such as marital status, or how the form was filled in. Was it neatly filled in? Was it typed? What colour ink was used? Did the candidate use words like 'ambition', 'career', 'motivation', 'leadership' and 'responsibility'? Are there long 'gaps' in educational or work history? Has the person frequently changed jobs or schools or colleges? Some research by Herriot (1989) showed that different British companies and recruiters used different criteria to accept or reject applicants for interview. These included:

- whether applicants wrote a lot;

- whether they used certain key words;

- whether the form was clear and legible;

- area of residence;

- marital status;

- sex.

The problem here is that none of these criteria may be related to successful job performance. Candidates may be accepted or rejected on subjective, idiosyncratic grounds. As we have seen earlier, recruiters may be subject to a variety of perception or attribution biases and will have certain implicit personality theories which they will bring into play. They may also be likely to search for candidates like themselves. One solution adopted by some large organisations such as the Civil Service, armed forces, banks and building societies has been to use biodata.

Biodata about individuals are typically gathered from a biodata form a 'biographical questionnaire'. This includes both 'hard' verifiable items, such as the number of siblings the candidate has, and 'soft' attitudinal items such as leisure interests or values. Candidate reponses to this form are objectively scored to generate a total score. This is used to make decisions about that candidate. For instance, a cut-off point may be set at, say 215, and only candidates who score above this cut-off point may be invited to proceed to the next stage of the selection procedure, such as an interview.

Biodata are often used by large employers to process large numbers of applicants quickly. The organisation typically attempts to ensure that the items it uses are associated with successful job performance – at least historic job performance. The principle here is that past activities, interests and achievements should predict future behaviour. Typically, a biodata questionnaire will be constructed through:

- a job analysis to identify relevant skills, abilities and characteristics associated with successful job performance in current employees;

- generation of a pool of items thought relevant to these characteristics, such as items on leisure interests to assess sociability or team-work, achievements to assess achievement motivation, or projects to assess organising skills;

- completion of the questionnaire by existing employees;

- statistical analysis of the responses to see which items best predict job performance, as measured by output or supervisory ratings or peer ratings;

- giving the revised form to applicants, with their responses scored, and selection decisions taken;

- making periodic checks on item validity and possible unfairness against women and minority groups.

(taken from Smith et al, 1989)

American studies have repeatedly shown that biodata do predict job performance moderately well. Concern has been expressed about some items disadvantaging women or minority groups such as having an inner city address, though these can be monitored and eliminated. In Britain, biodata scores have been shown to predict training success in the Royal Navy, and they seem to predict voluntary withdrawal and motivation to pursue a career in the armed forces. For example, Prince Edward, with his father and older brothers enjoying successful Army or Navy careers may still have found that his biodata would have got him into the Marines. Other items on school or leisure interests, however, showing an interest in 'drama' rather than 'uniformed youht organisations' may have lowered his score somewhat!

Since biodata scoring is very easy, biodata are cheap to employ though costly to develop as they need constant updating. They are useful for sifting through large numbers of applicants, and for specific jobs it is now possible to enter biodata directly into a personal computer. They may be less useful in the 1990s, as fewer people, especially young people, will be applying for more jobs, and organisations may not be faced with such an excess of applicants over jobs.

## Case study – Natco

One example of how biodata have been used in selection and assessment is in the financial services organisation we studied earlier (Natco). In this organisation, a biographical questionnaire was used to sift internal applicants for their suitability for a management development programme. It was used to assess three groups of people:

- A level entrants, external candidates;

- internal applicants for the programme;

- graduate entrants, external candidates.

The biodata form was used to pre-screen applicants, and successful applicants went on to a situational interview before entry to the programme. Biodata were used in part because a high percentage of applicants needed to be efficiently and objectively screened out. Applicants were assessed against the following criteria:

- achievement;

- career commitment;

- alertness;

- commitment to the organisation;

- adaptability;

- flexibility;

- self-monitoring;

- impact;

- leadership;

- self-organisation;

- social skills;

- communication.

The first part of the questionnaire asked for personal details such as age of joining, educational qualifications, sex and ethnic origin to monitor the organisation's equal opportunity policy. The second part asked for details of schooling, such as time spent in school, number of schools attended, the kind of school attended, age on leaving, prizes, positions of responsibility, sports captaincies and examination performances. Some items assessed more 'attitudinal' areas, such as the following.

- How difficult was secondary school work for you?
- How did you usually prefer to cope with meeting deadlines?
- How much do you believe each of the following (luck, study talents, interest, memory, teacher influence) contributed to your school success?
- How many friends did you have at school?
- How strict was your school?

Other sections looked at leisure activities, including kinds of leisure activities, elected positions, and friendships and career choices, including such questions as these:

- How often did you change your mind about possible careers?
- Which of the following elements in career choice was the most important to you?
- Which was your primary goal in choosing a career?

The final section focused on self-description asking about friendship consistency, interest in current affairs, magazines and journals, goal setting and planning, personal qualities, ways of working and things that made the applicant happy. It also asked about risk-taking and moving house, and such questions as these:

- When something powerful stands in the way of your plans, which of these would be most typical of you?
- Overall, how satisfied do you feel with your achievements to date?

In general, though biodata have been shown to be quite predictive of job success and seem useful to screen external applicants, their use in this way to screen internal staff seems more questionable. We found that candidates who failed to gain entry into the programme through the use of biodata felt very negatively about it, seeing it as unfair, inaccurate and invalid. It appeared to be demotivating to internal staff, given the difficulty of changing one's life history or doing anything about 'weaknesses'. It might be possible to improve your communication skills following feedback from an unsuccessful interview. It seems rather more difficult, short of falsifying your CV, to do much now about how many sisters you have, whether you joined the boy scouts or girl guides, and whether you attended Pond Lane Comprehensive or St Wilfred's Academy. Given these feelings of resentment, unfairness and injustice, counselling such applicants and giving them feedback seems rather problematic.

Another problem with biodata is its 'backward-looking' tendency, with the likelihood that organisations will select 'clones' similar in life history to already successful job incumbents. This is likely to lead to less diversity and creativity, a tendency of 'like to recruit like' and a tendency to select for existing rather than future jobs. The kinds of skills and experiences required in the future in the rapidly changing, turbulent environment of the 1990s are unlikely to be identical to those required in more stable times.

## EVALUATING PRIOR ACCOMPLISHMENTS

There are variants of the biodata approach which also obtain life history data, but in a different format geared more clearly to work-based competences and relevant work or work-related accomplishments. One such approach is the accomplishment record developed in the USA. Another is assessment of prior learning (APL), often used for accreditation purposes, and stimulated by the Management Charter Initiative (MCI) and the managerial competences movement in the UK.

### The accomplishment record

This method involves the following steps:

- job analysis through the critical incident method to derive effective and ineffective job behaviours and the categorisation of the behaviours into 'dimensions';

- development of an accomplishment record inventory where applicants are asked to describe major accomplishments illustrative of competence in the critical job dimensions, along with the name and address of persons who could verify the accomplishments;

- administration of the inventory to candidates;

- development of rating scales and principles to score the inventory;

- the scoring of the accomplishment record inventory.

This method is designed to obtain complete definitions of the important dimensions of a job, key characteristics to look for in determining the level of achievement demonstrated and actual examples of accomplishments. In American research it appears to be a good predictor of job success and to be fair to under-represented groups and women (Hough, 1984).

## Assessment of prior learning (APL)

Under the auspices of the MCI, there have been several initiatives designed to enable the assessment and accreditation of prior learning. The aim is to enable participants to claim, verify and obtain credits for competences they already possess. These might have been acquired through work experiences, training, and voluntary, leisure and community exercises rather than within formal educational settings. As with MCI generally, the focus is on the out-comes or achievements of learning, rather than the process of learning. If successful, participants receive a record of achievement and are in a position to receive a qualification such as a certificate or diploma. The process typically involves:

- reviewing past and present achievements to generate a profile of present competences;

- matching achievements to the MCI units of competences so that a claim to competence can be made;

- collecting and organising evidence to support the claims, presented in portfolio form;

- assessment of the claim and portfolio by a subject assessor, who may require additional evidence;

- certification of competence and opportunities for further progress.

The competences used in the management area will typically, for approved accreditation purposes, be the nationally agreed competences and perform-ance criteria developed through the MCI or through other industry-led bodies in other occupational areas. These qualifications will be brought together under the auspices of the NCVQ.

However, such an approach is in danger of neglecting the transferability of learning or the ability to 'learn to learn' in its emphasis on specific prior accomplishments.

## USING SELECTION INTERVIEWS

The typical selection interview has long had bad reviews for its poor reliability and validity. Interviewers have been shown to be prone to a variety of errors and biases, some of which we have reviewed earlier. These include interviewers doing the following.

1. Making their minds up in the first few minutes, and then searching for evidence to confirm their initial impressions.

2. Making these early impressions on the basis of candidates' non-verbal behaviour, especially their degree of eye-contact, head nodding and facial expressions. Interviewees would be wise from these findings to make sure they maintain eye contact, smile, look interested and nod their heads at appropriate points!

3. Interviewers often try to assess candidates' personality rather than skills, often on the basis of these non-verbal signals. They try to assess such difficult traits as confidence, assertiveness, integrity, maturity and initiative. These are often assessed against their stereotype of the 'ideal candidate'.

4. Interviewers remember early information and late information better than what goes on in the middle, ignoring much important information.

5. Interviewers tend to put more weight on 'out of the ordinary' behaviour, whether good or bad.

6. Interviewers are subject to typical rating errors such as contrast and halo effects – candidates are assessed against each other rather than against relevant criteria, and if interviewers rate you highly on one attribute, they are likely to rate you highly on others – or vice versa if you are rated poorly!

7. Interviewers are liable to make a variety of judgements on grounds unrelated to job performance such as:

   —*accent* interviewees with foreign or regional accents are often rated less favourably;

—*physical attractiveness*  attractive candidates are typically rated more positively;

—*dress style*  female candidates wearing 'appropriate' dress (moderately masculine) seem rated more positively than those with 'extremely masculine' or 'feminine' style;

—*scent*  candidates of both sexes wearing attractive scent seem to be rated more favourably by female, less favourably by male, interviewers;

—*age*  older candidates are often rated less favourably than younger candidates;

—*gender*  female candidates are often rated less favourably, especially when applying for 'out of role' jobs such as management or engineering jobs;

—*race/ethnicity*  black applicants may be rated less favourably than white applicants;

—*disability*  disabled candidates seem rated less favourably than able-bodied candidates;

—*personal liking*  an interviewer's personal liking for the candidate seems to affect their ratings and recommendations;

—*'similar to me'*  candidates with similar demographic or educational backgrounds, attitudes and personalities to the interviewer are rated more positively than 'dissimilar' candidates, resulting in a tendency of 'like to recruit like' which may perpetuate 'cloning'.

All these findings suggest that the interview is wide open to subjective bias, inaccurate assessment and unfair discrimination. The 'physical attractivess' finding is particularly interesting in showing the complexities in this area. A very pervasive finding is that physically attractive people derive many benefits in life, including better interview ratings, compared to their equally qualified and experienced but less attractive peers. However, recent American research has shown that this seems to depend on the gender of the candidates and the type of job they are applying for. If the candidate is male, good looks seem to help him for any job and in promotion decisions too. If the candidate is female, good looks seem to help her in getting 'typically feminine' jobs such as clerk or receptionist, but hinder her in getting managerial jobs and recommendations for promotion or pay rises in these jobs. This seems to be because physical attractiveness, enhancing 'perceived femininity', seems to make her perceived as less suitable in jobs stereotyped as needing 'masculine' characteristics like decisiveness, assertiveness and competitiveness.

The fact that management may not necessarily require such characteristics, in comparison with listening, counselling and nurturing for instance, and that men do not necessarily have more of these desirable qualities than women, is of course overlooked by many interviewers.

## Limitations

It might be argued that many of these findings, though disturbing, have been obtained in artificial laboratory settings. The 'candidate' is often represented by a photograph or CV, or a brief videoed extract from a role-played interview. The raters are often American college students. The situation almost screams out for them to use stereotypes – what other information have they got on which to base their judgements? How applicable is this situation to real-life, face-to-face extended interviews conducted by trained, professional British and European interviewers?

Some field research suggests that though such a 'real-life' setting may reduce the impact of such factors, it does not eliminate them entirely. Interviewers still seem to go by subjective, impressionistic information. For example, recent field studies of professional recruiters have shown the following.

- Interviewers' assessments of candidates' suitability for hiring were better predicted by personal liking (how attractive they seemed as a potential colleague), the impression the interviewee made in terms of appearance, drive, job knowledge and ability to express ideas, and to a lesser extent gender similarity than by relevant work experience or academic achievement.

- Interviewers were still influenced by demographic factors such as age and sex, but mainly through their effects on candidates' physical attractiveness. This in turn seemed to affect how likeable the candidates were rated, which affects the interviewers' judgements of intelligence and skills.

- Whether a graduate student was recommended for a job seemed to depend on the interviewer's personal liking for the candidate, which was affected by their similarity to the interviewer in terms of attitudes and beliefs, and by the interviewer's subjective impressions of the candidates' intelligence, interest, initiative, knowledge, experience and ability to express ideas. Recruiters were more likely to hold positive impressions of these if they liked the candidate and saw them as similar to themselves.

So it seems that though professional interviewers may take 'objective qualifications' into account, they are more influenced than they realise by:

- physical attractiveness;

- their liking for the candidate;

- the apparent similarity of the candidate to themselves;

- their subjective impressions of the candidate, especially of their personality, which, as we have seen, is strongly affected by the candidates' non-verbal behaviour.

## How to improve the interview

However, a number of findings also suggest that we can take steps to improve the interview in several ways. Such steps might include the following:

- *Training interviews* Training interviewers seems to improve their behaviour and reduce rating errors, but does not necessarily improve interview validity.

- *Using panel interviews* These are generally found to be more valid predictors of job performance, if a typical 'unstructured' interview is employed, though attention needs to be given to internal group dynamics.

- *Using mixed panels* Panels composed of mixed age, sex, race and other demographic variables will reduce 'similar to me' biases.

- *Taking notes* This improves the recall of information.

- *Structuring the interview* Providing an interview schedule seems to improve both inter-rater reliability and data recall.

- *Training interviewers in equal opportunity issues* This may enable interviewers to avoid the effects of discriminatory stereotypes and illegal discriminatory questioning.

- *Using structured job-related interviews* These include situational, criterion-related and patterned behaviour description interviews, which will be discussed next.

## Structured, job-related interviewing

There are basically two extreme approaches to selection interviewing. One approach might be termed the 'unstructured, personality-related' approach. Here the interview format is completely open, and interviewers are free to pursue whatever they wish, asking whatever questions of candidates in whatever order. Such interviews have often been found to be poor predictors of job performance.

Another approach might be to use a structured, job-related approach, where the interview format is carefully structured and candidates are asked similar or identical questions in the same order, with their responses assessed against job-related criteria obtained from prior job analysis. Such an approach is much more geared up to assess skills accurately rather than to assess personality inaccurately .

## Situational and patterned interviews

The patterned behaviour description interview and the situational interview are both structured, job-related interviews. They involve, like most structured interviewing, a series of job-related questions with pre-determined answers, consistently applied across all interviews for a particular job. Both involve a thorough job analysis; only job-related questions are asked, and all interviewees are asked the same questions, and pre-determined scales are created on which to score interviewees' answers.

The difference between the two lies in the orientation of the interview. The patterned behaviour description interview is past oriented; it asks how candidates have responded in the past to the situations presented to the candidate. The situational interview is future oriented; it asks how the candidate would respond to a hypothetical, realistic, job-related 'what would you do if' question.

| Patterned interview | Situational interview |
| --- | --- |
| Thorough job analysis revealing critical job situations | Thorough job analysis revealing critical job situations |
| Job-related questions | Job-related questions |
| Same questions to all candidates | Same questions to all candidates |

| Pre-determined scale to score candidate response | Pre-determined scale to score candidate response |
| How did candidate respond in the past to these situations? | How will candidate respond in the future to these situations? |

## The patterned behaviour description interview

Let us look more closely at the patterned behaviour description interview, initially developed by Janz in Canada (Janz, 1982).

This involves the following steps:

- Using the critical incidents technique to analyse the job in question and obtain critical incidents of effectiveness;

- Constructing behaviourally defined 'dimensions' from these incidents, such as 'problem analysis' or 'planning' or 'oral communications skills';

- Assembling questions from this list of critical incidents that suggest specific occasions in the applicants' life experience to predict future job performance;

- Selecting appropriate questions from this pattern and assuring that the interviewee does not stray from or evade the question;

- Recording interviewee responses by taking copious notes (though this may get in the way of the flow of interview);

- Rating the responses on each of the behavioural dimensions developed from the critical incidents.

Janz compared the patterned behaviour description interview with an unstructured interview for the position of teaching assistant in a Canadian university. The validity of the patterned interviewer was much higher. Comparison of the two kinds of interview in an Australian study also showed that the patterned interviews were considerably more predictive both of supervisors' ratings of life insurance sales people's performance and of the actual total value of life insurance sold one year later.

## The situational interview

This kind of structured interview was originally developed by Latham and Saari in the United States (Latham et al, 1980) to assess applicants for textile jobs. It is based on the premise that a person's expressed intentions are related to their subsequent behaviour, and asks applicants to describe how they think they would respond in certain job-related situations. It is therefore particularly useful for applicants who have never been confronted with tasks similar to those found in the new job, unlike the patterned interview.

It involves the following steps:

- identification of which behaviours contribute to successful job performance through job analysis;

- collecting critical incidents for the focal position – that is, issues currently found in the work environment which are critical to job success or failure, or events that are very likely to arise;

- generating a pool of situations that exemplify these critical incidents which

  —present a description of the situation to the candidate
  —ask the question, 'How would you handle that situation' or 'What would you have done in that situation'? 'Is there anything else you would like to add?';

- developing a rating scale for each question, such as a rating scale with scale points anchored with indicators exemplifying below average, average and above average performance;

- training interviewers in assessing and rating candidates;

- scoring candidates' responses using the scales.

An example item from a situational interview developed for the position of sales associate is presented in Example 5.3. Candidates are not given a set of choices but their answers are scored against a set of model answers. Studies have shown that the situational interview has good validity for predicting job success in entry positions, and also appears to be fair to black workers.

*Situational interviews in Natco*

We have examined the use of situational interviews in the large UK financial services organisation referred to earlier. These were given to internal candidates (in their early 20s) for promotion and accelerated career development within the organisation. Each interviewee was presented with 10 or 12 interview questions which described specific work situations and problems, read aloud and also presented on cards. Interviewers were given a two-day training course to introduce them to the situational interview, how it was developed, and the scales and forms used. They were also shown how to establish rapport

---

*Example 5.3*

A customer comes into the store to pick up a watch he or she had left for repair. The repair was supposed to have been completed a week ago, but the watch is not back yet from the repair shop. The customer becomes very angry. How would you handle this situation?

1. Tell the customer it isn't back yet and ask him or her to check back with you later. (poor response)
2. Apologise, tell the customer that you will check into the problem and call him or her back later. (average response)
3. Put the customer at ease and call the repair shop while the customer waits. (very good response)
4. Other

*Source*: Weekley and Grier (1987)

---

and how to ask the questions, with practice role-play sessions to record behaviour, categorise it and rate it on the relevant dimensions.

The situational interview questions and rating scales were developed through first identifying the dimensions or criteria of effective job performance. This was done through the critical incidents technique, the repertory grid technique with questionnaire follow-up and diary/observation studies of managers. The resultant behaviours were then grouped into clusters or dimensions.

In this organisation, the following criteria were used, each with summary definitions of behaviour that would exemplify it:

- *adaptability*
  —self-organisation
  —self-monitoring
  —behaviour flexibility;

- *positive outlook*
  —leadership
  —alertness;

- *career commitment*
  —need for achievement
  —career control;

- *adaptation to others*
  —social skills
  —team work

- *organisational commitment*
  —commitment
  —work ethic

The second step is the identification of critical situations in the target job grade for which applicants were applying, in this case managerial jobs. These covered difficult situations faced by current managers in their job. Structured interviews were held with 15 of these managers to allow them to describe 'times when they felt stretched and had to use all their skills'. These situations were then content-analysed and categorised under the five major dimensions (adaptability, positive outlook, career commitment, adaptation to others and organisational commitment) by independent experts.

Then follows a matching of dimensions and situations where the 50 situations were mapped on to the 5 dimensions to produce 10 incidents per dimension.

The next step is the identification of effective and less effective responses to these situations. These were obtained by presenting the critical incidents to 40 people at the target job level, who were asked what they would do. The responses of the above average, average and below average performers, as rated by their managers, were then compared and analysed so that the responses of each group to each question could be compared. Synthesising this with information obtained from 10 managers about how they believed top performers would behave provided descriptions of the responses that high, medium and low performers might give to each of the 50 situations.

The final step is the preparation of indicators for the rating scale so that interviewers could judge candidates' responses – that is, using rating scales with the various points anchored with a behavioural definition of performance level (behaviourally anchored rating scales).

Example 5.4 gives descriptions of typical situations and responses of high performers to some of the critical incidents used in this organisation.

---

*Example 5.4*

**A – Dimension – Adaptation to others**

*Situational question*
Following a reorganisation, a member of your staff must be offered a job which is lower in status, but which will allow him to retain the same salary level. You have looked at all alternative opportunities for redeployment and

this is the only option open. You anticipate a negative reaction to the job offered. What approach would you take to present the new job to your member of staff?

*Responses of effective performers*

- Talk to the staff member diplomatically and in private.
- Be completely honest – it *is* a drop in status.
- This *is* the only option.
- Salary will not be affected.
- Your talents, skills and experience are particularly suited to this job and highly valued by the company.
- Examine together longer-term career possibilities.

(adapted from Gratton, 1989)

## B – Dimension – Adaptability (flexibility)

*Situational question*
This involves a customer coming along with an interesting idea for a new business proposition.

*5 – High response*

- The organisation is enthusiastic about you as a customer.
- What is the legal side like?
- Do you have a prototype?
- We will contact the Patent Office.
- This seems a big growth area at present.
- We need information from you, and would recommend our own accountants.
- Come and talk about it when you have thought some more.

*3 – Medium response*

- Here's some information.
- Recruit a business expert.
- An accountant will prepare a cost report.
- Come and see our company experts.

*1 – Low response*

- Contact someone else such as an accountant for information on cash flows.
- Do not go ahead, its' too risky.

(adapted from Robertson et al, 1990)

In this particular company, candidate situational interview scores seemed a good predictor of ratings of job performance and future potential, obtained from the applicants' managers 12–18 months later (Sharpley, 1991).

This process is clearly time consuming and costly, and there are clearly problems in applying it to small organisations.

There is also the important question of the impact of this technique on candidates. In our own work in Natco we found that:

- situational interviews were seen by candidates as less adequate than assessment centres – that is, less fair, less accurate and less valid and in general candidates were less enthusiastic about their use;

- those who failed as a result of using situational interviews were particularly critical of them, and showed less organisational commitment and more thoughts about changing career;

- those who felt assessment to be inadequate were less likely to show commitment to the organisation after assessment and more likely to be thinking of changing their careers (Robertson, Iles, Gratton and Sharpley, 1991).

Hence, using situational interviews might have its costs in terms of using a relatively poorly regarded technique with possible declining commitment, performance and turnover from those rejected by its use. The same, of course, may well be true, or even more true, of the use of unstructured interviews.

It is also the case that such a procedure may seem rather artificial and prevent the benefits of the traditional interview from being realised. These include:

- face-to-face contact to assess suitability and fit;

- giving candidates the opportunity to ask questions and make decisions about acceptance of the job;

- allowing some negotiation to take place between parties;

- allowing the company or organisation to sell itself.

Another structured interview technique which allows the interview to retain some of these other benefits, is the criterion-referenced interview or criterion-based interview.

## Criterion-referenced interviews

These are also known in America as 'targeted selection' interviews, as they are targeted to such job-related dimensions as 'planning' or 'oral communications' derived from prior job analysis. These dimensions are explicitly defined in behavioural terms and interviewers are trained to obtain information related to job performance. Like the patterned behaviour description interview, such interveiws focus on past behaviour on the assumption that past performance on job-related dimensions predicts future performance on these same dimensions.

The steps involved in conducting a criterion-referenced interview are to:

- analyse the job in terms of critical incidents or repertory grid techniques to identify behaviours critical to job success;

- organise these behaviours into 'dimensions', usually 10–12 in number;

- provide each dimension with a comprehensive and understandable definition, with examples of job-related behaviours to illustrate desired behaviours;

- obtain examples of behaviour in the interview that are relevant to the dimension, drawn from the candidate's past experience;

- categorise these behavioural examples into dimensions;

- evaluate the categorised behaviour in terms of its ability to predict job performance.

For example, if one of the key dimensions or criteria of effective performance identified is 'analysing problems', the interviewer will need to seek past examples of successful or unsuccessful analysis of problems in situations resembling those likely to be encountered in the new job. This means:

- asking relevant questions;

- following up questions to enable actual behaviour to be specified;

- asking 'why'?

For example, if 'communication skills' are an important aspect of effective performance as identified in the job analysis, candidates might be asked the following.

- Describe a time when you had to give a formal presentation.

- What were your objectives and how did you go about realising them?

- Describe why you think you were relatively successful or unsuccessful in meeting these objectives.

If problem analysis is identified as a major area, candidates might be asked these questions.

- Describe a time in the last two years when you faced a particularly difficult problem.

- Describe when you first became aware of the problem and its origins.

- Describe how your understanding of the problem developed.

Notice that criterion-referenced, behavioural questions use a lot of 'did' and 'have done' or 'currently doing' phrases to elicit responses in terms of past behaviour, stated in such terms as 'I did', or 'I carried out', or 'I recommended' or 'I set up'. In gathering examples of relevant past behaviour, the interviewer is in a better position to predict future behaviour in the job. Candidates' answers may be scored against behaviourally-anchored rating scales where each point on the scale is marked with a behavioural indicator of level of performance.

## Redesigning the interview?

Given the poor record of the traditional interview in predicting job performance, three options seem open:

- drop it altogether;

- redesign it along more structured, job-related lines;

- redesign it to be less about selection and more about negotiation.

This last course of action is recommended by Herriot. He suggests that instead of eliminating most applicants through such unreliable methods as perusing application forms and employing unstructured first-round interviews, followed by using more accurate selection devices such as tests or assessment centres, organisations should allow much earlier self-selection to take place through providing much more 'realistic' information about the job and the organisation. Cognitive tests and assessment centres could then be used to sift applicants, especially graduates. The 'interview' would then come at the end of the process, and would be less about the 'selection' of a candidate and more about exchanging information, negotiating expectations and drawing up a 'psychological contract' between both parties. This takes the burden of acting as a 'selection vehicle' away from the interview, and allows it to act as a vehicle for mutual feedback, accommodation and decision-making (Herriot, 1989).

Of course, it may be desirable to go in both directions at once, that is:

- make one kind of interview more structured, to serve as a selection device;

- make another kind of interview less structured, to serve as a vehicle for negotiation.

The strategy used will depend on such factors as the stage of application reached (structured interviews for earlier stages, negotiation interviews for later stages), the status of the candidate (structured interviews might be used more often with external candidates) and the senority of the candidate. Trying to cram 'selection' and 'negotiation' functions into the one 30-minute interview will mean that neither function is carried out properly.

## TRAINING IMPLICATIONS OF DIFFERENT INTERVIEW STRATEGIES

Interviewers will require different training in how to operate each of the interview techniques discussed.

### Patterned behaviour description interviews

Interviewers will need training in:

- *Patterning* – how to assemble questions based on specific incidents in the candidate's past experience, derived from the job analysis and associated personnel specification;

- *questioning* – how to ask appropriate questions;

- *recording* – how to note the candidate's responses;

- *decision-making* – how to use a rating scale to attach a number to each response.

### Situational interviews

Interviewers will need training in:

- the aims of the process;

- how to use the dimensions, recording forms and scales;

- how to establish rapport and respond to candidate questions;

- how to record responses, categorise behaviour by dimension, compare the behavioural indicators to the observed behaviour, and rate the interviewee on the dimension.

## Criterion-referenced interviews

Interviews will need training in:

- how to use the job-related target dimension;

- how to use definitions and behavioural indicators;

- how to categorise behaviour by dimensions;

- how to evaluate the categorised behaviour;

- how to ask relevant questions, with follow-ups to determine 'what' and 'why'.

## Flexible interviews

It is possible to use interviews somewhat more flexibly so as to enable assessors to obtain behavioural evidence from the candidate and allow an assessment to be made of the candidate's skills in the criteria or dimensions derived from the job analysis. This will enable the strengths of the structured interview to be retained – the use of job analysis, the derivation of job-related criteria through a person specification, the eliciting of relevant behavioural evidence, the reliable categorisation of behaviour by dimension, and the evaluation and rating of that behaviour. However, we feel it is not necessarily desirable to use such rigid frameworks, where all candidates are asked exactly the same questions in the same order, to gain such evidence and make such judgements of candidates. The need for flexibility, the need to allow individuality and the need to meet candidates' expectations means that some deviations may be permissible, and even necessary, as long as evidence is reliably collected and an accurate rating of candidates against criteria is made.

To do this successfully, interviewers will need to be thoroughly trained. The authors have devised training courses for flexible interviewing which incorporate substantial amounts of practice with role-play sessions with video-tapes, tutor and peer feedback, using as far as possible 'real' candidates and jobs as close as possible to the people and jobs likely to be encountered by the organisation's interviewers and recruiters. Such courses have been run with local authorities for example. One particular course is shown in Example 5.5.

---

*Example 5.5*

*Flexible interview training in a construction company*

*Day 1*
    The stages of systematic selection
    Job analysis and job description exercise
    Personnel specification exercise
    Selection criteria and methods
    Interviewing skills 1
    Practise interviewing, in trios, with CCTV (closed circuit television) and feedback, on participants' careers

*Day 2*
    Selection exercise – from job description
    Candidates devise person specification
    Preparation for interviews, given application forms
    Practice interview with candidates, with closed circuit TV
    Presentation of rankings, and discussion of rankings
    Feedback from interviewees

Delegates are supplied with a number of handouts, with practice in their use, eg:
    job descriptions
    personnel specification
    interview structured guides
    questioning patterns
    question types and uses
    assessment forms
    listening skills
    non-verbal communication skills

---

One area where flexibility is necessary is in interviewing candidates of different ethnic, racial or cultural backgrounds. Such candidates may have a different style of presenting information, and interviewers may evaluate the information presented differently. Such interviewees may not be aware of the 'rules of the game' that interviewers take for granted – such as 'selling oneself', maintaining eye contact and flattering the interviewers by telling them how wonderful their organisation is when asked 'and why did you apply to us'.

Not knowing such rules may mean that asking the same candidates the same questions may put specific candidates at a disadvantage. Interviewers may need to rephrase their questions and probe differently to get the information they are seeking. Similar issues arise with interviewees with disabilities.

Some interesting national differences in how interviews are used have been uncovered. Shackleton and Newell (1991), for example, have found that British companies are more likely to make use of only one interview, whereas French companies typically use a series of interviews. Such interviews are likely to be with one interviewer only, whereas British companies often use panel interviews.

## SUMMARY

In this chapter we have looked at the following.

- A variety of assessment procedures have been developed. They can be evaluated in terms of such criteria as reliability, validity, bias, utility, acceptability and impact.

- Judged against such criteria, some methods such as graphology perform badly, whereas self and peer assessment come out quite well.

- In the assessment of skills and competences, rather than the assessment of traits, interest or motives, certain assessment methods seem particularly useful. These include criteria-related application forms, biodata or life history information, prior accomplishment records or portfolios, and structured job-related interviews such as situational interviews, patterned behaviour description interviews and criteria-referenced interviews. More flexible, but still criteria-related, interviews are appropriate in some instances.

- All such methods are based on a thorough job analysis which identifies the critical skills and competences necessary for present and future effective performance, and all require users to receive thorough training in how to employ the procedure.

# 6

# Using the Assessment Centre Method

## WHAT IS AN 'ASSESSMENT CENTRE'?

Despite its name, the 'assessment centre' is not a place but a method or process designed to assess skills or potential in as comprehensive and rigorous a way as possible. A properly designed 'assessment centre' involves the assessment of groups of participants by a team of trained observers. Candidates take part in a series of specially designed exercises or activities. These may involve psychometric tests or interviews, but generally focus on situational exercises designed to resemble critical job situations as closely as possible. In this way participants can be rated on how they handle situations that resemble the job or job family they are being assessed for. Their performance in these situations or simulations is assessed against a set of job-related skills (generally called dimensions or criteria) derived from a prior job analysis of the target job.

For example in one assessment centre we studied in a major clearing bank (which we shall call MCB) used to identify managerial potential among clerical and administrative staff, the following skills were assessed:

- intellectual power;

- business skills;

- communication skills;

- use of time;

- relationships with others;

- creativity;

- motivation

In this centre 78 candidates, 19 of whom were women, attended the centre in mixed groups of 12. Candidates were assessed by 6 assessors, that is each assessor observed and evaluated 2 candidates. Assessors were drawn from a pool of 12 assessors, who included 5 women. Any assessment panel always included some women in order to take some account of equal opportunity issues, and candidates always received feedback and counselling on their performance, as well as an overall rating. We found in this centre that assessment centre ratings were unrelated to candidate gender or to candidate physical attractiveness in contrast to the situation found in many studies of the interview (Iles, 1989).

## ORIGINS OF THE ASSESSMENT CENTRE METHOD

American authors like to emphasise the roots of the assessment centre in the use by the Office of Strategic Services (OSS) in the Second World War of work simulations to identify potential agents. However, the use of multiple exercises and simulations, and the assessment of performance by multiple observers has its origins in pre-war German military efforts to identify leadership potential, and similar efforts by the British War Office Selection Board in the Second World War.

This British military usage remains important in the assessment-centre type activities conducted by the Army, Navy and Air Force. It also seems to have influenced other British public sector selection procedures, such as those in the Civil Service Selection Board (CSSB) and the police.

However, this tradition makes greater use of extended interviews, long, written reports and physical tasks and exercises which do not always simulate current job demands, such as using ropes and planks to build bridges. Assessment centre practice as it has developed in America was first developed as a research programme within the American company AT and T. This was later taken up operationally in the Bell System in 1958 and has subsequently become the classical model for centre design and practice in the USA, Britain and elsewhere. It was this model which was reimported into Britain in the early 1970s.

## HOW IS A CENTRE CONSTRUCTED?

The Task Force on Development of Assessment Centre Standards, set up to establish good practice in this area, lays down the following seven conditions that need to be met if an assessment technique wishes to be regarded as an assessment centre.

- Multiple assessment techniques must be used. At least one of these techniques must be a simulation. (A simulation is an exercise or technique designed to elicit behaviours related to dimensions of performance on the job which require the participant to respond behaviourally to situational stimuli. The stimuli present in a simulation must parallel or resemble stimuli in the work situation. Examples of simulations include group, in-basket and fact-finding exercises. The in-basket exercise involves dealing with items that arrive in a simulated 'in-tray'.)

- Multiple assessors must be used. These assessors must receive training prior to participating in a centre.

- Judgements resulting in an outcome (ie, a recommendation for promotion, specific training or development) must be based on pooled information from the assessors and the techniques.

- An overall assessment of behaviour must be made by the assessors at a separate time from the observation of behaviour.

- Simulation exercises are used. These exercises are developed to tap a variety of pre-determined behaviours and have been pre-tested prior to use to ensure that they provide reliable, objective and relevant behavioural information for the organisation in question.

- The dimensions, attributes, characteristics or qualities evaluated by the assessment centre are determined by an analysis of relevant job behaviours.

- The techniques used in the assessment centre are designed to provide information which is used in evaluating the dimensions, attributes or qualities previously determined.

## The stages of centre construction

A centre is typically constructed and operated through the following steps:

- identification of the purpose of the centre;

- job analysis of the position under consideration;

- generation of a set of 'criteria' – categories or clusters of behaviour, skills or attributes, usually around 12 in number, thought to be necessary for effective performance in the job based on the job analysis and used as performance criteria;

- generation of an 'activity by criteria' matrix;

- construction of a set of 'activities' to allow assessment of these criteria;

- training of assessors;

- selection of participants;

- provision of pre-centre information;

- running the centre;

- recording and rating of behaviour against criteria;

- assigning an overall assessment rating (eg select, promote, develop etc);

- report back to management on recommended actions/decisions;

- feedback to participant.

## Identification of the purpose of a centre

The original purpose of the assessment centre was to select for supervisory or managerial positions from a pool of non-managerial staff or to select for administrative or leadership potential from graduates or recent recruits in British-style Civil Service or military centres. Selection remains an important use of assessment centres and has been extended to include, among others, middle and senior managers in public and private sectors, engineers, salespersons, police officers and R&D managers etc. We will go on to discuss some assessment centres we have designed for the selection of managerial staff in local authorities and the health service.

Centres have also been used to identify long-range potential for development and promotion. In this they have shown a remarkable ability to predict the managerial level participants will obtain many years later. This use often combines assessment and development functions, since those identified as having potential often gain access to accelerated programmes of management development which involve training, coaching, counselling, mentoring and job assignments designed to realise and develop potential, and enhance upward mobility. There are of course dangers in creating a 'self-fulfilling prophecy' in such a programme, and participants' self-esteem and need for achievement may well be raised. We will also look at how such a programme was operated in a major UK financial services organisation in some detail.

Assessment centres seem to perform very well in direct comparison with other predictors such as personality tests, interviews and supervisor ratings. However, some doubts have been cast over this apparently rosy picture. A major problem has arisen over the criteria selected to represent effectiveness. Many criteria found useful in other jobs, such as the number of sales made or objects produced, are inappropriate at managerial levels. Many studies have used criteria of job performance as they have been rated by supervisors, which is not necessarily the most appropriate measure of effectiveness.

One problem with using promotions or level achieved as a criterion is that many studies have suffered from 'criterion contamination', whereby job promotion is not an independent measure of effectiveness. If centre ratings have been used operationally as part of the promotion process, the oberved correlation between predictor (centre rating) and criterion (management level) will be artificially inflated. However, some studies controlling for this have still found that assessment centres make impressive predictions.

## Equal opportunity issues

A major question is the degree to which bias or potential for unfair discrimination exists in assessment centres. Most studies have shown that similar proportions of women to men have been identified, and that overall ratings and specific criterion ratings are equally predictive of subsequent managerial success for women and men. Indeed, in MCB, referred to earlier, we found that males and females scored equally highly on the overall assessment rating produced at the end of the centre. There were also no significant differences in rating on any of the individual skills or criteria on which candidates were assessed.

However, some race and gender effects have been noted. Black women were less highly rated on a number of dimensions in one US study. In another, black women were rated lower as the number of white males in the group rose. A recent US study of a financial centre has shown that women were rated more highly than men, not by mixed assessor groups but, perhaps surprisingly, by all-male assessor groups (Walsh, Weinberg and Fairfield, 1987).

It is also important to remember that the whole centre process needs to be studied, not just the event itself. For example, if women have had to survive potentially discriminatory pre-screening hurdles, the proportionately fewer women who make it to the centre are likely to be highly skilled and highly able, and will score more highly on average than those men who were less stringently selected. Conversely, a company which, as part of a positive action effort, sends all its women managers to a centre but pre-selects its male managers more stringently may find that its women managers, on average, score less highly.

Therefore, the assessment centre process as a whole needs to be examined carefully for bias, as suggested by Alban-Metcalfe (1989). She suggests examining:

- how the criteria are defined;

- how the exercises are designed;

- how the assessors are selected;

- who composes the participant group and the assessors' group;

- how the centre is publicised;

- how candidates are nominated and screened;

- the quality of feedback given to candidates; and

- the kinds of personal development plans recommended.

## Development and diagnosis

This mention of feedback and personal development planning leads to a third use of assessment centres, that of development and diagnosis of strengths and weaknesses or development needs. In this kind of centre, the emphasis is less on an overall judgement and more on specific development needs as revealed by the centre. A profile and a personal development plan is often derived which may build on strengths and/or address development needs. This plan may incorporate, for example, job assignments, training, coaching, counselling and mentoring. The use of centres for such purposes seems to be growing, especially in the UK, and such centres are often termed 'development centres' or 'career development workshops' rather than assessment centres, since their focus is on participant development. The feedback participants receive after the centre can itself be a developmental experience.

## Other uses of assessment centres

Centres can be used, for many other purposes, for example:

- career planning;

- self-development;

- succession planning

- management development; and

- organisation development.

The skills or competencies the organisation may require in the future can be identified to build up an audit of strengths and needs. This can help appropriate recruitment, selection, promotion, training, development and redeployment programmes to be implemented. Training as an assessor and participating as an assessee may also help to build a common language and assist in programmes of cultural change. It may also enable transfers, secondments and developmental projects to be arranged more easily. The assessment centre process can bring assessees and assessors from different parts of the organisation together and enable them to acquire a common language and conceptual framework.

This team-building function can be particularly important where managers may come from very diverse professional disciplines and backgrounds, with very different and conflicting assumptions and perspectives. This fragmentation can contribute to making inter-agency or inter-professional team working very difficult. We found this fragmentation to be the case in a consultancy project designed to help a community drug team composed of five members of different professional groups employed by three different authorities work more closely together as a team.

## Identification of the participants

Participants may nominate themselves, or be nominated by their supervisor or a nomination committee. They may be selected through a variety of pre-screening procedures or through a combination of such procedures. It is important to monitor ideally, from an equal opportunity perspective, the nature and targeting of publicity material, who does and does not apply, and their reasons for so doing. Such monitoring should be extended to any pre-screens used to sift candidates such as prior interviews, biodata scores or ability tests. All of these are likely to display some potential for adverse impact against women, black people and other groups.

Participants may be rejected in the pre-screen tests in ways they consider unfair and inaccurate, and this may well affect their work motivation, commitment and work performance. For example, we found that internal candidates rejected from entry to an accelerated development programme in a UK financial services assessment centre through biodata and situational interviews regarded both techniques very negatively, seeing them as unfair, inaccurate and invalid. This seemed to affect their commitment to their work and intentions to stay with the organisation, and perhaps also their performance. We also, found, however, that such feelings were much less expressed towards the assessment centres used, a finding we will explore further in a later section (Robertson et al, 1991).

## Job analysis

A thorough and systematic job analysis is regarded by most assessment centre practitioners and researchers as necessary to ensure the content validity of a centre, that is the degree to which it represents important parts of the job. Through job analysis it is possible to identify those qualities, skills, characteristics or abilities required for effective job performance, and to specify the 'criteria' against which centre participants are to be assessed. Job analysis will also enable activities to be selected or designed that adequately sample the job in question and allow the observation of the criteria.

It is interesting to note a difference between American and British practice here. Most American centre designers use a combination of standardised check-lists and questionnaires, interviews and the 'critical incidents technique'. The 'critical incidents' technique is often used in British centres too, but extensive use of the repertory grid technique is also made.

The criteria selected are often drawn from samples of white men, and they may represent rather a 'macho' view of management, emphasising such attributes as planning, directing, controlling, leading and formulating 'strategy', rather than the more guiding, directing, enabling aspects of the managerial role. We have elicited from samples of women managers dimensions which 'feel' differently from those elicited from male managers, and have used them as criteria in assessment centres. We will go on to discuss such criteria in more detail below.

## Which criteria and dimensions are to be assessed?

There appears to be some degree of interchange between the words used to specify the behaviour to be assessed. It is important to distinguish between them. The 1979 Task Force in Assessment Centre Standards defined the technique as 'the standardised evaluation of behaviour,' but an earlier report talks about 'dimensions, attributes, characteristics or qualities'. It is important that centre designers know what they are defining. A job analysis can result in descriptions of desired skills or 'competences' which may, for example, include skills such as communications skills or personality traits, or qualities such as emotional stability. Some centre designers use the term 'dimension' as a description under which behaviour can be reliably classified and as a convenient label for observed behaviour. If the description of behaviour is to prove the basis for the design of the simulations and of what is to be assessed, the meaning of the term being used must be clear and consistent. Many organisations are unclear exactly what it is they are seeking in employees. Even if they use the same terms (eg leadership), they often disagree as to what these terms mean. Consequently, it is important to be clear over the definition of the criteria used.

Often around 8–12 competencies are used in centres. If assessors are to be able to observe accurately, and then record and evaluate levels of behaviour, it is essential that criteria dimensions be precisely defined and indications given as to what constitutes effective and ineffective performance. Centre designers differ, however, in their approach, some providing assessors only with a list of competencies with short summary definitions, others providing specific descriptions of effective and ineffective performance on that dimension.

In our practice we use summary definitions and specific indicators of performance levels, assessed on a six-point scale, used to prevent assessors focusing on the mid point. If only summary definitions are provided, assessors may find it difficult to recognise whether relevant behaviour has been displayed, and may find it difficult to differentiate between levels of performance. If dimensions are not behaviourally defined or are multidimensional, unclear or ambiguous, assessors cannot be expected to be able to obtain reliable measurements.

## Assessment strategies in practice

We will now look more closely at some of the ways organisations have used assessment centres to identify staff competence in specific skills identified as critical to the organisation through prior job analysis. Example 6.1 shows the performance criteria adopted in two different assessment centres used at two different career stages by Natco, the UK financial services organisation we looked at in Chapter 5.

---

*Example 6.1*

As we have seen, Natco, the financial services organisation, used a mixture of biodata, situational interviews, assessment centres and panel interviews to select internal staff for an accelerated management development programme.

In their mid 20s, staff selected for the programme through biodata and situational interviews had their potential for further promotion and career development assessed by means of a one-day assessment centre after around two years on the management development programme. It assessed candidates against the following criteria:

- self-organisation;
- adaptability;
- problem-solving;
- leadership;
- alertness;
- social skills;

---

- team skills;
- commitment;
- communication skills;
- need to achieve.

Candidates took part in five exercises:

- in-tray exercise;
- a group discussion exercise on allocating staff time;
- a one-to-one 'difficult customer' discussion exercise;
- a one-to-one 'difficult employee' discussion exercise;
- a self-appraisal questionnaire on achievement motivation.

After around ten years on the programme in their early 30s, candidates' potential for obtaining executive levels was assessed in a five-day assessment centre against the following criteria:

- desire to excel;
- adaptability;
- leadership;
- adaptation to others;
- communication skills;
- intellectual/analytical skills.

Candidates took part in the following exercises:

- an in-tray exercise;
- a business exercise;
- five outdoor activities;
- a presentation exercise;
- a group discussion exercise;
- a group decision-making exercise.

*Source*: Iles and Robertson (1989); Gratton (1989)

Similar performance criteria have been employed in other organisations outside the financial services sector. Organisations in industry and in the public sector have also made extensive use of assessment centres. Example 6.2 describes assessment centres used in Cadbury Schweppes after a trip to McBers' consultancy in the US. Interestingly the competence language employed has not only become used in designing assessment centres, but also in the performance appraisal and management development functions.

---

*Example 6.2*

In Cadbury Schweppes steps have been taken to 'find better ways of describing managers' in order to make more effective decisions about their future, as Tony Glaze has put it (1989). As the organisation has stripped away managerial layers, focused on mainstream activities, and 'bought in' specialist services, managerial competence has become more important, and has been assessed through:

- Belbin's team roles;
- psychometric tests;
- competence data.

The organisation was 'set on the competence road' through the introduction of assessment centres, which set out the first 'language of competence' and introduced managers to a more objective approach to selection. Centre technology was seen as:

- improving the quality of appointments;
- defining job needs more clearly;
- objectively evaluating candidates;
- helping managers gain 'behavioural literacy', improving feedback on job performance.

In 1982, the competence language became incorporated into performance appraisal and development activities. The competence framework was used also in 'graduate recruitment' and in career counselling with graduates and in 'profiling' high potential managers. The framework used involves the following key dimensions:

- strategy;
- drive;
- relationships;
- persuasion;
- leadership;
- analysis;
- implementation;
- personal factors – integrity, ambition etc.

---

Assessment centres have also become popular in the National Health Service, and Example 6.3 describes two different kinds of centre employed to identify candidates for a general management training scheme – that is, internal 'identificatory' centres.

*Example 6.3*

With the introduction of general management into the NHS in 1984, there has been increasing interest in ensuring a supply of appropriately qualified people to fill general management posts. The NHS Training Authority (NHSTA) in 1985 argued for a three-stage national accelerated development programme to accelerate the career development of high potential individuals for general management. Stage 3 of the general management training scheme was designed to prepare people for 'board level' posts. This was acknowledged to be difficult because of problems in the NHS in making judgements and comparisons between different professional groups without a common language of managerial competence and a common methodolgy for identifying potential, involving more systematic, standardised and objective methods. Such methods would:

- aid selection;
- aid self-development;
- generate information on human resources;
- help individuals identify alternative career paths;
- identify individuals in non-mangerial roles with management potential.

Some health authorities began using assessment centres to identify candidates for the general management training scheme Stage 3. One kind of centre used by two health authorities used repertory grid and critical incident techniques to analyse the jobs of general managers, as well as the professional and managerial position questionnaire. It identified ten criteria or performance dimensions as critical to performance of this role:

- leadership;
- communication;
- influence;
- people orientation;
- strategic planning;
- innovation;
- analytical reasoning;
- decision-making;
- achievement orientation;
- resilience.

Candidates were assessed against these criteria in a two-day assessment centre consisting of:

- an assigned role group exercise on resource allocation;
- an 'unassigned' group exercise on proposals for a performance review;
- an in-tray exercise;
- verbal and numerical critical reasoning tests;

- a productive thinking test;
- a personality questionnaire;
- an oral presentation;
- a career development interview.

Another health authority employed a different set of consultants who also employed critical incident and repertory grid techniques to analyse general management jobs. The following criteria were identified.

Managing change

—strategic vision
—leadership
—initiative
—personal characteristics.

Communicating

—interpersonal skills
—written work
—presentations

Developing the unit

—planning and resource allocation
—delegation
—management control
—development of people

Decision making

—analysis and judgement
—decisiveness

Candidates took part in a one-day assessment centre, consisting of the following exercises:

- a meeting with a medical consultant on attracting staff;
- a group exercise on strategy for running down large hospitals;
- a one to one briefing exercise with a district general manager;
- an in-tray exercise;
- an interview on the in-tray.

*Source*: Alban-Metcalfe (1989)

Note that both the NHS work and the Natco example describe how criteria are often assessed by means of various activities. We will explore the way activities are designed and employed in the next stage of the discussion.

Alban-Metcalfe's work also casts light on good practice in this area. One consultancy merely gave assessors a label for the criteria being sought such as 'influence', and a short summary definition of what was meant by that label. For instance, in one centre influence was defined as:

> The ability to influence up, down and across. The ability to gain co-operation and agreement through the skills of persuasion and negotiation; to gain respect and credibility in particular to gain the confidence of medical staff. The ability to maintain a balanced independence and handle difficult people and conflict.

This short summary definition gives very few indicators of what specific behaviours assessors should look for in each exercise in order to make judgements. It gives no description of what effective or ineffective managers would actually do to merit a high or low score on the dimension. Assessors are left somewhat in the dark as to what exactly they are looking for. It is likely that many assessors will find it difficult to use many of these criteria, and indeed Alban-Metcalfe found that their returns contained many missing values. In addition it is likely that assessors will be unable to distinguish successful from unsuccessful performers and indeed this is what Alban-Metcalfe found.

We feel that assessors need to have very clear understanding of what to look for in each activity – what the criterion actually refers to, in terms of specific behaviours, things that the assessors can actually see the participants doing. We also feel that the assessors need to be shown how to differentiate clearly poor from good performance – that is, what would they see effective performers actually doing, and how would this differ from ineffective performers?

What this means is that adequate behavioural frameworks need to be provided. In the first place, the definitions of the criteria themselves need to be clear, unambiguous and concise. Note that in the above example, not only was the definition of 'influence' rather lengthy, it also seemed somewhat tautologous ('the ability to influence') and seemed to mix up together rather different things:

- gaining agreement;
- persuading;
- negotiating;
- earning credibility; and;
- handling conflict.

We feel that criteria definitions need to be more precise, and that asesessors need to be given not just summary definitions, but specific indicators of effective and ineffective performance on that dimension in each exercise. Such indicators should be derived from the job analysis. For example, the critical incidents technique will reveal specific examples of good and poor performance, as will the repertory grid technique.

Providing a framework is likely to help assessors avoid missing values and nil returns, as they will be able to recognise specific examples of the criterion from participant behaviour. They are also more likely to be able to discriminate between good and poor performers. Indeed, Alban-Metcalfe found this to be the case in the second of her samples, where the consultants this time provided definitions, examples of what good and bad unit general managers would do, and specific indicators of effective and ineffective performance. We use criteria that are not only concisely defined, but also provide guideline definitions of effective and ineffective performance, anchored on a 1–6 scale. Example 6.4 gives some examples of how criteria used in our assessment centres have been defined and how participant behaviour is rated.

## WHAT ACTIVITIES, EXERCISES OR TESTS ARE TO BE USED?

This stage covers the exercises or activities used to provide opportunities to observe performance. Commonly, participants' behaviour is assessed by several trained assessors as they engage in various activities. These may take the form of in-tray exercises, leaderless group discussions, case studies, pen-and-paper tests, questionnaires, role-plays or interviews. These can be bought 'off-the-shelf' or designed specifically for the organisation in question. They are designed to be multiple – that is, they should provide varied kinds of activity, some analytical, some interpersonal, some solo, some group, some pencil and paper, some oral, some collaborative, some competitive.

### Reflect not simulate

The activities should reflect and not just simulate the job in terms of content and context. To achieve this requires:

- a high degree of congruity between the test environment and the actual work environment;

- a high degree of response freedom; and

- minimising of inferences drawn from a set of observations.

*Example 6.4*

*Planning and organisation*
Ability to plan ahead, determine priorities and organise resources for the achievement of an objective.

| Score | Guideline definitions |
| --- | --- |
| 1 | Creates chaos out of order |
| 2 | Completely random behaviour – no attempts to plan or organise. |
| 3 | Attempts to plan are ineffective through poor organisation or prioritisation. |
| 4 | Develops clear plans and priorities but not aimed at objectives. |
| 5 | Is clear about objectives, develops plans, sets priorities but does not use all resources. |
| 6 | Develops clear plans and priorities directed at objectives. Utilises all available resources. Draws up contingency plans. |

*Assertiveness*
Ability to confront others calmly but firmly, without aggression, sarcasm or discourtesy, irrespective of rank or position.

| Score | Guideline definitions |
| --- | --- |
| 1 | Makes no effort to confront a situation or to sort it out. |
| 2 | Reacts to criticism with anger, sarcasm or meekly accepts what is said. |
| 3 | Attempts to be assertive are clumsy and backs off when the going gets tough. |
| 4 | Attempts to be assertive are more skilful but withdraws if challenged directly. |
| 5 | Is assertive and is able to confront difficult situations. |
| 6 | Is assertive and remains calm even when faced with others' anger, sarcasm and discourtesy. |

The work behaviours, the associated tasks and work products needs to be completely described and the link between a knowledge, skill or ability and the appropriate work behaviour established. The method used to determine this link must also be specified. A centre is more than a collection of exercises, it is a process which should be highly congruent with the work environment.

## Involvement of managers

Managers should be involved in the design process as a means of increasing ownership of the centre. This provides development for the managers themselves, as well as ensuring that the activities are relevant to the organisation. This implies the use of tailor-made exercises, but off-the-shelf packages which clearly contradict the principles of assessment centre technology are still used. This could well be due to cost and resourcing. Generic activities may have their place, as the purpose of the centre is to assess management ability rather than knowledge of an organisation, but the simulations should contain elements that reflect the specific organisation's situation. The exercises should be designed to elicit the behaviours being sought and should be balanced in terms of type of activity. It is important to see the centre as one activity comprised of different elements as experienced by the participants, rather than a series of several different exercises, as experienced by the designer.

## Kinds of activities

Let us look more closely at the kinds of activities that are used in assessment centres. Such activities are commonly samples of the job in question, or simulations of situations commonly encountered in the target job or likely to be met in the foreseeable future.

### Group situations

The activities also often include various kinds of situations. These may be group situations; a common example is the leaderless group exercise. This exercise may be job-related, such as the discussion and ordering of relevant managerial competences or a management team strategy meeting. Other centres use less job-related exercises, such as classic group decision-making exercises involving consensus rankings or tower-building exercises. Some exercises may involve putting people in assigned roles, where they play parts linked to particular briefs. These can involve somewhat more competitive and rather less collaborative group activities. Again they may be job-related, such as discussions of new accommodation or resource allocation, or may be less job-related, as with discussions about alternative options for a run-down hotel. Another favourite exercise is to use a business game of some kind, often with assigned roles.

## Individual exercises

Other activities may involve *individual* work, such as reading a complex report to provide a position paper for management or a set of strategy recommendations. Other individual activities may involve analysis of a dilemma, or individual face-to-face discussions. These may be focused on the centre itself, such as on strengths and weaknesses in performance. They may be focused on job and career history, on behavioural events, or on personal hopes and aspirations. Often a criterion-referenced interview might be used, exploring aspects of the candidates' work history that might cast light on the same criteria used in the rest of the assessment centre.

A classic individual exercise is the in-tray or in-basket exercise. In this exercise, candidates are often presented with a scenario such as, 'It's a Sunday morning and you have to work through the contents of your in-tray before leaving in two hours' time to catch a plane to Zurich. No one else is in the building.' Participants' handling of the in-tray, containing 'typical' items such as memos, invitations, reports, letters, complaints, requests and arrangements is scored in terms of how they organise their time, how they prioritise the items, how they delegate, how tactful they are, and how lucid and concise are their written communications.

Candidates may also have to write reports on situations or cases where they have to prepare for a critical meeting, or produce written conclusions or recommendations.

## One-to-one exercises

This scenario might then lead into the next set of activities involving one-to-one exercises. For example, after working through written materials the participants may actually have to go to the meeting with the colleague (role played by an assessor), to defend their position and ensure a successful outcome. After examining a strategy report and making recommendations for a meeting with their boss, candidates may then actually go to attend a meeting with the 'boss', again role-played by an assessor. The boss may require briefing for a critical meeting later that week and may ask probing questions on both scenarios. The assessor will score candidate performance on such criteria as vision, influence, assertiveness and negotiation.

Other one-to-one activities might include role-play discussions with difficult customers or subordinates or colleagues, who might be played either by assessors or other participants, or by trained role-players. Others might involve counselling or coaching sessions with employees, or conducting a disciplinary interview.

## Oral presentation

Finally, a classic activity in many assessment centres is the oral presentation made usually to both fellow candidates and assessors. This again may be job-related or unrelated, and candidates may have varying amounts of notice and be allowed various kinds of audio-visual aids. In many cases questioning on the presentation from assessors or other participants will be included.

## Case study – Natco

Let us look more closely at the kinds of exercises used in Natco, the financial services organisation. This organisation used a one-day assessment centre consisting of the following activities:

- *In-tray exercise*   this simulated the contents of a first-line manager's in-tray. Candidates had to make decisions about what to do with this information under tight time constraints.

- *Group discussion*   in this exercise the six candidates attended a meeting concerned with the allocation of staff time.

- *Customer discussion*   This was a one-to-one exercise where candidates had to deal with a (role-played) customer who has made a complaint about deposit charges.

- *Staff discussion*   This was again a one-to-one exercise where the candidate had to interview a 'difficult' member of staff who was taking too much time off work and whose work was suffering.

- *Self-appraisal inventory*   This was a personality questionnaire designed to measure need to achieve, work interests, goals and motivations.

In our research we found that participants had a high regard for this centre. They tended to see it as fairer, more accurate and more valid than the other techniques such as biodata, situational interview and another kind of assessment centre. They also regarded its developmental value highly, seeing the feedback and recommendations they got as accurate, worth while and motivating. This was in many cases true of both groups – those who failed the centre and were not selected for further progress and development, and those who passed the centre and were selected for further promotion.

At a later stage, a more complex, five day assessment centre was used. This involved the following.

- *As in-tray exercise* candidates first ordered the importance and urgency of the items included in the in-tray, and then worked on nine items to demonstrate the quality and appropriateness of their responses and their written communication skills.

- *Business exercise* in this exercise, candidates first completed a short report on the key issues facing a fictional company. A planning meeting was then held to develop a group summary of key issues. This was then followed by a final presentation to assessors, who questioned the group on their recommendations.

- *Outdoor exercise* these involved five separate activities with each person acting as group leader for one activity. Candidates were assessed as both leader and team members.

- *Presentation exercise* candidates delivered a presentation which they had prepared beforehand.

- *Group discussion exercise* individuals identified key issues to which the organisation should be paying attention in the next five years, and then the group arrived at a consensus ranking of the items.

- *Assigned role exercise* participants were given a problem concerning the allocation of salaries and briefs from which to argue a case.

- *Decision-making exercise* as a group the participants made decisions over financial expenditure and the size of the advertising budget.

Example 6.5 shows how these two centres were integrated into Natco's total management development programme.

In our research on the second centre we found that it was not in general as positively regarded as the earlier assessment centre. In particular, those who 'failed' the centre were particularly critical; this was not found with the earlier centre. This is important, for if candidates feel inaccurately assessed by invalid methods presented in an insensitive way, they may well leave or show lower commitment to the organisation in other ways. Certainly our research at Natco showed that subsequent commitment to the organisation and thoughts about leaving jobs or changing career were often strongly linked to the perceived adequacy of the assessment procedure at this stage. Those who thought the procedure fair, valid and accurate were often most likely to report greater commitment and fewer thoughts of leaving several

*Example 6.5*

Natco has developed a sophisticated range of assessment procedures to identify, track and develop potential at all stages of an individual's career. Though some posts are specialised, most career paths are broad and assessment is centralised. Most managerial requirements are met through internal identification and development from a large pool of potential recruits at various career stages. The company realised in the mid 1980s that bank managers traditionally had been seen as technicians, but with new technology needed other skills. It wished to identify people faster, push them forwards more rapidly compared to the past, and retain talented people.

This was accomplished through the 'tiering' of people at various points in their career according to the potential they were seen to display. Initial screening for internal staff to an accelerated management development programme was carried out through biodata and a situational interview. The situational interview was developed through a series of critical incidents faced by managers and hypothetical situations. Both methods are valid predictors of potential and both cost-effective with large numbers of staff, given the need to reduce numbers entering the programme from 3,000 to a few hundred. Graduates entered the programme directly, 150 being sifted from 5,000 applicants, reduced to 800 at first interviews, 400 at second interviews with 150 receiving job offers. One-third of those offered jobs were taken away for a special assessment weekend, and if successful offered 'special entry' to the programme.

As the pool of potential 'high flyers' is reduced in number, increasingly expensive but more valid techniques generating much more developmental information are employed. An initial one-day assessment centre at around 24 years of age targeted on junior managerial competencies was used to grant entry to a personal development programme, which included a development centre at around the age of 28. It culminated in a further five-day assessment centre targeted on middle management competencies at around 30. Successful performance led to a structured group panel interview targeted on executive competencies.

This is a very systematic, integrated approach to identifying and developing future managers using a series of standardised, reliable techniques with high validity and utility. However, there is the important question of impact. An assessment technique may be a highly valid predictor, yet be seen negatively by staff, who may lose commitment and motivation if rejected by such a technique.

*Source*: Gratton (1989); Iles and Robertson (1989)

months later. Consequently, it is important to get the assessment centre right from the perspective of the candidates.

## Comparing the two centres

What has caused this difference in reactions to these two centres run in the same organisation? It is not possible to be certain – further research on this area is needed. But it seems likely that the one-day junior centre was more job-related, more accurately targeted on junior managerial competences, and more adequately tailored to the content and context of a junior manager's job in the organisation. The range of activities was comprehensive, involving one-to-one, individual and group work. The competences were accurately targeted, involving basic managerial skills appropriate to this level – adaptability, self-organisation, problem-solving, leadership, alertness, social skills, team skills, organisational commitment, written and verbal communication skills and need for achievement. The actual content of the activities was clearly organisation-related – the in-tray contained relevant items, and the staffing discussion, the customer complaint discussion, and the fact-finding interview with an under-performing employee all seemed relevant and likely to be encountered by managers in this organisation. The only question-mark concerned the self-appraisal inventory, as assessors appeared to be unsure how to use the information generated.

In contrast, the later centre employed what appeared to be standard, off-the-shelf exercises not customised or tailored to the organisation's needs. The salary allocation exercise, for example, contained many names which were clearly American in origin. The business game did not seem to lead to involvement or ownership by participants, and in many cases it was unclear as to whether it was individuals or teams who were being assessed. Given that many of the activities were carried out by teams, but that assessors scored individuals, feelings of unfairness may have arisen. Again, many of the exercises, such as the outdoor activities, did not seem to have much to do with the business skills required in the organisation. The competences being assessed were perhaps more appropriate to junior management, appearing to neglect the strategic and representative functions of senior management. In addition, the exercises involved only group or individual activities – no one-to-one negotiating, counselling, influencing or discussion exercises were included.

From this research, our own practitioner experience, and Alban-Metcalfe's work with NHS assessment centres, we can draw up the following guidelines for good assessment centre practice:

- conduct a thorough job analysis;

- target the selected competencies at the appropriate job level;

- use behavioural frameworks that not only give summary definitions of each criterion, but also give specific indicators of good and bad practice;

- use a comprehensive range of exercises – individual, one-to-one and group;

- use a set of exercises so that each exercise leads naturally and logically into the next to form an integrated whole, not a series of discrete events.

We feel that in general it is preferable to try and aim for an 'integrated day in the life of' kind of design as far as possible, especially with development centres run for developmental purposes with internal staff. A centre we designed for senior nurses at a large psychiatric hospital illustrates how this might be achieved.

## A development centre for health service operational managers

In this one-day centre, participants were given the opportunity of taking part in a 'management development workshop' so that they could demonstrate their skills against 11 different criteria. These criteria were:

- decision-making;

- communication;

- interviewing;

- leadership;

- delegation;

- feedback;

- vision;

- acumen;

- assertiveness;

- social skills;

- managing complexity.

Each criteria was behaviourally defined with indicators of effective and ineffective performance. Trained line managers in the organisation assessed participants against these criteria on a six-point rating scale. They took part in five different activities during the day. Example 6.6 shows the timetable for this centre, while Example 6.7 shows how it was described.

The first exercise was an in-tray exercise termed 'the morning mail'. It contained various typical items likely to be found in the mail on Monday morning – letters, resignations, announcements, requests for assistance, telephone messages, memos, notice bulletins and agendas. Candidates were assessed on how they dealt with this post, in terms of skills of decision-making, communicating, delegation, acumen and managing complexity.

Participants then went on to draft a report on an urgent move into temporary accommodation (See Example 6.8).

They then went on to a meeting of senior sisters to make recommenda-

| | *Example 6.6* |
| --- | --- |
| | *Senior nurse manager assessment centre* |
| | *TIMETABLE* |
| 9.15 | Start |
| 9.30 | 'Morning Post' |
| 11.30 | Meeting 1 (Situation Interview) |
| 12.00 | Meeting 2 (Situation Interview) |
| 12.30 | Lunch |
| 1.30 | Working Party |
| 3.00 | Meetings re Interview |
| 3.45 | Tea |
| 4.00 | Small Group Review |
| 4.30 | Final Review |
| 4.45 | Close |

*Example 6.7*

*Mental Health Unit – Management Development Workshop*

*Introduction*

You are taking part in a workshop designed to allow you to demonstrate your managerial abilities against a number of different criteria. During the course of the day, you will be asked to take part in a number of different activities, individually or as part of a group. The activities are designed to be stretching but enjoyable. So please do not worry about being observed, be yourself and just follow the instructions. If anything is not clear, the workshop staff will help if you ask.

Attached is a diary sheet. Imagine you have just arrived at work on Monday 23 May and are thinking about the tasks for the day . . .

---

*Example 6.8*

*Mental Health Unit – Management Development Workshop*

*Report*

Recent fears regarding the condition of the roof have just been confirmed. It would seem that the main structural supports are in a weak condition and need to be replaced urgently. This means moving your service totally into temporary accommodation for at least three months.

Fortunately, the local authority has just closed a residential home a mile away from your hospital. While the accommodation is not ideal it will do. As one of the reasons for closure was the fact that the building consists of very large rooms, which would not easily provide for the kind of private rooms the social services want to make available.

Nevertheless, the move is going to cause some upheaval and it has been seen as an opportunity to review how your particular part of the service is run. You had a discussion with your manager yesterday and agreed that this was the chance for a 'no holds barred' look at staffing levels and mix.

You said you would prepare a draft report outlining your ideas on how to reorganise the staffing of the service to improve coverage of holidays and sickness, allow for training time, take account of different care programmes, changing patterns of skill mix and recruitment problems, and any other factors that influence the provision of care, running the service and the staff/patient ratio. (The personnel department has the historic and other relevant information.)

You also agreed to provide some thoughts on the cost of the move. It is likely that some capital work will be needed. You have not been able to see the home, but have been asked to say what essential requirements need to exist for safety, mobility and fire prevention etc. And you know you will need some more basic equipment. (The unit accountant has the supplies catalogue and you know she has some information regarding the costs of building work.)

The other factor that is causing some concern is the effect the move will have on the unit's performance indicators. The region (and so the district) is concerned about the length of stay and occupancy levels. Your manager has asked you to think about how the upheaval might effect these and other measures of performance since you know your patients the best. (Information regarding last year's indicators is available from your manager, if you need it.)

Because of the urgency of the move, you agreed to prepare a draft report on each of these three aspects and any other relevant issues this morning. Your line manager has half-an-hour free later on to discuss it with you.

---

*Example 6.9*

*Mental Health Unit – Management Development Workshop*

*Group activity*

(Ward-based working party)
This activity is designed to explore your ability to work with others and to make decisions.

The general manager has asked that efforts are made to improve the public image of X Hospital, following some poor press regarding services to the mentally ill in general. He also thinks it will be a good opportunity for the senior sisters to do some work together.

Consequently, he has suggested that groups of eight sisters meet for 45 minutes to make some recommendations. This is a topic close to your heart and you have an idea you would like to see adopted. The meeting is due to start in 15 minutes – you can use this time to prepare your case.

---

tions to improve the public image of their hospital, following time to prepare their case (see Example 6.9).

They also took part in a working party to deal with the problem of 'disappearances' of patients' property, and came up with some recommendations for the general manager (see Example 6.10). After this exercise participants ranked their own and their colleagues' performance during the meeting.

---

*Example 6.10*

*Mental Health Unit – Management Development Workshop*

*Group exercise*

(Day hospital – based managers working party)
This activity is designed to explore your ability to work with others and to make decisions.

You are asked to imagine you have been asked to attend the first meeting of a working party set up to consider how to deal with a potentially sensitive situation. Increasingly, reports are being made concerning the 'disappearance' of patients' personal property (including money). There seems to be no pattern, but the general manager wants to deal with the situation – whatever that might be – before something really serious happens.

A group of nurse managers, consequently, has been asked to make some recommendations on what should be done. The general manager has suggested that you give some thought to this matter – spending say 15 minutes jotting down some thoughts and ideas, and then meet for no more than 45 minutes to agree some recommendations and an indication of the implications.

---

They next engaged in another small group meeting to produce a checklist/code of practice on how to conduct an interview and recruit staff. This was followed by a small group review where candidates assessed their performance, giving and receiving feedback from each other. At the end of the day, candidates undertook a final self-assessment using a prepared form and at the end of this exercise received a feedback form containing both general and specific feedback.

There are other points to note about this centre; in particular the assessor training, the way assessors rated performance against criteria, and the use of a matrix to integrate exercises and dimensions. These points will be covered in later sections. Note also that it is a 'development' centre and incorporates rather more self and peer assessment and feedback than is normally the case with selection-oriented 'assessment centres'. We will explore the differences between assessment and development centres more fully in a later section, but first let us look at a more 'selection-oriented' centre.

## A selection centre designed for a senior post in higher education

The centre was to last one day and involved a series of activities, beginning with individual work on a series of issues:

- a business plan;

- an industrial relations issue;

- a letter of complaint;

- access issues;

- ideas for income generation.

Example 6.11 gives the day's programme.

---

*Example 6.11*

*Programme*

---

| 9.00am | Open |
|---|---|
| 9.30am | Private work<br>  Business plan<br>  IR problem<br>  Letter of complaint from student re dangers of<br>  working late<br>  Income generation |
| 10.45am | Access<br>Coffee |
| 11.00am | COPOL meeting |
| 12.00 noon | Meeting assessment |
| 12.15pm | Lunch |

| 1.30pm | Business plan meetings | | | | | | |
|---|---|---|---|---|---|---|---|
| | | 1.30<br>1.45 | 1.45<br>2.00 | 2.00<br>2.15 | 2.15<br>2.30 | 2.30<br>2.45 | 2.45<br>3.00 |
| | AP | 3 | 2 | 1 | 5 | 4 | 6 |
| | DP | 6 | 5 | 4 | 3 | 2 | 1 |
| | DR | 5 | 4 | 3 | 6 | 1 | 2 |

| 3.15pm | Final assessment |
|---|---|
| 3.30pm | Tea |
| 3.45pm | Close |

The candidates were invited to write their replies, comments, letters and recommendations in response to a file of information, requests and instructions. This included a draft business plan and an executive summary of the organisation's strategic plan.

After coffee, candidates attended a task group meeting on the implications of resource-based learning. This meeting with candidates was followed by a self-assessment of the meeting and the extent to which agreement was reached.

The afternoon was taken up with the business plan meetings with two other senior managers (role-played by assessors) to discuss the candidates' ideas. At the end of the day, candidates were asked to note their final reflections of the day on a pre-prepared form, to be considered by the assessors during the overall rating.

In this assessment centre, candidates were assessed against the following criteria:

- communication skill;

- assertiveness;

- resourcefulness;

- perception;

- negotiation;

- decision-making;

- planning and organisation;

- technical competence.

Each of these criteria was behaviourally defined, and candidates rated on six-point scales.

## ACTIVITIES AND CRITERIA

The way that activities relate to the criteria being assessed has been the subject of some controversy. The theme running through much of this debate focuses on claims about the level of the content and construct validity of the assessment centre technique. The main contention has been over whether the dimension scores correlate more highly across the different exercises, or more highly within each self-contained exercise, and the significance of this.

A crucial difference between work sampling and assessment centres involves the identification and use of criteria as the basis for activity design in assessment centres. In work sample testing, the activities are derived directly from job analysis without the intervening stage of developing dimensions or criteria.

Most of this controversy stems from recent British and American research which has shown that the average correlations of ratings on the same criterion in different activities, such as 'leadership' as rated in a role-play, a leaderless group discussion exercise and a personality inventory, are often near zero. It was contended that this meant that assessors did not seem to be in fact assessing the constructs of leadership they were supposed to be assessing. Even more significant was the finding that ratings of different criteria within an exercise (such as ratings of such criteria as interpersonal skills, analytical skills and oral communications made in a role-play) often correlated more highly than across exercise ratings of the same criterion (such as 'oral communications') as assessed in a group exercise, role-plays and oral presentations. This, it is contended, means that assessment ratings are almost entirely situation-specific and assessors do not seem to be assessing general skills, but specific task performance.

## Changes in practice

This has led to some changes in British assessment centre practice. 'Task-based' assessment centres, for example, use observer checklists to assess task or exercise performance, not dimensional or criterion performance. Critical job tasks are sampled and represented in situational exercises, and candidate performance is scored in terms of exercise specific checklists or behaviourally-based rating scales. However, though this may be appropriate for external selection, it seems less appropriate for internal candidates needing feedback on their skills. For 'developmental' purposes, assessment by criterion and feedback on criterion performance seems appropriate in addition to feedback on performance in an activity.

We feel that assessment centres never were designed nor should be used to measure stable personality traits, but situation specific skills. The multiple exercises used in centres are not simply there to provide multiple opportunities for the measurement of the same stable trait. The assessment centre as a whole needs to resemble the target job, and needs to be an integrated whole, not a collection of separate exercises. If the assessors are adequately trained, and if the criteria are behaviourally defined with specific performance indicators, then assessors are able to support their ratings with observable evidence. The exercises chosen should sample both content and context, and we should not necessarily expect stable performance across exercises. Clearly some people perform better in some situations than others – some people communicate well in small groups or in one-to-one interviews, for example, but perform badly with large audiences when giving oral presentations. Others may show good group skills or interpersonal skills in a co-operative group activity, but rather poor ones in a competitive task with assigned roles. A well-defined assessment centre should use multiple exercises that sample the job comprehensively, not just use different exercises merely as vehicles to provide repeated opportunities to observe the same behaviour.

The overall guiding principle of assessment centre design is the link between job-required skills and activities designed to enable the demonstration of those skills. In the design process the use of a matrix ensures that each skill is elicited several times in several different activities. We will discuss the use of the matrix in the next stage.

## Generation of an 'activity by criterion' matrix

A matrix helps bring together the activities and the criteria, and helps design the activities. In a 'matrix' activities form the columns, and the criteria or dimensions the rows. Not every criterion is measured by every exercise. Typically, each criterion is measured at least three times, and each activity contributes to the measurement of at least three criteria.

For example, we devised an assessment centre (called a 'diagnostic day' to emphasise its 'developmental' focus) with laboratory service managers employed in a district health authority (see Example 6.12). In all, 12 criteria were drawn up following a job analysis to profile the key managerial skills needed by this group:

- planning and organisation;

- interviewing;

- decision-making;

- perception;

- self-awareness;

- learning abilities;

- assertiveness;

- resourcefulness;

- feedback;

- communication;

- social skills;

- assimilation.

Activities were then constructed which would expose these managerial skills and which were:

- diverse;

- equally unfamiliar to all participants not requiring specialist or technical knowledge;

- testing managerial processes, not technical expertise;

- fair in terms of content and timing;

- realistic and relevant to both context and content of job;

- reflective of the appropriate level of skills required for the job.

---

*Example 6.12*

*Department of pathology – manager skills profile*

**Managing the job**
PLANNING AND ORGANISATION
Is able to plan ahead, prioritise, utilise and organise resources.

INTERVIEWING
Is able to gather information from an interviewee by building a rapport, asking appropriate questions and observing and listening to the responses. Is able to satisfy the interviewee's requests for information.

DECISION-MAKING
Ability to identify and investigate problems. Knows when to make considered decisions. Is prepared to amend them in the light of new, relevant evidence.

**Managing the environment**
PERCEPTION
Is aware of the broader context in which the role is performed.

**Managing oneself**
SELF-AWARENESS
Is able to conduct oneself with confidence in new or difficult situations. Is aware of one's strengths and weaknesses.

---

---

LEARNING ABILITIES
Is able to seek actively new ideas and opportunities, adapt them and find ways of putting them into practice for one's own and others' learning.

ASSERTIVENESS
Is able to confront others calmly but firmly, without aggression, sarcasm or discourtesy, irrespective of rank or position.

RESOURCEFULNESS
Ability to find other ways of doing things and to act on initiative.

**Managing others**
FEEDBACK
Is able to appraise others' performance accurately and give feedback tactfully and in a way which helps the other.

COMMUNICATION
Is willing and able to express oneself clearly and concisely, verbally and in writing. Checks understanding and can be seen to listen.

SOCIAL SKILLS
Is able to develop and maintain constructive relationships with one or more people, demonstrating sensitivity to their moods and needs.

**Conceptual abilities**
ASSIMILATION
Is able to grasp the essential points and summarise them for others.

---

Each activity was designed to expose more than one dimension, and each dimension was to be exposed in at least three activities throughout the length of the centre, allowing a comprehensive picture of each participant to be developed by the assessor panel. These activities, designed to simulate workplace situations for the participants, consisted of:

- a *written test* on the implications of a fire;

- an *in-tray exercise* with a follow up interview;

- a series of *investigative role-play interviews* where a resource person (assessor) was interviewed to investigate some interpersonal incidents;

- a *small group discussion* to discuss these findings and agree recommendations;

- a *presentation* on the findings and recommendations;

- a *group review of the case study and feedback* session to discuss the events and reflect on performance;

- an overall reflective review.

A grid or matrix was constructed with each of the 12 dimensions against which behaviour was to be observed listed down the left-hand side and each of the activities listed across the top (see Example 6.13). This was used to aid the design and act as a basis for the final assessment.

Another matrix of criteria by activities this time for a centre designed to select a public sector manager for Sheffield City Council, is shown in Example 6.14. In this centre, ten criteria were assessed in five activities:

- a memo on an audit commission report;

- a meeting on the memo with the director;

- a meeting with a junior manager over a disciplinary problem;

- a group discussion on accommodation issues;

- a strategic planning meeting; and

- a self-assessment inventory.

## HOW TO CHOOSE AND TRAIN ASSESSORS

The choice of assessor in a way is dependent on the choice of method used to assess the participants. If highly sophisticated techniques are to be used, obviously the assessors need to have some degree of competence in their use. The accepted practice is that line managers perform the role and that assessors should be trained. The standard of assessment ability is more difficult to specify, and using checklists may be one means of overcoming assessors' lack of abilities or training.

### The best choice

Accepted wisdom states that assessors should be drawn from a population knowledgeable about the job but not directly involved with the participants. This gives the centre some of its high face validity, as the assessors can be seen to have some expertise, either from their role as a line manager (content knowledge) or some other involvement in the organisation (context knowledge). In some situations it is appropriate to use 'stranger' assessors, as in graduate recruitment or for external candidates.

*Example 6.13*

Laboratory service managers' 'diagnostic day'

| | Test | In-Tray/ Interview | Problem Interview | Group Meeting | Presen- tation | Feed- back | Group Feed- back |
|---|---|---|---|---|---|---|---|
| PLANNING AND ORGANISATION | / | / | / | / | | | |
| INTERVIEWING | | | / | / | | / | |
| DECISION-MAKING | / | / | | / | | / | |
| PERCEPTION | / | / | / | / | | | / |
| SELF-AWARENESS | | / | / | / | / | | |
| LEARNING ABILITIES | | / | | / | | / | / |
| ASSERTIVENESS | | / | / | / | / | | / |
| RESOURCE-FULNESS | / | / | / | / | | | |
| FEEDBACK | | | | Review / | | / | / |
| COMMUNICATION | / | / | / | / | / | / | / |
| SOCIAL SKILLS | | | | / | / | / | / |
| ASSIMILATION | / | / | / | / | / | / | / |

An external observer familiar with the process, such as a chartered psychologist or personnel manager may prove a very useful member of the panel to ensure that good dispassionate practice is followed and adequate evidence for ratings produced by assessors. Such a person need not be an actual assessor.

In centres used as part of a larger development programme it might be

*Example 6.14*

Overall assessment criteria

Manager, public sector development

| Criteria | Audit Memo | Dir. Meeting | Junior Manager | Accommo- dation Discussion | Strategy Meeting | Self- Assessment |
|---|---|---|---|---|---|---|
| Strategic thinking | | | | | | |
| Mental scope | | | | | | |
| Assertive | | | | | | |
| Resourceful | | | | | | |
| Managing complexity | | | | | | |
| Negotiate | | | | | | |
| Perception | | | | | | |
| Decision-making | | | | | | |
| Leadership | | | | | | |
| Assimilation | | | | | | |

better to use managers who can have some continuing relationship with the participants.

Practice has indicated to us that it is preferable not to use a manager who is the direct supervisor of a participant, nor should a subordinate and a manager be assessors on the same panel. However, in certain situations, it is difficult to avoid this. It would be almost impossible, and perhaps undesirable, to keep the boss out of a selection centre. And if the centre is for developmental purposes, the involvement of the line manager can be seen as essential to ensure ownership and follow-up action.

The relationships within the assessor panel also need to be considered where it is not possible to avoid involving those with a hierarchical or some other relationship. The person chairing the panel needs to be aware of potential difficulties as well as be sensitive to the dynamics of the panel as a whole.

## Assessors' skills

Assessors need to have some knowledge of the job in terms of its context or content. They must be skilled in:

- observing behaviour;

- recording accurately;

- reporting clearly;

- suspending judgement;

- giving constructive feedback.

Ideally, for an internal development centre line managers two steps above the post in question should be involved, but without previous knowledge of the participants. Information gained from contact outside the centre should never be used to make an assessment. Ideally also the ratio of assessors to participants should be 1:2 or 1:3.

In the pathology laboratory service manager centre (see Example 6.13), the centre was run on three separate occasions with eight participants on each occasion. A total of 12 assessors was needed, selected from a large pool of managers throughout the district with previous involvement in management development initiatives. Assessors were taken from a broad range of professional disciplines and organisational cultures. In this light, it was necessary for all assessors to have a common understanding of how each dimension was defined and what constituted effective or ineffective performance. Two weeks before the first of the centres was run, a two-day training and briefing session was held to ensure all observers were familiar with the centre objectives and exercises, and the role of the observer. The observers were also provided with an information and documentation booklet.

Assessors require training in each of the five stages of observation; recording; classification; evaluation; and feedback. They need a common understanding of:

- the purpose of the centre;

- the relevant dimensions;

- the behaviour to be identified for each dimension;

- examples of behaviours that reflect the ratings within each dimension;

- the kinds of behaviour likely to be exhibited in each activity;

- how a particular exercise relates to important aspects of the job under question;

- how to rate the behaviour exhibited;

- how to integrate the data into the final assessment;

- how to give specific relevant, confidential feedback to candidates.

### The benefits of line manager assessors

If line manager assessors are involved in the centre, a number of benefits can ensue:

- a common competency language and framework becomes established;

- it can complement other initiatives such as performance appraisal, training and development and succession planning;

- reduced conflict through increased understanding and contact;

- cross-organisational sharing, resulting in easier arrangement of secondments, in-company projects, task forces and the like;

- increased commitment to and 'ownership' of the centre and the process, including the developmental activities which may result;

- increased pay-offs for the assessors themselves, in terms of improved skills in observation, categorisation, and evaluation and better skills in interviewing and giving feedback, all of which are likely to improve the assessors' performance away from the centre in appraising, interviewing, coaching and counselling.

## RECORDING AND RATING BEHAVIOUR

A major variation found in different assessment centre practices concerns how the dimensions are rated. Examples include:

- behaviour scored against a pre-specified criterion in ascending order of desirability;

- checklists used to assess performance during each separate exercise;

- behavioural rating scales with points giving examples of 'good' and 'bad' performance;

- absolute scales that judge individuals;

- judgement of individuals relative to one another.

Performance might be rated both on dimensions and on activities. In some centres, candidates are rated on each dimension after each activity. In others, the rating of dimensions is left to the end of the centre when all the information has been collected.

These alternatives conceal important issues such as:

- the difference between personality factors that are unique and particular to one individual and are difficult to change, and skills which are behaviours that can be learned and changed;

- the difference between a rating scale which spans a set of dimensions, a scale that covers self-contained value judgements, and a checklist of behaviours displayed in one exercise;

- the number of critical behaviours used is significant. Twelve seems to be a workable maximum as assessors find difficulties in differentiating between too many dimensions. Practice has indicated to us that assessors are just about able to manage up to 12 dimensions, if they are precisely defined and similar criteria clarified, with overlap being eliminated. It must also be remembered that each exercise should not be intended to expose every dimension.

It is possible to weight the dimensions according to degrees of importance, and to classify them depending on whether they are desirable or essential. This should be decided in advance. Alternatively, they can be clustered into 'meta' criteria, as was the case in Cadbury Schweppes (Example 6.2).

## Timing of the rating

The timing of the rating can affect the way the assessors organise and process the information. In some centres, the assessors are trained to rate the participants after each exercise against a number of prescribed dimensions. In others such as in AT and T, the assessors record behavioural information from all the exercises, then rate each participant on each dimension across the various activities. These ratings are later pooled to arrive at an overall rating. The earlier discussion on the ways in which people perceive and assess each other has obvious relevance here.

Recent uses of assessment centres for development purposes use highly participative rating procedures. Consideration needs to be given to how the timing and use of the rating influences the overall, final assessment.

## Variance in the ratings

It is difficult to distil from the final overall rating how much variance is due to each contributing source of information and much expensively acquired information may not be used. Checklists may be one way of dealing with this by enabling assessors to focus in on specific, recognisable pieces of behaviour in an exercise.

One danger in rating individual behaviour in this way is that other influential factors, such as the situation, the behaviour of others and the presence of assessors are also taken into account during the rating process. It is difficult to ensure in practice that the assessors are assessing the behaviour of the participants, and not revealing their own implicit personality theories.

When a matrix is used, questions arise regarding the acceptability of nil returns if inadequate evidence of behaviour is reported. Practice has shown that the purity of completing the matrix must come second to the quality of the information being obtained.

There has been some controversy over the different methods of arriving at an overall rating and in particular consensus/discussion methods against calculated/weighted scoring. Many researchers have found that averaging the various ratings to arrive at an overall rating predicts subsequent performance as well, if not better than that achieved through a consensus of the assessors after discussion in the 'assessors' conference'. The conference might be employed to discuss only 'borderline' cases, rather than every candidate.

## The use of the final rating

Concern has also been expressed in discussions about the use of the final rating. This can be one overall assessment, a rating against each component skill dimension, an assessment of performance in each exercise or a combination of all three. Most of the research has concentrated on the validity of the overall rating as a predictor of potential, and on the process as a whole having content and construct validity.

The whole purpose of running a centre is to gather information about participants to aid a decision process, whether for recruitment purposes, admission to a training scheme, diagnosis of an individual's development needs or as an aid to organisation development. In some settings, it is appropriate that this decision is made on the basis of one piece of information, such as a final overall score. In others, a large amount of qualitative information needs to be used, such as observations on the competency and effectiveness of an individual's skills, performance or behaviour in different situations, so that appropriate development actions can be planned. Consideration must also be given to the subsequent use of the information. If the results of the centre are to be disclosed to the individual, the value and impact of a score as opposed to a potentially lengthy report needs to be taken into account.

### Rating at the nurse manager centre

Let us look more closely at how behaviour is recorded and rated, and how an overall assessment rating is made, with reference to the senior nurse manager centre (see Example 6.6). If you recall, candidates began their day with an in-tray exercise termed 'the morning post' containing a series of letters, messages and other material. Candidates were rated on how they approached these items and dealt with them, in terms of the criteria of decision-making, delegation, acumen and communications (and for day hospital sisters 'managing complexity').

The next activity was the 'removal report' exercise. Again, candidates were assessed on a variety of criteria by means of the rating form. This exercise also provided observers with guidance as to things to note at the beginning and end of the activity, as well as in the main body of the exercise.

Candidate performance in the group meeting was also rated with guidance provided to observers to help them focus on participant behaviour. Similar checklists were provided for the small group meeting.

At the end of the centre, an overall summary of each participant was made, in both qualitative and quantitative terms using the matrix. Ratings on each criterion were aggregated to form an overall rating, and specific comments were made on performance on each dimension, as well as on overall performance. The participants may also be scored in terms of their written communication skills.

We will now look at the feedback stage.

## HOW SHOULD FEEDBACK BE GIVEN?

A commonly heard criticism of assessment centres made by participants concerns the quality of the feedback they have been given. The participants are also making an investment in the process, so they deserve some consideration and it is reasonable for them to expect to get some return. Even if the centre is being used for selection and involves external candidates, some access to the resultant information should be provided. This is even more critical for internal candidates. We have examined the impact that selection processes, including centres, have had on individuals, and how this has affected their subsequent perceptions of their employer and their careers. The quality of the feedback received seems to play a major role in forming these perceptions.

Decisions need to be made, preferably during the design stages, about who is to give the feedback, and when this is to be done. Ideally, participants should be given dates with the pre-centre information. The role the line manager is to play needs also to be clarified. These decisions vary for different types of centre but should be made consciously.

Decisions consequently are needed regarding access to such information and the use of it for other purposes. Confidentiality should be of prime concern. Designers and client managers need to be informed about the limited value of this sort of information and have a clear code of ethics about its use for other purposes. Participants should be informed if the information is to be made available or used for other purposes.

Supplying feedback is as skilled a process as any other part of the assessment centre technique, so it should also be covered in the initial training assessors receive.

The person giving the feedback should ideally be a member of the assessor panel, for the choice of feedback provider can influence the acceptability of the information. It can be done on a diagnostic basis with the participants being encouraged to reflect on their own performance, using the exercises and dimensions as a framework. Alternatively, and less helpfully, the assessor can appear to take an omniscient stance, appearing to have an overall view of the individual's personality.

Participants have a right to see any test scores or assessment ratings and to receive feedback on their performance. Full and detailed feedback at a time close to the original assessment is necessary. Given the risks to self-esteem it is felt that just giving the test scores or ratings is insufficient. Full oral feedback is necessary, with an emphasis on strengths as well as weaknesses, and a focus on how those weaknesses can be addressed.

Example 6.15 gives the feedback report used in the senior psychiatric nurse assessment centre already discussed.

---

*Example 6.15*

Feedback report

Participant's name _____

Date _____

Observer panel _____

_____

| *Criteria* | *Feedback* |
|---|---|
| Decision-making | |
| Communication | |
| Interviewing | |
| Leadership | |
| Delegation | |
| Feedback | |
| Vision | |
| Acumen | |
| Assertiveness | |
| Social skills | |
| Managing complexity | |

*General feedback and recommendations:*

Signed _____

Participant's comments:

Signed _____

## Report and recommended actions

Some regional health authorities have found that the way their centres were being used to select candidates for 'fast track' programmes was having a negative impact on capable but unsuccessful participants. This has led them to change the timing of the selection decision until a later date and to use the centre technique as a means of development for all the candidates, from which everyone can emerge a winner. This is done by paying attention to the climate in which the centre is run, the degree of participation and assessment built into the design and the quality of the feedback. Follow-up action is guaranteed.

## HOW CAN CENTRES BE USED AS A DEVELOPMENTAL TOOL?

It has been shown that a centre can be an end in itself – for assessment of need, potential or appointability – or it can be a means to the end.

These means can be diagnostic tools by which appropriate action can be taken to help an individual and/or group of individuals to upgrade their managerial performance against an agreed set of criteria. If these criteria have been drawn from the job through thorough job analysis, and the current level of performance assessed against them in job-relevant but unfamiliar situations, good quality information can be gathered from which to draw up development/learning plans. This enables resources to be targeted towards the acquisition or development of needed skills. Developmental applications of assessment centres represent an emerging and exciting area for practitioners interested in maximising the benefits of assessment centres.

If the centre has been well designed and closely related to the needs of the job and the organisation, it should generate follow-up action which:

● is acceptable to the individuals and organisation; and

● is readily applicable.

While these may seem to be obvious conclusions, they are not necessarily followed. The strength of the assessment centre technique is the rigorous discipline that it needs to be successful. The process demands energy and commitment from the participants as well as the assessors and organisation.

Follow-up actions do not have to be restricted to traditional training solutions. The involvement of line managers enables them to act as coaches and mentors, secondments can be easier to arrange, action learning sets can be established and learning contracts drawn up. The whole process can be used to contribute to the development of the organisation, in addition to the intended individual and management development.

Most research seems to be focused on the validity or the predictability of the technique as a selection device, rather than the usefulness of the information gathered for development.

## Development centres

Development centres often depart from traditional assessment centre design and practice in several ways, as they often take a more 'collaborative' approach to assessment and decision-making. Feedback may be given after each exercise, rather than at the end of the centre. They also involve much more self and peer assessment than is usually used in selection-oriented assessment centres.

The developmental centre designed for use with senior nurses also contained substantial amounts of self-assessment of the candidates' performance as a whole. Candidates were invited to assess both their own and other participants' performance in the group activity. Both sets of assessments were used as inputs to the overall rating and to the developmental actions recommended.

We have studied development centres operated in the major clearing bank, MCB, and in a major telecommunications company, as well as in Natco and several departments in a local authority. In general, such centres were very well regarded by participants. In particular, participants found that the observations made about them were accurate and acceptable, and that the developmental recommendations made were worth while. They felt that participation in such a centre motivated them to address their weaknesses, and that the feedback they received was clear and helpful, although a little too general and insufficiently specific at times. Participation in a centre run in MCB also seemed to affect how participants saw their careers, often bringing about changes in career plans and strategies, and precipitating thoughts about career change (Iles et al, 1989).

## THE FUTURE OF ASSESSMENT CENTRES

It would be very easy for a good technique to become discredited by people exploiting an organisation's desire to improve on its selection/development processes. The danger signs are already there. All the research evidence shows that centres need to be designed for the organisation/job in question.

It therefore follows that the use of generic criteria and off-the-shelf activities cannot either be properly described as an assessment centre or claim necessarily to have the predictive validity or acceptability of one.

Assessment centres are described as being expensive to set up and run, involving costs in consultancy, administration, training, and assessors' and participants' time. However, they have high validity in predicting job performance and potential. Their contribution in generating profiles on participants' developmental needs and in allowing further training and development to be accurately planned makes them extremely good value. Recent developments in utility theory have shown that investments in human resources are among the most effective investments organisations can make. The cash benefits of using valid selection techniques can be considerable, and recent calculations have estimated that using assessment centres in the British police and armed services has generated benefits for these organisations running into millions of pounds a year. Assessment centres also generate considerable developmental benefits. Since our research shows that people often like them and feel less likely to leave when assessed by them than by some other techniques, such figures are likely to be an underestimate.

## Assessment centres and strategic change

Assessment centres have proved very useful in facilitating organisational change and strategic management. Example 4.2 described some of the new skills required by managers in the UK financial services sector. One organisation we have been associated with, the National and Provincial Building Society, has begun to use development-focused assessment centres employing criteria competences that reflect these new managerial requirements:

- entrepreneurship;

- strategic orientation;

- achievement orientation;

- leadership;

- information-handling; and

- values, including the value of commitment to customer care.

Participants were assessed against these criteria in the course of a three-day centre which included psychometric tests of ability and personality, a non-assigned group exercise, a personal interview, an assigned role group exercise, and a series of presentations. All participants received feedback and the opportunity of a personal development plan, which included access to internal and external development programmes and opportunities.

Other organisations have used centres strategically in other ways. For example, Bass plc, faced with a Monopolies and Mergers Commission Review which lessened the control of brewers on distributors, found itself required to change its culture away from its family firm, secure, long-term employment-oriented one. Bass Brewers and Bass Inns and Taverns were separated, and Bass Systems, dealing with IT issues, was also split into two. Both sections wanted certain people, and assessment centres, called here 'IT skills workshops', were used to select who would go into which new job. Participants were assessed on technical skills, numerical reasoning, verbal reasoning, diagrammatic reasoning, oral communications, written communications, planning and organising, decisiveness, leadership, initiative, judgement, negotiating/persuading, and problem analysis. In the course of a one-and-a-half day centre, the participants undertook verbal and numerical critical reasoning tests, a diagrammatic reasoning test, the occupational personality questionnaire, a technical interview, a general interview, a case study based on a strategic business plan, an in-tray exercise, and two group discussions, one specifically focused on IT topics (Lurie and Watts, 1991).

One final example takes us back to the financial services sector, this time to a middle-sized British based firm called 'Finserv' by the consultant (Shackleton, 1992). Again, faced with a more competitive environment and high client expectations, Finserv realised it needed to 'manage its business' more effectively, focusing on targets, fee generation, profitability, marketing, internal controls and accountability, and the development of a more 'entrepreneurial' culture which identified selling opportunities, offered a range of services, networked with prospective clients and offered services in new areas. To help make this transition, it used a development-oriented assessment centre to assess partners against the criteria necessary for success in the future and to help plan development programmes which might bridge the gap between present competence and future needs.

The eventual centre consisted of a group discussion, a client-meeting exercise, a coaching role-play, a strategy and leadership talk and discussion, and psychometric tests. All participants again received a personal profile and feedback, and were given a personal improvement plan designed to 'close the gap' between present performance and what was needed in the future (Dale and Iles, 1992).

# SUMMARY

In this chapter we have looked at the following.

- The assessment centre, where groups are assessed by trained assessors against criteria derived from a job analysis as they engage in a series of activities including job simulations, is a particularly useful way of assessing skills at work. Centres can be used for selection, for promotion, for the identification of potential, for the diagnosis of training and development needs, for career development and for organisational development.

- Assessment centres have been shown to be a highly valid indicator of future job performance and to be generally fair to minorities and to women, though care needs to be taken to avoid bias at all stages of the assessment centre process.

- Assessment centres can be used for training and development purposes, and for organisation development. In these contexts, they are often termed development centres, or career development workshops. Such centres often place more emphasis on self and peer assessment, on feedback and action planning, and on the involvement of the participant at all stages of the centre procedure.

- Not all so-called 'assessment centres' fully deserve the title. The number of competences employed, the way they are defined, the way ratings are made and the way assessors are trained have all been shown to affect the quality of the overall process.

- A number of assessment centre programmes either studied or designed and implemented by us in banks, building societies, hospitals, and higher education institutions, as well as studies of assessment centres in British industry and in the National Health Service, have been described. Guidelines for good practice over how jobs should be analysed and how criteria should be defined, how activities should be designed, how ratings should be made, how feedback should be given, how action planning should be conducted, how assessors should be trained, and how assessment and development centres can be used as a developmental tool and in the process of strategic change have been presented on the basis of these studies and from our own experience in designing, running and evaluating assessment and development centres.

# 7
# The Assessee's Perspective

How people are assessed will significantly affect the way they think about themselves, their careers, the people acting as assessors and the organisation which is carrying out the assessment. External candidates who feel that they have been inadequately, insensitively or unfairly assessed are likely to express their displeasure by helping to foster a negative impression of the organisation's competence, courtesy and professionalism. Even if offered a job, they may well turn it down, believing that if that is how the organisation will treat them at interview or assessment, then that is how it is likely to treat them when they start work. Now that the demographic changes in the 1990s mean that there is a drop in the numbers of young people coming on to the market, competition between organisations for skilled labour may increase, despite the recession of the early 1990s. Candidates, despite continuing high unemployment in some sectors and areas, may realise that they are beginning to have more labour market power. Increasingly, they will be selecting or rejecting organisations, not vice versa. One of the factors that will lead them to join organisation A rather than organisation B will be how they are treated at every stage of the recruitment process, from their initial contacts when asking for details right through to the final interview. Even if it remains a buyer's market for labour, organisations ought to adopt more 'user-friendly' selection methods (Herriot 1990).

There is quite a lot of research evidence to support these propositions. Candidates often feel that the glossy recruitment literature put out by organisations is too generalised, and is often misleading and inaccurate. They often feel that more informal sources of information, such as word-of-mouth recruitment, or friends or relatives who work for the organisation, are more useful indicators of what the organisation is like as a employer and what a career there may be like. There is also evidence that if candidates get 'realistic job previews' of what the job is really like, those that decide the job is still for them often join up with less rosy expectations and stay longer.

However, we feel that it is questionable how 'realistic' a preview can be if conveyed by films, videos, brochures and presentations, even if the organisation is careful to include 'pen' pictures of the early careers of new entrants and even if it makes sure that a few are around to chat informally with prospective employees about 'what life is really like' in the company. One of the advantages of using an assessment centre or a work sample test in selection is that the candidate can get an accurate picture of the job. The candidate has then received more realistic information on what it might involve, and can take the decision whether or not to go on with the application. Non-managerial employees wishing to consider a managerial career may decide for example that it is not for them after all, after going through a day of job simulations designed to represent a typical day in the life of a manager. The research evidence suggests that those who decide it is for them once selected are likely to be more committed to their employers and less likely to leave due to finding that their expectations of the job and the organisation's expectations fail to match.

## THE INTERVIEWER

There is also a lot of evidence to show that if candidates form a favourable impression of their interviewers, they are more likely to accept a job offer. This is particularly true if the interviewers are seen as typical or representative of the kinds of people who generally work in the organisation. They are more likely to form favourable impressions of interviewers who seem competent, courteous and interested in them as people. Interviewers who seem sensitive, show empathy, listen and show good counselling skills, as well as knowledge about the job and company, seem to be particularly well regarded.

Such considerations of course apply to internal candidates too. It is likely that in the 1990s organisations will need to place an even bigger value not just on attracting employees, but on retaining them and winning their continued commitment. In part, such commitment will be affected by how and why they are assessed. Employees who feel that they have been assessed unfairly, or that they have been rejected by an invalid technique, are likely to 'vote with their feet' and leave the company – or at least think about leaving, while doing their job less whole-heartedly than they did before. On the other hand, candidates who feel they have been assessed accurately in ways that help them get a better picture of themselves and have received constructive feedback, which has helped them identify ways they could address any weaknesses, may even feel a rise in self esteem, an enhanced sense of well-being, a greater sense of commitment to their organisation and their career, and an increased sense of motivation to undertake further training and development. This will have positive benefits not only for them but for their employers too. The kinds of assessment techniques that applicants are exposed to and the ways these are used will increasingly come to play a part in the competitive edge that organisations seek.

## CANDIDATE'S PREFERRED TECHNIQUES

There is evidence that candidates seem to like certain techniques more than others. They do not seem to particularly like psychometric tests, nor do they seem to like peer assessments unless these are carried out for developmental reasons. They see peer assessment as suffering from friendship biases. They also seem to dislike what they consider to be unnecessary intrusions into their personal privacy, concerns which are likely to be particularly evident with some kinds of personality tests, biodata and interviews. They seem less hostile to the use of productivity data or to work-related tests, questionnaires and exercises. They are also likely to feel that their privacy has been invaded if the information they divulge about themselves is outside their control, and likely to be disclosed to other people. Organisations have often claimed the right to ask for all sorts of personal information from candidates and employees, but have often refused to divulge information themselves, claiming such data to be 'confidential'. This is increasingly going to be seen as a very unbalanced situation, and steps will be taken to redress the balance. In Continental Europe there has long been an interest in the candidate's rights to privacy and in the candidate's vulnerable position *vis à vis* the employer. Increasingly, the candidate is seen as a 'client' and 'partner' with rights and interests which need to be met through mutual collaboration, negotiation and decision-making. And of course the Data Protection Act 1984 has given candidates the right to see copies of information held on file and to know about the assessment criteria used in selection.

### *The move to assessment and development centres*

Our own research shows that applicants do not particularly like the use of biodata or situational interviews. Our research, and that of many others in many countries, does seem to confirm, however, that they do like work sample tests, and they particularly like assessment and development centres. Many studies, including our own, have shown that such centres are often regarded as a fair and valid way of assessing potential, and as presenting participants with opportunities to display their potential in ways that paper and pencil tests or interviews do not. Participants often feel that they receive a helpful and realistic picture of their strengths and weaknesses, and few adverse effects have been reported.

One adverse effect that has been noted is that low performers may be discouraged and demotivated because their career prospects have become negatively affected. This is one reason why many organisations have begun to move from assessment centres to development centres so that all participants, not just the 'high fliers' can get something positive from the experience. If all participants get a realistic and helpful picture of their strengths and weaknesses, useful feedback, valuable training and development opportunities, and opportunities for reassessment, then these negative impacts are likely to be less marked.

## Prospective and collaborative procedures

In general, it must be remembered that any selection procedure is catalytic as well as analytic – it stimulates changes in the candidates' self-esteem, self-image and relationships to their organisation, job and career. Candidates generally seem to prefer procedures which are prospective rather than retrospective – that is, procedures like assessment centres which point forwards to the future, rather than procedures, like biodata, which point backwards to the past.

They also tend to prefer procedures which are collaborative rather than controlling, where are able to participate in the assessment and in decisions made on the basis of that assessment (Mabey and Iles, 1991).

These findings on impact have been confirmed by us in research on Natco's assessment programme, in collaboration with Professor Robertson of the Manchester School of Management at UMIST. These impacts may be affected by such variables as the decision itself, whether pass, fail, or fail with feedback, the importance of the decision to the candidate's career, the candidate's beliefs about the accuracy of the technique and the prior degree of involvement of the candidate. In addition, various features of the technique itself may affect the impact of the selection experience.

Clearly, the way in which assessment decisions are taken is within the control of the organisation. Organisations should consider the extent to which their assessment techniques possess desirable or undesirable features. Features of likely importance include the following:

1. *Preparation*

- Motivation of assessees to attend. Is attendance voluntary? What consequences flow from it?

- Assessee understanding of the procedures used, the rationale for their use and their validity for the task at hand.

- Pre-counselling of assessees on likely outcomes and coping procedures.

- Organisational/social support networks.

2. *Assessment experience*

- Perceived relevance of the assessment method.

- Perceived level of procedural justice involved.

- Amount of control vested in assessee.

- Intrusiveness of the assessment method.

3. *Follow-up*

- The quality of the feedback given.

- Supervisor/other social support.

- Relevant training/counselling/developmental support.

- Opportunities for reassessment.

Recent research by Fletcher at Goldsmiths College (Fletcher, 1991) on the uses of assessment centres in a leading British company to identify management potential and development needs has confirmed that experiencing an assessment centre in particular can have significant impacts on participants. Assessment centres are likely to be particularly potent in their effects since they use a wide variety of activities, are long lasting and have high acceptability to participants. All of this will make it harder for participants to rationalise away the effects of poor performance. In his study the experience of going through a centre did have a significant impact on candidate's need for achievement, job involvement and psychological well-being, but some elements of this impact tended to diminish over time. If there is such an immediate impact, organisations should try to capitalise on the learning potential of the experience by providing feedback and action planning as soon as possible after the assessment centre.

## FACTORS INFLUENCING INDIVIDUALS' USE OF THEIR SKILLS

The research we have discussed on the acceptability and impact of assessment procedures shows that some seem better regarded than others, and that assessment centres in particular are generally well thought of by participants. In addition our own research in Natco has shown that the assessment decision has an impact on participant's commitment to the organisation and career plans, and that the perceived adequacy of the procedure also has such an impact (Robertson, Iles, Gratton and Sharpley, 1991). Participants, after experiencing an assessment centre run in MCB, also reported changes in their career plans and intentions (Iles, Robertson and Rout, 1989). However, this is an area that has only just begun to be explored, and it is likely that many other factors will affect not only the assessees' commitment, career planning and well-being, but the extent to which the assessees will make use of their skills. Such use is likely to depend on the degree of person-organisation fit.

## INDIVIDUAL ASPIRATIONS

What individuals want from their working lives – what they want from their jobs, career, organisation and profession – is likely to be of crucial importance. This situation is likely to be dynamic and influenced by their perception of their own strengths and weaknesses, their self-image and their self-efficacy (the degree to which they feel able to perform successfully). These factors are also, of course, linked to access to education, feedback, support, opportunities and role models. Within work people's choices tend to be made on the basis of their whole lives, not just their working lives, and factors such as leisure pursuits and personal commitments have a bearing on their choices. They also influence how much energy they can devote to their work tasks and goals. Such questions are clearly not gender-free. Most themes of job design, job satisfaction and job motivation focus on the internal world of work, but other factors need to be considered. Assessment of skills and potential can become outdated due to factors completely external to an individual's level of task ability.

Many trades, occupations and professions, not just those commonly recognised as such with an agreed and formally stated body of knowledge and code of conduct, have a set of clear expectations about the role of the individual, with prescribed career paths and choices. The culture of the profession, as well as of the organisation, can constrain an individual's development by indicating what is 'the done thing' and what is not. The professions' codes and practices may impose conditions that inhibit individual skill use and development. A profession's culture can condition individuals' expectations of developing, defining and realising their potential, and hence the amount of energy they are prepared to devote to it in relation to their other life activities. Examples might include a clash between a night-class and a pub quiz night, or between attending a residential weekend and leaving one's dependent parent. Professional arrogance may also mean that it can often be difficult to assess areas of weakness, given an ethos of 'equal competence' once qualified.

## THE ORGANISATION'S ABILITY TO MEET INDIVIDUAL NEEDS

How far individuals feel able to commit or invest skills in an organisation also depends on their personal needs and agendas as these evolve over time. This can be as true of newly appointed staff as those who have been employed for a long time. New staff may well have high expectations of success, and high hopes of being able to align their own goals with the organisation's goals. This matching, as we have seen, is likely to depend on:

- prior information on job, organisation and career;
- the selection event itself;
- the picture painted by the organisation and any promises made;
- the induction/inclusion phase;
- the matching of reality to expectations;
- the quality of relationships experienced;
- the culture of the organisation;
- the degree and quality of feedback provided on performance and success;
- equity of rewards and resource allocation;
- the degree to which the individual's changing needs can be recognised and accommodated;

- the career plans of individuals and how they perceive the organisation and the job, as a stepping stone elsewhere or as a job for life;

- the commitment of the individuals and their identification with organisational goals;

- the degree to which the organisation satisfies other needs outside work;

- the challenges, rewards, kudos offered;

- the opportunities offered to use existing skills and develop new ones;

- the assessment of the probability that individual aspirations can be achieved.

## WHAT THE ORGANISATION WANTS FROM INDIVIDUALS

In the first place, the organisation may not know or be clear about what it wants from its employees, and may for example put graduates into clerical jobs. It may not pay sufficient attention to job design, overloading jobs with unrealistic expectations that build failure into a job. Or it may underload jobs, oversimplifying them so that they do not satisfy employee needs and aspirations. The organisation needs to be clear and realistic about its performance expectations, the standards required and its criteria for success. These criteria need to be specified in terms of realistic outputs rather than in vague abstractions, and they need to define the kind of person needed to perform the role effectively in terms of personnel specifications. Organisations also need to engage in strategic planning and to have a clear, if flexible, vision of the future, which links recruitment and development programmes to future operational and business needs as well as accommodating current requirements.

Organisations and professions need also to consider carefully access to professional updating through journals, conferences, meetings, and grant opportunities to transfer skills to new projects, reskilling in rapidly changing areas, revitalising dormant skills, and providing job and career development. Such development might include unfocused, individually initiated development such as part-time courses, but should also include focused, planned programmes of development linked to performance review schemes and learning contracts, linked to the needs of the job, the individual and the organisation. The organisation will also need to consider fostering self-development, as it is unlikely that managers and other employees will be able to develop relationships with others and contribute to their workplace development if they are not first able to understand and develop themselves. Organisations will also need to consider utilising and developing the skills of people out of work due to illness and injury, those taking career breaks, and those caring for dependents. Such concerns will become increasingly important as the 'demographic downturn' takes effect and the number of young people coming on to the labour market declines significantly.

## A FRAMEWORK FOR DEVELOPING SKILLS AFTER ASSESSMENT

It is important to have a framework in place for developing skills and competences after assessment has occurred. Below we will look at developing individuals and organisations in more detail. However, it is appropriate here to outline a model which we have found particularly useful in our work on developing individuals, teams and organisations in a variety of private, public and voluntary sector organisations. It is called 'Framework' and has been developed with Lynn Downs, Viv Whittaker and Vida Pearson. The model as applied to management and organisation development first distinguishes between:

- *manager development*   the development of individuals;

- *management development*   the development of teams, management processes and skill applications;

- *organisation development*   the development of the organisation's ability to meet changing conditions and threats to its survival and effectiveness.

We will take up the themes of management development and organisation development below. At this point all we need to note is that organisational performance depends not only on individual managerial skills and competences, but on joint effort between managers at different levels, and their relationships with the rest of the workforce. Our focus here will be on individual manager development.

### Individual manager development

Management development as traditionally conceived and practised in business schools and  companies has tended to concentrate on managerial tasks and on the techniques used to perform those tasks effectively, especially on analytical and quantitative techniques. Less attention has been devoted to the skills of applying the techniques and to the interpersonal skills necessary to 'get things done through/with other people', which after all is the essence of management. Often interpersonal skills, personal effectiveness, leadership, team-building and communication skills have been seen as rather 'trendy' and 'airy-fairy', and not properly coupled with the application of techniques nor linked into organisational effectiveness. Despite the popularity in the 1980s of books on culture, excellence and leadership, their lessons are in danger of being forgotten, and the more recent focus on visioning, forward planning and strategic thinking may be in danger of going the same way.

It is difficult to link all these concerns into a simple conceptual image of the managerial role – attempts to do so tend to create long lists of everything that could conceivably come into the definition of a manager's job. Such lists would be so comprehensive as to become indigestible and unusable, as well as rapidly outdated and inflexible in the face of changing situations and new demands on the managerial role. Such a list may also not be very transferable between organisations of very different size, type or sector.

## An MCI national framework

The Management Charter Initiative (MCI) has attempted, as the operating arm of the National Foundation of Management Education and Development, to develop a national framework for management development that distinguishes three levels of management – equivalent to certificate, diploma and masters level; or junior, middle and senior management. At each level, there are moves to define occupational standards of competence, in terms of the ability to do the job at the level expected by lead bodies in industry.

At certificate level, for instance, there are four key roles (managing operations, managing people, managing finance and managing information), nine units of competence, and one element of competence, each of which must be assessed.

At diploma level, there are still four key roles, but there are ten units of competence, and even more elements! In addition, there are numerous performance criteria by which evidence of competence is to be judged, and a multitude of 'range statements' indicating the kinds of contexts in which competence is to be expected. There are also 'knowledge and understanding specifications' specifying the contexts, principles, methods and data appropriate to the kinds of knowledge and understanding thought necessary to 'deliver' the competences, and a 'personal competence model' which indicates the kinds of personal skills required in using intellect, planning and organising, relating to others, and self-management thought necessary to achieve the 'functional' competences.

Such a model, at present at an early stage of development and application, clearly has benefits in terms of rigour, systematisation, and national authority. Its very weight, complexity and generic nature also make it vulnerable to some of the problems we discussed earlier, however.

We have found that Framework, conceiving as it does of the managerial job as consisting of 'managing the job', 'developing the organisation', 'interacting with the environment', 'knowing oneself', and 'working with others', provides a very useful transferable model of managing organisations that can be used in many different organisations for many different puposes.

Each major heading can be broken down into a variety of behaviourally-defined elements, which can serve as criteria for assessment. For example, 'working with others' can be seen as involving guiding, directing, and enabling others; 'directing others' can be seen as involving motivating, delegating, and giving and receiving feedback, among other behaviours (see Figure 7.1). Each of these terms can be behaviourally defined in terms of a six-point rating scale. You will have come across examples of this in Chapter 6, when we discussed the assessment centres we designed in the health service and other organisations. We have found this model to be robust and transferable, to make sense to managers and to provide a useful starting point for assessment and development programmes.

## SUMMARY

In this chapter we have looked at the following.

- How candidates are assessed affects their acceptance of job offers, their commitment to their employer, their career plans and goals, and their well-being and self-image.

- The need to treat applicants competently, sensitively and courteously at all stages of a recruitment or assessment process.

- Interviewees like interviewers who are sensitive, competent and informative, who listen, and who display good counselling skills. They are more likely to accept job offers from such interviews.

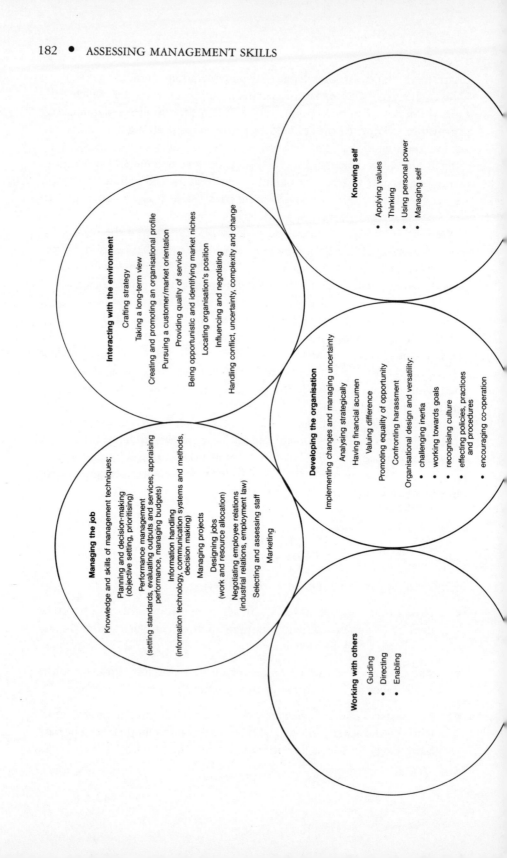

**Interacting with the environment**

Crafting strategy

Taking a long-term view

Creating and promoting an organisational profile

Pursuing a customer/market orientation

Providing quality of service

Being opportunistic and identifying market niches

Locating organisation's position

Influencing and negotiating

Handling conflict, uncertainty, complexity and change

**Knowing self**

- Applying values
- Thinking
- Using personal power
- Managing self

**Managing the job**

Knowledge and skills of management techniques;

Planning and decision-making
(objective setting, prioritising)

Performance management
(setting standards, evaluating outputs and services, appraising performance, managing budgets)

Information handling
(information technology, communication systems and methods, decision making)

Managing projects

Designing jobs
(work and resource allocation)

Negotiating employee relations
(industrial relations, employment law)

Selecting and assessing staff

Marketing

**Developing the organisation**

Implementing changes and managing uncertainty

Analysing strategically

Having financial acumen

Valuing difference

Promoting equality of opportunity

Confronting harassment

Organisational design and versatility:

- challenging inertia
- working towards goals
- recognising culture
- effecting policies, practices and procedures
- encouraging co-operation

**Working with others**

- Guiding
- Directing
- Enabling

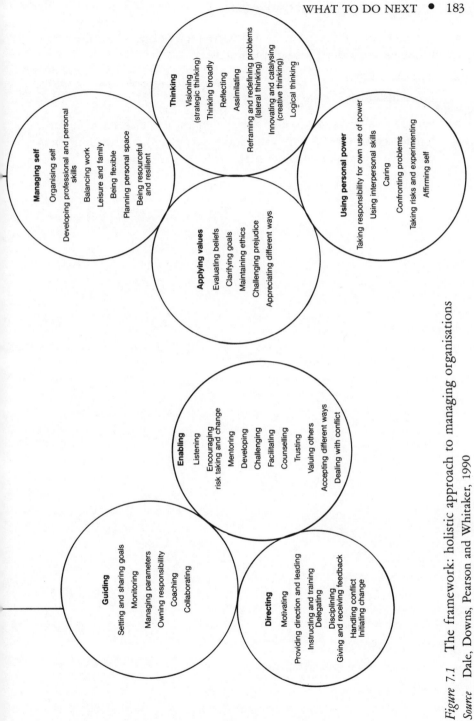

*Figure 7.1* The framework: holistic approach to managing organisations
*Source* Dale, Downs, Pearson and Whitaker, 1990

- A variety of factors, most of which are under organisational control, influence individuals' use of their skills.

- The 'framework' provides a helpful model for assessing and developing skills.

- Participants seem to regard work samples and assessment centres highly, seeing them as fair, valid and accurate, and as providing them with worthwhile developmental feedback, opportunities and recommendations.

# 8

# What to do next

A critical phase of assessment is the follow-up action that is taken as a result of whatever technique is used. Sadly, we have found that most attention is given to the assessment technique itself and, as we discussed in Chapter 7, the people being assessed are often neglected. They become part of the process instead of being the key actors with feelings, opinions and perceptions. The consequences of this neglect may affect the validity of the technique and have an impact on the acceptability and credibility of the outcome, their performance and their degree of affinity to the organisation. We will discuss this at greater length later. The design and running of the event, without attention to this impact, can become ends in themselves. The feedback and follow-up stages need to be treated as integral and as essential to the overall success as are the preliminary and operational stages. Thus, they require as much care and planning as any of the others.

In this chapter we will outline how quality can be achieved in the final stages of assessment and provide some guidance on how to avoid some of the pitfalls we have come across. We hope to provide some ideas on how the assessment, coupled with giving feedback and facilitating development can be made to be effective and produce positive outcomes for all involved.

The importance of getting these stages right cannot be stressed too strongly. For no matter how good the technique is in itself and how well it has been implemented, it has to be seen in its totality and the lasting impact rests on the action that results from the whole. If the assessment process is run as a seamless entity and each stage is well planned and run, the pay-off is known to include improved individual performance, clearer understandings of role and goals which are shared between the individual and the manager, spin-off development and learning for managers and increased contributions to organisational effectiveness. Getting it wrong, however, risks greater losses. The individual can actually be damaged by poor quality feedback given in an insensitive way.

Example 8.1 overleaf is an extreme which was probably influenced by other factors. However, it serves to show the power of the assessment process and the person giving the feedback. We will give other examples later that show other areas of impact.

*Example 8.1*

Take a situation where a young manager who had followed a graduate training scheme and had planned a career in his chosen field, was told that he was in the wrong job and should start again, simply because his psychometric profile did not fit the norms being used. These had been drawn from a very small and unrepresentative sample, and made up only a small part of the assessment technique being used. The person giving the feedback did not take into account the degree of investment already made by the individual, nor the stresses he was facing (even though these were known). Neither was any guidance given on what action could be taken by the individual to help him get closer to fitting the profile (if that was what was required), nor how he could improve his overall performance. Needless to say that individual was faced with a situation that undermined both his actual performance and his self-confidence.

The relationship between the assessor and the assessee is also a vulnerable one. This relationship is of particular importance if a line manager and subordinate are involved. During a feedback session, it is easy to make vague promises of training and development opportunities, and to raise expectations. Realising these can be a different matter as other factors intervene and the vagueness proves too abstract to bring to life. But then the damage will have been done, and the reputation and trust that is needed between the two will be eroded. The skills of managers as assessors will be subject, rightly, to question. But more seriously a commitment to development staff will be in doubt. Trust in the manager's word and the value of any promises will have been diminished. Once these aspects of a manager's performance become suspect it is very difficult to reinstate credibility. If the assessors are outsiders, any negative aspects of their performance tend to reflect more on the process than on them as individuals and on the organisation for having used them. Nevertheless, if the process is badly handled, some of these negative aspects will also taint the assessors' reputation (see Example 8.2).

Failure to deliver quality feedback and follow-up action also throws into question the validity of the technique. The best assessment techniques, as we have shown, produce information that is valid, reliable, acceptable and actionable. Vague generalisations help no one and can reduce the impact of the technique. Many experienced people have, over the years, been exposed to the latest management approach. Such a popular 'jumping on the bandwagon' use of techniques has rightly caused some cynicism and can lead to a feeling of having 'seen it all before'. Managers' professionalism will be

---

*Example 8.2*

One large employer used a firm of consultants to design and run a series of development centres to assist a management development initiative. The feedback was supplied in the form of a letter to the individuals, with a copy being sent to their manager. The participants were offered the facility of a feedback interview with one of the assessors, if they wished. The assessors were managers from other parts of the organisation. The letter consisted of one side of A4 paper which had been written by the consultant. The contents were thought, by the participants, to be very general and almost universally applicable. Only one or two sentences could be related directly to each individual's performance. The participants, with whom the reports were discussed, felt they had little new information to use in a developmental meeting with their manager and had experienced difficulty in getting hold of the assessors as they were now involved in the next series of development centres.

As the word spread the programme as a whole was regarded with increasing suspicion and the managers involved were seen to be playing games. The consultant was thought to be on to a 'good thing' and the employing organisation was seen by its staff as being unable to deliver. Not surprisingly willing participation in the initiative began to decrease. Eventually the whole programme had to be restructured. But at what true cost?

---

discredited and they can be seen as playing games with their staff. This is not a good way to go about establishing trust and a climate in which learning and development are accepted ways of operating. Many good techniques have failed and gone out of general usage because of poor application.

Another common failing is weak action to implement findings. The different uses made of appraisal (ie to reward and review performance, identify potential and development needs etc) provide an example of how management techniques go in and out of vogue; management by objectives is another such technique that gets picked up and put down.

If a technique does not gain the acceptance of participants as a whole very quickly, the desired outcome will not be achieved. The best way of gaining the assessees' commitment and interest and the enthusiasm of others is by ensuring that those who go first gain something positive as a result of their involvement. This involvement, if it is to have long-term credibility, needs to be more than an enjoyable experience. Participants need to feel and be seen to have gained some relevant, personal, applicable, developmental and actionable outcomes.

The consequences of failure to follow up can have varying effects on the organisation. At the very least a minimal impact can be more confirmation, for the staff, of the organisation's culture. However this is rarely the only impact. The involvement in assessment raises the hopes and aspirations of the assessees. It may not necessarily be viewed as the dawning of a new age, but certainly there will be the expectation that something will happen as a result of the initiative. If this does not occur, demoralisation and negative perceptions can be the outcome. If, on the other hand, the assessment and the implementation of the agreed action plans goes well, the pay-off can be enormous for everyone – including the organisation. The introduction of the new approach, in itself, is organisational development in its full sense, and will alter the organisation's culture.

As a final word, any manager contemplating the introduction of any form of assessment must include, while making the decision, an evaluation of their own and the organisation's ability to provide quality feedback and deliver on the defined and expected developmental actions. Any doubts in these areas should throw the whole idea of introducing any assessment technique into question. Sometimes it is better to do nothing than introduce an approach, especially one which can be very personal to those involved, that is thought of as being limited in its chances of success. It is very important that managers should conduct a realistic risk assessment of their own and their organisation's abilities to conduct each stage of the chosen technique properly. In this way weak areas can be identified and isolated, and corrective action or some other form of damage limitation taken.

## FEEDBACK

### Giving feedback

Feedback involves the supply, receipt, exchange and use of information gathered to help improve performance. It should not be merely the manager telling subordinates where they are falling down. The process should be concerned with accumulating, sharing and agreeing an understanding of the individual's effectiveness, based on a realistic assessment which is specific without being too detailed and forward-looking without being star-gazing. The information on which the assessment is made should have been gathered systematically and transmitted to the individual with care and sensitivity.

The information should be as factual as any information regarding behaviour can be and, ideally, it should be possible to provide evidence of the behaviour in question. The individual should not be seen as a passive actor in the process of giving feedback. As the focus of attention, assessees have the right to an opinion, and to question and challenge that of the person providing the feedback. Assessees may also have valuable information which helps to complete the picture. It must also be stressed that once the feedback has been given, it becomes the property of the recipient, who as owner, has the right to use it as desired.

We regard the provision of quality feedback as an essential and integral part of any assessment process. Quality needs to apply equally to both the content and the method of transmission. Like all the other stages of assessment, this requires skill which may – as all other skills – be acquired and developed through learning, practice and the receipt of feedback.

In this chapter we will give some general guidance on the factors that should be given attention. However this stage is highly personalised and each individual manager will need to work out a style that best suits the situation, the people involved, the organisation's culture and the manager's own preferred way of relating to others.

## Timing of feedback provision

Providing feedback too soon after assessment means that it is difficult to step back to reflect; providing it too far away from the assessment means that relevant points can get forgotten or distorted by the passage of time. The purpose of the assessment in part will determine the timing, which may also be influenced by the need to gather data from other sources, activities or people. The following example shows how assessments from multiple sources, using a variety of techniques, can contribute to the selection of participants for a management training scheme:

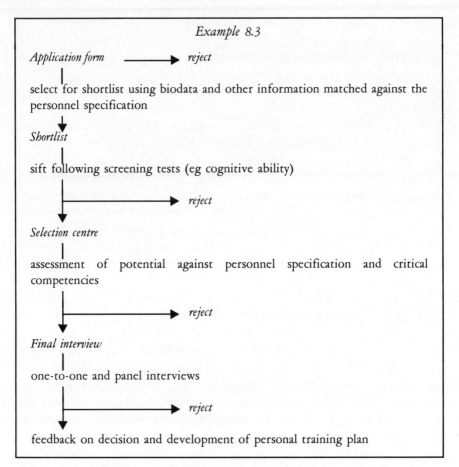

*Example 8.3*

*Application form* ⟶ *reject*

select for shortlist using biodata and other information matched against the personnel specification

*Shortlist*

sift following screening tests (eg cognitive ability)

⟶ *reject*

*Selection centre*

assessment of potential against personnel specification and critical competencies

⟶ *reject*

*Final interview*

one-to-one and panel interviews

⟶ *reject*

feedback on decision and development of personal training plan

The timing of the provision of feedback to rejected applicants can be fixed at each stage. The organisation can also decide how much information it wishes to make available to participants and when it will do so. However, one can question how much should be given to the successful candidates as they pass through the process. Will the information help or hinder their performance? Will it give what may be incorrect or misleading messages about what is being assessed and required of them? The gathering of information in a systematic pattern is aimed at gaining as full a profile of an individual as possible. A manager running such a process is able to decide whether to maintain the integrity of the whole or to see each separate technique as producing stand-alone information that can be disclosed without contaminating any other stage.

## Media used for feedback message

There are varous ways in which feedback can be given. We know of an example of a letter being sent. Other media used are face-to-face discussions and feedback reports, ranging in length from a dossier to a brief, factual summary. Each technique produces outcomes in different shapes and forms which need varying amounts of interpretation and explanation.

Some psychometric tests produce quite complicated charts and graphs which need careful explanation. Merely sending these out in the form of the raw data is not particularly helpful without some supporting material. The assessee deserves some clarification and the opportunity to question the results and the meaning of the assessment.

Face-to-face discussions alone can be less than satisfactory, despite being potentially the best and most commonly used method. Receiving feedback can be stressful and under such circumstances it is easy for verbal messages to be distorted, misunderstood, forgotten and misremembered. Some sort of written back-up can therefore be a valuable supporting medium. Examples of how this can be achieved can be found in some performance review schemes.

Preliminary assessment of past performance would be made by both the assessor and assessee, and exchanged in advance of the meeting. During its course agreement should be reached on the assessment against the previously set goals. A record of the meeting should be made which includes the agreed assessment, the following period's goals and the development plan. This should be drawn up jointly and be aimed at helping the individual improve on the current level of performance and achieve the next set of goals. The record then serves as a report of the meeting, an aid to the implementation of the plan, a monitor of achievement and the basis for the next review.

By linking the personal and written provision of feedback in this way, the assessee is given the opportunity to question, challenge and/or disagree with the assessment. This can help redress the balance of power by enabling the assessee to have their own assessment of performance formally included. The role of a manager is to guide, develop and enable staff to perform their role effectively. A member of staff cannot be held accountable for failing to achieve objectives if these have not been done. This also allows situational factors to be taken into account. As we saw from person perception theories, these factors are often excluded and events are often wrongly attributed to the individual.

The amount of written information provided is dependent on what the technique generates and the assessor's decision on how much detail to give.

Too much fine detail can detract from the main messages; too little can mean that the feedback is too general and non-specific. This can inhibit the creation of follow-up action. More will be said about the content of feedback messages later.

## Who should give the feedback?

If the first line manager is the assessor, there is no question to answer. The manager's role as mentor is very much in vogue at the moment and so we will discuss it at greater length below. However, if other people are involved as assessors, consideration also needs to be given to who should provide the feedback to the assessee and to subsequent roles in any follow-up action. If an associated manager from another part of the organisation or another person is to act in a mentoring capacity, attention needs to be paid to their relationship with the assessee *and* with the manager.

One organisation we are aware of has adopted a cascade approach for the development of its managers. Senior managers go through a development centre and, as part of the follow-up action and their learning, act as assessors in subsequent centres run for the next tranche of managers. They provide the feedback to the assessees and help them to formulate their own development plans. These are then negotiated with the relevant line manager with the assessor providing assistance and support if required. A learning contract is drawn up and the assessor changes role to become a mentor, helping, supporting, coaching and counselling the assessee during the implementation of the plan.

This approach can work well as long as everyone keeps to their part of the contract. Sadly, it is easy for the mentor role to become a low priority, especially if the two parties are not physically close to each other, if their workload does not give proper acknowledgement of the time required or if the organisation is experiencing a high level of change. The latter situation, however, is the very time when supported learning is most needed. Another difficulty can arise when the three corners of the learning contract triangle are not in full accord. This relationship needs to be managed very carefully so that the assessee does not suffer or lose as a result of interpersonal conflict between the other two parties.

The relationship also begs the question of confidentiality. How much information should be given to the line manager following an assessment to which they have not been a party? How much should be contained between the assessor or the person giving the feedback and the individual concerned?

These questions posed very real problems for us during the running of a series of development centres. The line manager commissioning them was very keen to act on the outcome of the centres and ensure that the development plans were implemented. However, one candidate's performance suggested that there might be some deep-rooted problem areas for the individual concerned. The assessors felt very strongly that the feedback discussion should exclude the line manager. Obviously he was not very happy with the situation. He wanted to know what to do to assist the individual's development and felt that he should have an understanding of all their needs. The situation was eventually resolved after long debates by agreeing to hold a two-stage feedback discussion. The first stage was held in private between the individual and the assessor. The line manager joined them later to hear the conclusions of the discussion and anything the assessee wanted to share. The development plan was then drawn up between the three.

If external assessors are involved, consideration needs to be given to whether they should give feedback to the line manager, to the assessee or to both. If the information is to be given to the manager, consideration needs to be paid to how this information is to be interpreted. This is particularly important in the case of psychometric tests. The line manager should have an understanding of the technique used and the implications of the results for the individuals. Some of the tests result in the production of graphs, charts or profiles. If this raw data is to be supplied to the managers, the person responsible for the centre should ensure they have an understanding of their meaning and the terms used. Some of the dimensions and phrases have very specific meanings. There have been situations where assessment data has been supplied to line managers and then used for other purposes. Clarification and perhaps guarantees are needed from line managers regarding the use of this information. We will discuss impact of this and confidentiality later.

## Where and when feedback should be given

One organisation we know called their appraisal scheme 'Job Assessment Review' – going for a 'jar' had a very different meaning for its employees than for the rest of us.

The accepted wisdom is that feedback should be given in private, in comfortable surroundings in which both participants can be at their ease and where interruptions can be avoided. Frequently, these discussions are held in the boss's office. If the organisation's culture and the manager's style is open and relaxed, and the employee is used to working in this location, this setting can be ideal. However, if these conditions do not exist and the relationship or atmosphere is judgemental and punative, one would hardly expect the boss's office to be a conducive location for a frank and open sharing of perceptions of performance.

Enough time should be allowed for both parties to have opportunities for reflection and questioning. It is important that areas of doubt or conflict are resolved during the discussion. Unfinished business can leave an unnecessary taint simply because the next appointee arrived 15 minutes too soon.

The physical layout of the room used can help or hinder the feedback session. A desk can be a barrier – especially if it is loaded with files, trays, telephones, photographs and the other litter of the everyday working life. Alternatively, an empty desk can be very threatening. The size, relative height and position of the chairs also gives out messages. Thinking about the arrangement of the furniture does not take a long time but layout can have an important, if unintentional, impact on the discussion.

## Preparation for giving feedback

Both the person giving the feedback and the one receiving it need adequate time to prepare themselves for the discussion. They also require space to reflect on the assessment, reach conclusions, plan the discussion's content and context, and generate ideas for follow-up action. If the timescale between the assessment and the feedback session is too long, ideas will become fixed. But if it is too soon, the assessee's performance could be seen to be out of perspective or context. Around a week seems to be about right from our experience, but the timespan obviously needs to reflect the requirements of the organisation and the people involved.

Inadequate preparation does not necessarily mean that the feedback session will not be productive, nor does thorough preparation guarantee success. However, according to script theory, the individuals involved will predict and go through some mental rehearsal of the likely scenario. Training for both the assessor and the assessee, which includes some role-play and structured preparation can help avoid distortion or fantasising about the impending discussion. The assessor's preparation should include consideration of the following.

- The physical environment, as mentioned above.

- The style of the discussion. Is it to be formal or informal, an exchange or a telling session?

- The way in which the discussion is to be conducted. Who will open, who will be 'in charge', how will agreement be reached?

- What role will each adopt? Will both be equal parties or will the boss–subordinate roles be perpetuated, and who will take responsibility for what?

- The content of the feedback. Which messages *have* to be given and which *should* be given if the 'right' opportunity presents itself, how will the messages be received and how best should they be transmitted?

- How can the right opportunity be created so that the more sensitive messages can be given constructively?

It can be helpful for the preparatory thinking to be recorded and notes made. The assessor should avoid, though, creating a fixed agenda. Some flexibility will be needed if the assessees have also prepared, for they will also have ideas on what the discussion will be like.

Assessee preparation is more likely to be reflective, but again some notes may prove to be useful. This reflection should include:

- how they performed during the period being assessed;

- what influenced that performance, including internal and external factors;

- how it compares to their 'normal' behaviour;

- reasons for any differences;

- areas in which improvements could be made and how they can best be achieved.


## Role and style of assessor during feedback discussions

Three stances can be identified from which the assessor can choose to operate. While behaviour can be controlled and a particular way of giving feedback adopted, this should be married with the assessor's preferred and normal way of working. Play acting, as new or different behaviour patterns can seem to be, may appear to be false and can be more damaging to the overall intent than behaving normally.

The three stances are:

1. Telling the assessee what the results of the assessment were:

    —pointing out what was good and where the strengths were seen;
    —indicating which aspects of performance were not good or which were seen as being weaknesses;
    —illustrating ways in which different actions could be more effective.

2. Listening to the assessees' perspective on their performance and experience during the assessment and hearing the results of their reflections and introspection. Very little, if any, information is supplied unless requested and the assessor does not offer any opinion or guidance. The role is to aid the reflective process, and the search for insight and understanding of the assessees' behaviour. It may also be necessary to guide the assessees and help plan any development needed to increase effectiveness.

3. Synthesising both the assessor's and the assessees' perceptions of performance. From the two angles (complemented by those of other assessors during the assessment), a fuller picture can be drawn. Contributing factors, unknown to either party, can be added. This joint discussion enables perceptions to be questioned and a deeper understanding gained. From this a development plan can be created and ways of implementing the plan considered and agreed.

Theoretically, the third style should lead to a greater commitment from both to the outcome, than either of the other two styles.

Different techniques, because they produce information in different formats, tend to determine, in part, the role the assessor can adopt. Psychometric profiles require the individual to be told the results of the tests or questionnaires. On the other hand, performance counselling could require more listening. Similarly, different uses to which the techniques may be put influence the role. Recruitment and selection tend to produce a specific decision which has to be communicated and explained to the assessee. Career guidance is more amenable to synthesis, while personal development tends to involve the assessor more in a counselling role.

The individual style and preferences of both parties also have bearings. We referred above to the style of the assessor. Assessees also have preferred ways of hearing the outcome of assessment. Some may prefer to be told, given the opportunity to reflect on the information and to return with questions and areas for clarification. Others will want to make sure the assessor fully understands their perspective and has all the possible information surrounding their performance during the assessment. These assessees may need help to hear what has to be fed back to them.

There is considerable scope for choice and the improvement of skills in the feedback process. We tend to focus on the skills needed by the assessor for giving the feedback. As indicated above, receiving feedback also requires skills, which can be learnt and improved with practice. Training for assessees, therefore, also should be considered and unless there are very good reasons for not doing so, should be provided as a matter of course.

## Content of feedback

### Focus on behaviour

It is now accepted that an individual has a comparatively stable personality which may not easily be changed. However, behaviour can be changed or modified. It may require hard work and effort, but an individual can take action that results in changes or improvements to performance. Assessment of performance, as it is largely aimed at improvements in behaviour at work, should focus on what an individual does and how. Assessment of personality, if done at all, should still, in the context of work, be concerned with the effect the individual's personality has on behaviour.

### Focus on observation

In Chapter 2 we discussed the process of perception and outlined the sources of bias, especially attribution. If the feedback concentrates on what has been seen or heard during the course of the assessment, there is less chance of these errors being made. Anyone supplying feedback should be careful not to draw inferences or attribute motives from their observation. They should also be aware of their own attempts to confirm their implicit personality theories. When the feedback is being put together from the observations and assessment made by other observers, checks should be made to ensure these can be evidenced and are not the product of the others' prejudices.

### Focus on description

Value judgements of behaviour are not necessarily helpful. Even when decisions are being made about individuals or when assessees are being ranked in relation to each other, the assessment and feedback should centre on effective or ineffective performance. In the case of disciplinary action, the concern should be whether the performance is appropriate and in line with the organisation's requirement rather than whether it was 'good' or 'bad'.

In selection, the decision should be made on the basis of the 'best fit' between the individual, the job and the organisation. What is 'best' in one set of circumstances may be the 'worst' in another. Even when the same people and the same organisation are involved, depending on the circumstances, what could be an unproductive relationship can produce very different outputs when the 'right' job is added to the equation. When being used for development purposes, the focus of the feedback should be placed on how strengths can be maintained, improved and built upon, and how weaknesses can be improved, minimised or accommodated.

## Focus on the specific

This does not mean that fine, precise detail should be fed back. Rather, identifiable examples that can be recognised by the individual and used constructively should be used. Generalisations and/or abstractions should be avoided if at all possible. It is difficult to make a general overall point without it being so broad that the point gets lost. Similarly, it is not easy to avoid being so specific that the discussion concentrates on the narrow aspects and loses sight of the overall message. This is why giving feedback requires skill.

## Focus on alternative models of behaviour

It does not help anyone learn if they are told only how 'to do it good'. Building ways from experience and actual performance to how performance can be improved is an integral part of the learning process.

Kolb's learning cycle (1974) can be used to underpin development planning. It identifies four phases of learning which start from:

Concrete experience
1. (doing the job)
2. (trying them out)

Active experimentation (trying out other patterns of behaviour)

Reflective observation (thinking and talking about it)

Abstract conceptualisation (drawing meaning and understanding implications)

*Figure 8.1*   Kolb's learning cycle

The feedback session should aim to help the reflection and the conceptualisation of ways in which performance can be improved based on actual experience. Demonstration of different ways of completing a task or performing a set of skills contributes to experimentation and exploration of which mode of behaviour best suits the individual, the task and the situation.

Coaching also makes a positive contribution to the learning cycle. The demonstration of more effective ways of performing is a central feature of the process.

I do it normal,
I do it slow,
You do it with me,
Off you go.

(Nursery rhyme)

But a skilled coach recognises that the learner needs to adapt what they are being shown into their own repertoire of behaviours. Presenting a set of alternatives enables the assessee to select which is likely to work for them and avoids the 'I know best' approach. Sharing ideas and synthesising them, rather than giving an answer can also be more beneficial. And, sometimes, even the coach can learn something.

## Focus on information that is beneficial to the recipient

The person giving feedback should ask themselves how the piece of information will help the person being assessed. Care should be taken to avoid feeding back information for the sake of it, or for the satisfaction of the personal needs of the assessor.

Similarly, the feedback should deal with aspects of behaviour that individuals can do something about and that are within their power to take action. For example it is not reasonable to expect staff to maintain effective management of the overall photocopying budget if they are not able to influence the amount of copying done by staff from other offices.

## Consider the quantity of feedback being given

An individual can only cope with a limited number of ideas at any one time. It is generally accepted that this is about seven discrete items.

The amount of detail being given during the feedback session should also be considered. If there is a large quantity to be given it may be better to find some way of grouping the information and/or organising several separate sessions. Perhaps the first session could be used to indicate general areas and to plan how other sessions are to be conducted. The aim, after all, is to help the person to act. Too much information can leave the assessee in the position of not knowing where to start or trying to do everything at once.

The assessor has to decide, therefore, what to include and what to omit. All information that has an impact on overall success should be included, as well as all that is needed by the assessee. Sometimes it may be appropriate to ask the assessee what they *want* to know. This needs to be tempered with what they *should* know as a result of the assessment. Needless to say it is possible that the two may be different. Again these are difficult decisions that need to be made with skill.

### Focus on the content of the message

While giving feedback emphasis should be placed on what is being said, rather than why the assessment was conducted.

The reason for assessment should have been explained to the assessees during the preparation phase, the initial briefing and the start of the assessment. The way in which the intent of the process is communicated to the participants at the very beginning has a direct impact on the acceptability of the assessment and the feedback, and its perceived value to the assessees. Therefore the style, the transmission and the structuring of this initial message is critical.

Similarly, the content of the feedback message requires thought. Consideration ought to be given to how the assessee will hear what is being said and how the message will be interpreted. Any double messages or items that could be wrongly interpreted or misinterpreted should be clarified while the person giving the feedback is preparing for the session. Sometimes it may be helpful to check the content with one of the other assessors.

### Communication is a two-way process

It consists of giving and receiving ideas. As well as sending out a message, an assessor should check that it has been received correctly and understood. This involves:

- summarising each point clearly and concisely before moving on to the next;

- giving the assessees time to reflect on each point before moving on to the next;

- asking the assessees to repeat the message or summarise it;

- encouraging the assessees to ask questions if they are not clear or sure of what is meant;

- assisting reflection by using the techniques of active listening;

- concluding the discussion by providing and asking the assessees to give an overall summary of the main points and what has been agreed.

It also requires the assessor to listen closely to the assessees' reflections and summaries. Active listening can help but it may also be necessary to reopen a point if there is any doubt about the level of understanding. It would be more than a shame at this stage of assessment for the assessee to leave the discussion very enthusiastic about developing in the wrong direction as a result of a simple misunderstanding gained during the feedback session.

## Once given, the information is the property of the assessee

Assessees have the right not to act on the results of the assessment or change their behaviour. Neither do they have to learn another skill. However, if this decision is the end product of the assessment, the line manager and the organisation have to consider their position. Certainly questions should be asked as to why the individual should react in this way.

---

### Example 8.4

Take the following example, which is not untypical, and consider how you would respond to this employee.

It has been decided to introduce a performance review scheme. The organisation requires its managers to:

- have their current level of skill in conducting appraisal meetings assessed;
- partake in appropriately designed training to bring their current skills to the desired standard.

One manager, after the assessment, refuses to participate in either the training or the scheme. The reasons behind the refusal are not known . . .

---

The reasons for the refusal should be explored and if ultimately the decision is unchanged, the employee's future as a manager will need to be considered. All employees are implicitly required to carry out reasonable requests as part of their contract of employment. Is the refusal to use an accepted management technique and partake in the training and development opportunities being made available to ensure the technique is to be implemented properly, the refusal of a reasonable request?

## The end of the feedback session should not leave the assessee in the air

The meeting should finish with a clear, agreed conclusion. Ideally this should be a plan of action to which both parties are fully committed.

If the plan is imposed by the assessor, it is unlikely that any real, effective and lasting learning will be achieved. (We could spend a lot more time discussing the purpose and processes of learning than space here permits.) If the assessment has been made because of poor performance and the outcome is some form of punitive action, extra effort is needed to ensure that more than the compliance of the assessee is secured.

To be able to say that learning has taken place, something needs to be different. Either more or new knowledge is acquired or a skill developed, improved or put into practice. The assessee, in preparing for learning, should acquire an understanding of why it is needed and the reasons why their behaviour has to be modified. The desired outcome should also be clearly understood. It is the responsibility of the person giving the feedback to make sure that this state of readiness is achieved and that the assessees, at the end of the feedback session, know clearly:

- what they are being required to do;

- what resources are available to help them achieve the desired end result;

- how progress will be monitored;

- what future reviews will be conducted;

- how the effectiveness of the action will be evaluated.

Similarly, the assessors, especially if they are line managers, need to be clear about what their future roles will be, the degree of involvement, what action they are committed to taking and when. This can be a problem when using external assessors. The extent of the external assessors' involvement and degree of their commitment (within the limits of their resources) should be negotiated during the drawing up of the initial agreements regarding their participation in the whole of the assessment process. The internal resources available from other parts of the organisation should also have been identified and committed at the beginning. At least some moral commitment should be made, even if the precise resources needed to help the assessor provide the feedback and follow-up action are not known at the start of the process.

## Conclusions about giving feedback

Giving feedback is not easy. It requires:

- skill;

- courage;

- space;

- time;

- planning;

- understanding; and

- ability to empathise and respect others.

All of these, like any other aspect of the management role, can be acquired through learning, and can be improved with practice and developed. But as we have already said, skills need to be defined behaviourally, assessed against pre-determined criteria, the outcome of the assessment fed back to the assessee and an action plan created to develop and improve the needed skills. Should giving feedback be any different?

Two ways of assessing a manager's skills in providing feedback are possible. One way is to observe or video their performance during role-play of a feedback session. The other is for the recipient of the feedback to provide feedback in turn. The latter method calls for courage and a real willingness to learn – especially if the person giving the feedback is the line manager and the assessee is a subordinate.

## IMPLEMENTING AN ACTION PLAN

Before considering the sort of action that can be taken as a result of assessment, we want to look at some general principles. These concern planning and implementing the plan, monitoring its implementation and contribution towards the desired outcomes, evaluating its overall effectiveness, and conducting future reviews and assessments.

Regardless of the reason for assessing performance or the particular technique being used, these underlying principles always remain the same. While individuals are responsible for their own development and learning, managers cannot delegate their responsibilities for ensuring the development of their own staff. This should be a systematic process which marries the individual's aspirations with the needs of the employing organisation. Therefore, the plans made should be realistic, achievable, implemented and evaluated.

## Planning follow-up action

Action can be planned for individuals and/or groups and should consist of four key elements:

- *what*   the content of the plan and desired outcome;
- *who*   is responsible for making the plan happen;
- *how*   the plan is to be implemented;
- *when*   the action is to be taken.

The content should be as specific and as detailed as needs be. The plan should avoid being too rigid and unchangeable. Circumstances and people may demand changes that an inflexible plan cannot accommodate. A large amount of fine detail can lead to a lack of flexibility. However, a general plan can be too vague to have any real meaning in the future and provide no real guidance to aid enactment. The desired outcome of the plan, however, should always be precisely specified as general aims and specific objectives. Whenever possible these should be given in behavioural terms.

The plan should be realistic and achievable. Realism means that account should be taken of the organisation's circumstances and culture and the individuals involved. The achievability should be concerned with the abilities and capacities of the organisation and individuals to enact the plan, and turn its intentions into action. It should also take account of any impediments that are likely to arise within the plan's life-span.

The people responsible for enacting the plan should be named. They should be aware of this responsibility and be clear and agreeable to what they are being required to do. The subjects of the plan, the assessees and recipients of the action, obviously should be aware of their part in it, what it intends for them and who is responsible for what. Ideally, all concerned should have been involved in the plan's formulation and agree to its contents.

The way in which the plan is to be made to happen depends on a number of factors. The culture of the organisation determines which methods can be considered and which are feasible to implement. Its traditions, norms and aspirations have direct bearing on what the makers of plans can realistically contemplate. One almost classical phrase was uttered with regard to the introduction of assessment centres in an organisation we know: 'We can't do that, we never have before'.

Similarly, the resources available also constrain. Sometimes having too much money can be as much as a constraint as having too little. The need to spend can force the plan to be expensive and engage in action which is more concerned with being lavish rather than being productive and cost-effective.

The time-span of the plan can also determine choice of methods. 'Quick and dirty' solutions so designed to satisfy specific needs should not aspire to be academically rigorous, but they can be effective and fast. Alternatively, if time is not limited and external credibility is important, effort should be expended on making sure that content is valid.

The availability of the capabilities and skills needed to implement the plan, influence its formulation and the decisions about how it is to be enacted also influence the choice of what methods are possible and how, strategically, the plan can be achieved.

A plan should distinguish between the short, medium and long term. These time-spans should be reflected in the amount of detail given. Short-term plans ought to be detailed and specific with targets, dates for achievement and responsibilities being assigned. Medium-term plans are generally for one or two years and therefore should be more general statements of intent. It is possible that they will contain the steps planned to achieve the aims and should take into account predicted and intervening factors that may change the plan. Long-term plans can only hope to be general, but they should also contain goals and aims. Outlines of how these are to be achieved are needed and contingency plans should be included. It is advisable to include details of how the plan is to be reviewed and revised.

## Putting the plan into action

Plans should be visible. A plan hidden within clean, typed pages in a filing cabinet is dead. A plan that is being implemented is dog-eared and dirty. People refer to it regularly. They talk about it, enthuse or bewail its implications – and act upon it.

In our experience we have found that the lack of resources is rarely responsible for the failure to implement a plan. This is the excuse; not the reason. There is a lot of truth in the old saying 'where there is a will there is a way'. If people, managers and staff alike, want the outcomes to be realised then they will usually find a way of achieving it. If either party is not fully committed to the plan, it is unlikely to happen. This could be due to a failure to act just as much as delaying tactics, a refusal to participate or sabotage.

We will see in more detail below just how much can be achieved without needing any tangible resources. It is well accepted that the best learning at work results from real experiences, but these do not just happen. The opportunities need to be created and linked to desired improvements or changes in behaviour. It has to be remembered that development is being sought for reasons additional to individual benefit and enjoyment, therefore the opportunities should be targeted at the required job related as well as personal outcomes.

As these opportunities can arise through real operations, they do not necessarily require any actual outlay of money. (In fact they could actually save some, if improvements to methods occur as a result of the learning.) However, to be maximised, they need first to be recognised as such. Secondly, they have to be structured in a way that enables the learning to be related to the behavioural objectives. Thirdly, monitoring is required to ensure that the learning is being internalised and there is evidence of the new skills being applied and practised.

A manager needs to take the time to help the staff take the risks needed to work in new or different ways, encourage reflection and understanding of learning, and to reinforce the implementation of the changes. For most organisations the most expensive outlay is time. But can any manager afford not to invest in the sort of commitment needed to develop their staff's abilities and capacities? If needed, a cost-benefit or utility analysis can be carried out. This too takes time and we would encourage any manager who is dubious about the actual cost to take us on trust, rather than wasting time working out the sum.

## Monitoring the implementation of the plan

The need to find a way to accredit prior learning has reawakened interest in a well-known, but seldom used, device for aiding the implementation and monitoring of development and learning plans. The learning log or diary provides a semi-structured, flexible and personal way of recording progress. It enables objectives to be specified and kept by the individuals involved. This gives them direct ownership of the changes, improvements and development being sought. Opportunities that have been created, those which occur and other experiences can be linked to the pre-defined learning objectives. Interest is also growing in learning contracts. These provide ways of focusing development while tying the interested parties into semi-formal agreements to enact plans and create opportunities.

The maintenance of the diary provides a vehicle that can aid reflection. Summarising the learning and linking it into the objectives can contribute to the learner's understanding of what they have achieved. Its upkeep also gives the manager a record from which progress can be assessed. It creates a focus for discussion and can contribute to the longer-term review of performance and achievement. Such a log is very cheap to establish and use, and yet can be very beneficial to all involved.

However, techniques will not ensure enactment of a plan no matter how good it is. The key to successful implementation is determination and discipline. Managers who start their staff on development plans risk rapid demotivation and loss of credibility if they fail to honour their commitment. Establishing effective monitoring systems helps to ensure that plans are implemented according to their intent, to empower the members of staff concerned so they have a way of ensuring the manager responds and to give the manager a prop for their own discipline.

It is important that, during learning, progress is recognised. Changing behaviour can be demoralising and result in a loss of confidence. The individual moves from a state of competence in a well-known routine or pattern of behaviour to carrying out new tasks poorly or performing in a way in which their skill levels and competencies are low. Indicators of achievement and success are important to rebuild confidence and encourage staff to go on to achieve more.

## Review and reward of achievement

Reviewing the implementation of a plan has two important aspects. First, its purpose is to ensure that the action being taken is achieving the required objectives in terms of the changes or improvements to behaviour and the overall aims of the programme. Secondly, a review permits flexibility by taking account of any changes to circumstances.

If the plan is for a longish term, say a year or more, it can easily take on its own life unless it is reviewed regularly. The action being taken can overtake its purpose unless it is kept in context. Monitoring and review mechanisms, that should have been built into the plan during its formulation, help to ensure that action is subordinate to its aims and objectives. Changes do happen during the implementation of any course of action that can mean it is no longer appropriate for the individuals concerned or the circumstances. This, however, need not change the desired outcome, just the means of achieving it may need to be re-thought.

Any plan needs to have a degree of flexibility as part of its integral fabric. This should take into account, again, the individuals, their circumstances and the organisation's culture (or that which is desired). One organisation wished to change its development provision from being *ad hoc* and focused exclusively on individual development. It saw that a systematic approach more closely linked to organisational objectives would be beneficial to both parties. The use of assessment of performance and the creation of personal action plans was the way it chose to achieve its overall end. In this situation the plans, initially at least, were not very flexible. This was to help the organisation's culture absorb the more systematic method. At the same time it recognised that blueprint planning is not totally appropriate for human resources management. Despite many efforts to mitigate the effect and prevent it happening, people do change their minds and their behaviour.

The recognition and reward of achievement forms part of the review process. Learning is a risky business. People have to do things they have never done before or work in ways which are unfamiliar. They have to explore their existing perceptions and take on new ideas. This means that they are starting anew and do not have the same skill level they were used to expecting of themselves. Anyone managing a learning process needs to take account of this uncertainty and lack of confidence. Belbin (1981) wrote on the needs of the adult learner in training situations and this text is commended.

A way of minimising the negative effects of this uncertainty is to build in reviews and have tokens of reward for achievement. 'There is nothing that succeeds like success'. It is equally important to celebrate strengths just as much as it is to point out weaknesses, but we are not very good at doing this. In our society rewards are usually equated with money or payment, but these are not the only ways of recognising achievement. Research on motivation has long demonstrated that recognition can be more important and has a longer-lasting effect than just money. Yet we fail repeatedly to act on this knowledge. Yes, financial reward can have a short-term beneficial effect and is a common way of saying well done and thank you. But it is not the only way. These other ways should be used more and be given more value by organisations.

Peters and Waterman (1982) give examples of some American ways of rewarding achievement and contributing to improvements in performance. Some of these may seem over the top to British eyes, but celebration of achievement in the face of adversity has been used in our own experience to very good effect. The staff involved often gain the confidence and courage to go from strength to strength individually; the team draws more closely together and works productively and the level of the output increases dramatically in volume and quality.

Reviewing the implementation of the plans gives the individual some power in the process. Good learning contracts commit the organisation and the individual manager to the plan just as much as the individual member of staff. If the latter is clear about what each party is contracted to do, knows the required outcome and expected actions designed to achieve them, they are in a position to require and demand that things happen as a result of their assessment. This is strengthened even more if they have a mentor from another part of the organisation.

However, all this fails if there are no agreed indicators of performance that can be used to recognise and review achievement. These are usually quantitative targets, such as volume outputs, cost reductions, number of clients served. The total quality movement has introduced other ways of assessing performance. Approaches similar to the financial ratios permit comparative assessments to be made which provide alternatives to counting numbers. Behaviourally anchored rating scales and the kind of graded criteria we use for assessment centres also provide ways of reviewing achievement.

## Evaluating effectiveness

Some form of systematic evaluation of any managerial technique should be carried out periodically. The use of assessment techniques, especially because their use can be sensitive, should be evaluated so that their benefit can be demonstrated. The indicators of performance mentioned above can be of help in doing this. The following questions can also be asked.

The evaluation of intangible activities is often avoided because it is thought to be 'difficult'. It does need effort and application and, because qualitative judgements are involved, imagination is also needed. But these are excuses, not reasons for not evaluating the worth of the activity. If those involved as assessors have learnt anything themselves from the assessment of others' performance, it should help them carry out the evaluation of the process in which they have engaged and the techniques they have used. Questions for evaluating assessment techniques and the implementation of follow-up plans include the following:

- Has each component part of the plan worked:

  —as activities in their own right?
  —as contributors to the achievement of specific learning objectives?

- The behavioural objectives:

  —were they well specified?
  —were they achievable?
  —were the plan's objectives achieved (was it well made, did it work, did it achieve its objectives)?

- The overall process:

  —has it resulted in improvements in the performance for the individuals?
  —has it achieved improvements for implementation of the section/ department?
  —has it contributed to the organisation?
  —has it been cost-effective and added value?

## Future review

If the process proves its worth, assessment should become part of the organisation's culture and normal method of working. This will mean that assessments will be conducted on a regular basis. Future assessments need to be based on two principles. First, the same measures of performance should be used so that people are assessed against some important bench-marks that are well known and agreed. Secondly, these need to take account of changes to the organisation's culture, its environment, the involvement of different people, and the learning and growth of those previously involved.

It would be very interesting to repeat a development centre after the implementation of a development programme, employing the same criteria and activities and, if possible, the same assessors. However, such an exercise, while interesting academically and providing valuable information for validating the technique, does not provide a realistic reflection of the modern-day reality of organisational life. Things are changing and the truth is that this will continue. Assessing people against last year's criteria alone, is like wearing last season's fashions. And if part of the purpose of assessment is to equip people to cope with the demands likely to be placed on them in the future, assessing against historic factors seems pointless. This is not to say, however, that previous criteria should not contribute to re-assessment. These should, however, be reviewed and re-evaluated in the light of the organisation's context and requirements at the time.

Some consistency needs to be maintained if the organisation is going to progress. Growth is not achieved through constant, haphazard change for 'without a purpose it is the ideology of the cancer cell'. Lindblom's (1979) notion of disjointed incrementalism, we think, is probably a true reflection of organisational life. This implies therefore that the textbook version of strategic planning is more an ideal than a reality. Put simply, he proposes that plans are formulated starting from where people and organisations are. Rational strategic planning suggests that goals are identified and plans made to achieve them. While we accept Lindblom's notion, we still think there is a place for the planned development of individuals, management and organisations. For this to be achieved, practical planning and systematic techniques, which take change into account and are adaptable, need to be used.

## Keeping assessees informed

Regardless of why an individual's performance is being assessed, the assessment process cannot exist in isolation. Even when someone's performance and potential has been assessed for appointment to a new employer, the individual has a reasonable expectation to receive some feedback. If they are determined to gain employment with that organisation, one would expect them to take action as a result of that feedback to satisfy the desired criteria.

In most other cases, assessment is usually done by the employing organisation using assessors who are either employed themselves or contracted to carry out the process. The result of these assessments are used in some way to achieve a desired end. Even when assessment is part of formal disciplinary action, it should always be aimed at improving performance in some way to enhance the individual's contribution to organisational success and effectiveness. Unless there is only one specific area of improvement being sought, some form of an action plan needs to be formulated. Ideally, the assessee and the assessor should be involved, with the line manager if this person is not the assessor, in drawing up the plan and agreeing responsibilities, content, timing and review processes. At the beginning of the plan, consideration should be given to how it is to be monitored and evaluated. Methods of doing this, responsibilities and dates for achievement should be built in. It can also be helpful to include some ideas at least of possible measures of success.

It is important that people know what is being expected of them, what help they are going to be given to achieve the required ends and by when they have to complete the task. It is a must, we think, that they know what success looks like. So many people complain of shifting goal posts and sometimes not even knowing if they are playing water polo or croquet. This degree of uncertainty does not help learning, the catalyst to changing behaviour. The only time when there should be any uncertainty is when the individual's ability to deal with uncertainty is the behaviour to be improved.

The recognition and reward of achievement is so important it cannot be emphasised enough. Most organisations can improve their treatment of their staff. Many find it easy to use the stick, but not many know how to hand out the bouquets and carrots without being obsequious. We think this part of organisational behaviour could, in general, be vastly improved.

## EDUCATION, TRAINING AND DEVELOPMENT

We recognise that there are dangers in opening the following debate, but we think that there is some merit in clarifying the terms we are going to use. Education, training and development are very closely related and the concepts overlap to such a fine degree that sometimes it is impossible to distinguish one from the other. Nevertheless, there are some important differences that should be stated. In a way it does not matter if the reader does not agree with our usage. What is important is that we all understand what is being meant for the purposes of this book.

Education is taken to be concerned with general concepts and principles which are widely applicable, with only minor modifications being needed to take account of local circumstances. Most courses leading to recognised qualifications fall into this category. The syllabus may contain some techniques, but again these will be generally accepted. There is frequent criticism that qualification courses, especially those leading to vocational qualifications, are too theoretical. Newly qualified workers then, it is claimed by the critics, have to be trained in basic practices once they start work. It is also said that course content is often too conceptual and unrelated to the realities of the world of work.

The introduction of occupational competencies by the NCVQ is blurring the boundaries between education and training. In some ways this is being done in response to the above criticisms and is an attempt to rectify some of the recognised failings. The competencies require that an individual's performance and competency is assessed in relation to the application on the job. This approach contains its own weaknesses. It is possible that it will result in an inbalance between skills and background knowledge and understanding. One can foresee the situation where there will be a large number of 'technicians' but very few 'people with management potential'. Those planning the new qualifications will no doubt take these and other concerns into account.

Regardless of their level of qualification and expertise, a new worker will always need to be trained to do the job. The amount of training needed will differ depending on experience and competency. Training is concerned with the acquisition and application of skills and knowledge to a specific job in the context of an employing organisation. It can take place at an initial level, equipping the individual with the skills and knowledge needed to perform the basic job. The training could include the method of operating a particular machine (how to switch on the computer terminal); following a particular procedure (how to claim travelling expenses); using a particular technique (how to conduct a team briefing meeting) etc. Training can then be used to supplement those basic skills by the addition of others or the improvement of those already possessed. Additionally, the individual can be trained to develop and enhance their existing abilities.

The distinction between training and development is even finer and can provide a fruitful topic of debate. Rather than open that debate here, we will differentiate the concepts by using training as being specific to the current job or the next one to be held. Development is concerned with the realisation of potential. This could:

- deal with potential that is known, ie helping the individual get better in areas in which they already possess some abilities;

- be concerned with building up areas that are seen as being weaknesses;

- be focused towards the discovery and release of untapped or latent talents.

Therefore:

- recruitment and selection's contribution to strategic human resource management would be, in our terms, *education*;

- copywriting advertisements and interviewing skills in line with the employer's procedures would be *training*;

- understanding one's own perception processes and how that influences decisions made about others would be *development*.

As we are concerned here to describe what can be done to improve skills at work following the assessment of the current level of ability, we will concentrate here on training and development.

## TRAINING

Earlier we said that training mainly takes the form of organised events, rather than some of the other activities that are sometimes included within this term. A training event should have pre-defined, desired objectives and a programme which has been planned in advance, and organised to achieve them. The objectives should be behaviourally described in a way that enables the participants to decide whether they need to acquire the offered knowledge and/or skills, and know what they should be able to do at the end of the training event. Training should be relevant to the job and the context in which the individual is involved. As it should be applicable in that job and context, the training should be realistic and related. The event should be recognisable as training so the participants understand fully what they are doing.

## Learning objectives

The work of Mager (1984) has been useful in helping to write learning objectives in a way that describes the required behaviour. Even the 'fuzzies', the intangible aspects of performance, can be described satisfactorily.

It is worth the effort needed to distinguish between aims and objectives. Sometimes these are merged or muddled. Here aims are used to describe statements of intent. In training terms this would appear as a phrase such as:

'The programme is designed to help the participants improve their skills of communication.'

An objective is specific with a clearly defined outcome to be obtained. Mager goes further and says that it should contain an expression of behaviour, the condition under which it is to be demonstrated and the criteria by which an acceptable level of success will be assessed. Therefore, a complementary objective to the above aim would be:

The participants will be able to write clear, concise reports for submission to internal committee meetings:

write – behaviour;
clear – criteria;
concise – criteria;
committee meetings – condition.

Some of the techniques we have described above, such as job analysis, are valuable in helping to clarify what is required of an effective performer. It is essential that in areas where it is less easy to be precise about specific performance, some form of diagnosis is used. We all know when we have been given good customer service and when good interpersonal skills have been used. But what constitutes good service, and do we all agree on the same skills and the standards attained in their execution? Again Mager, with Piper, (1984) provides some help in 'Goal Analysis'. The blindingly obvious question 'How would you know one if you saw one?' is asked. Techniques other than those cited above are known to have been used by the Training Agency for the NCVQ competencies and by the likes of Boyatzis (1982) and McClelland (1965). The power of Mager's approach is its simplicity and accessibility. Every manager can differentiate between a good member of staff and one whose performance is less than satisfactory. Think for yourself, in your own organisation.

- What do my managers do that leads me believe their performance is good?

- What do my managers do that leads me to believe their performance is poor?

These two questions provide the dimensions that can be developed into poles for a rating scale. Any number of people can be involved in the process of drawing up such scales. This involvement enhances the quality of the dimensions through the effects of synergy and the inclusion of a range of perspectives. It also helps to develop the concept of ownership of the criteria.

## Contents

The contents should be determined in relation to their contribution to the aims and objectives of the training. This statement may seem obvious, but it is surprising how many times skills, ideas and activities are included because the trainers like running them. The relationship need not be a straight link, but each learning point should have some relevance to the aims and objectives and why the learner is attending the event. The activities should be designed or chosen to lead to that point. One hears the complaint that, yes the session was interesting, but no one could see why it had been included.

To achieve the above aims and objectives, a two-day report writing course programme could be as follows:

| **Day 1** | 9.00 | Assemble and welcome |
|---|---|---|
| | 9.30 | Getting to know you |
| | 11.00 | Coffee |
| | 11.30 | The purpose of reports |
| | 12.30 | Lunch |
| | 1.30 | Report contents and structure |
| | 3.00 | Tea |

|  | 3.30 | Plain English |
|  | 5.00 | Close |

| **Day 2** | 9.00 | FOG (free of gobbledegook) index |
|  | 11.00 | Coffee |
|  | 11.30 | Use and presentation of data |
|  | 12.30 | Lunch |
|  | 1.30 | Numbers and statistics |
|  | 3.00 | Tea |
|  | 3.30 | Examples for improvement |
|  | 5.00 | Close |

When asked why the first two hours are dedicated to 'getting to know you' on a programme that is primarily concerned with the transmission of information regarding good practice and the development of individual writing skills, the trainer might reply 'I always use it; it gets them going.' Wonder why? Perhaps the participants want to get on with the task in hand . . .

## Relevance to job and context

When we talk of training we normally understand this to mean courses. These, usually, are obtained from an external provider, or a consultant, or are provided internally. The amount of control an organisation has over the content of a course and its relevancy is directly in proportion to the proximity of the provider to the organisation.

An externally provided course is usually found through a brochure and perhaps a conversation with the provider. Then a judgement is made about its relevancy to the person, job and organisation in question. Because such courses are provided publically, one can only expect them to be general and universal in their coverage.

Perhaps the individual attending will benefit from the experience and will learn something they can apply to the job. Generally, however, these ideas have to be adapted so they can be transferred into the organisational context. Mainly, these courses can be interesting and can give the participants ideas for future use. One of the recognised dangers of sending people on such courses is that they come back with ideas, skills and aspirations that they are keen to use, but are not relevant to the work in hand at the time. An example is training secretarial staff to use desk-top publishing packages when the computer facilities do not have the capacity to take the programmes and no money is available to upgrade them.

Bringing in external experts to provide the training in-house gives the organisation more control over the relevancy of the content. Even when the consultant or trainer knows the organisation well, they need to be briefed regarding internal procedures, quirks, culture etc. If this does not happen the trainers can be left exposed and lose their credibility by seeming not to know what they are talking about, simply because they do not have a piece of local knowledge. On the other hand, sometimes it can be better to bring in an outside expert. One of the major problems of an internal trainer is being a prophet in one's own land. Having someone from outside with ascribed credibility speaking your words can give them added value. This, we have found, is sad but true!

Some of the barriers that can prevent the implementation of learning should be included in the content of any training event. Most programmes, now, cover action planning and consideration of how the learning can be used in the concluding session. One limitation of internal training is that some of the organisation's cultural features that ought to be challenged so that learning can be implemented and change effected can be seen by all concerned, including the trainer, as unquestionable, universal truths.

### Applicability

Following relevance we need to consider how applicable the training will be. The action plan referred to above should take account of individual abilities, capacity and will to implement the skills and knowledge, and the organisation's capability to allow that learning to be implemented. This concerns more than the cultural limitations. So often people are sent to be trained and come back and say the ideas are fine in theory but not in practice.

This expression, we contest, is used to shield a number of other underlying reasons for not implementing the learning. These may include failure within the training to ensure that the skills and/or knowledge are properly learnt. This means that the individual will not feel confident enough to try them out for real. It may be that the individual is resisting the changes that necessitated the training. It may be that they simply do not have the required time or space within their current work load. It must be remembered that performance generally falls off while the new patterns of behaviour and newly acquired skills are practised, and the previous levels of competence and confidence are reattained.

This is true for both manual and mental skills and these constraints should be considered before the training event is attended by both the individual and their manager. The use and implementation of the training, after all, should be the main reason for attendance.

While these considerations are important, it is even more important for the organisation to be sure it is prepared to live with the consequences of training its staff. Exposure to new ideas and approaches, and the acquisition of different skills, means that staff will want to use them. This requires the organisation to permit (and we hope encourage) this and to be able to manage with the resultant changes. Failure to do this can cause staff to become subversive, rebellious or disillusioned, which can be manifested by staff being turned off or even finding jobs elsewhere. Sending people off to be trained to keep them quiet can be an expensive exercise in the end. Conversely, we know of an organisation that pursued this tactic as a deliberate means of encouraging unwanted employees to leave! Promoting training and development, convincingly, as a practical way of working requires some form of evidence to show that the learning will be relevant and useful to the organisation and the individual.

### Recognisable

We have referred above to one subversive use of training. Often training, as a term, is used to encompass a number of activities that are not primarily aimed at the learning and development of the participants. The best example of this is conference-going. Papers given at conferences are presented to disseminate the ideas, approaches and experiences of others. These are interesting and possibly developmental, but often because of differences in circumstances and cultures much effort is needed to translate them from one organisation to another. It can be more difficult to make theoretical ideas work in practice. Often, the real reason for attending conferences is to meet other colleagues. While conferences do serve to inform and update, there is a high degree of social interaction. This is fine, but we should be honest about why people are going to conferences and stop pretending it is for training.

Conversely, we can give examples of events that are organised as other activities that are really intended to be training. While the conditions given above may not be met explicitly, it is possible to find that activities have been designed with specific learning objectives in mind. For example a manager may plan an absence so a subordinate has no option but to attend a meeting they have been trying to avoid.

### Reasons for training

The usual reason for training staff is to equip them to undertake a new task or assume a new role. A criticism often levelled at organisations is the failure to equip their newly appointed managers to do the job. It is assumed they will pick it up as they go along. Handy (1978) and the evidence of more recent reports have shown that most managers receive less than one day's training per year and that many had received none. Graduate trainee schemes are a way of addressing this failure, but there must be many thousands of managers who still need to acquire basic skills.

However, the experience of these managers means that some see training at a middle stage in their career as a loss of face or even an admission of failure. One big aim we all must have is to build training into work, as a normal feature of the job. Many see it as an add-on extra that has nothing really to do with everyday activity. This has to be taken into account and training has to be portrayed as a mandatory, essential part of effective performance. So many people fail to turn up or find excuses for getting out of being trained. An organisation aspiring to be known for its commitment to learning and development has to address this if involvement in training and development is to be a feature of its culture.

Thus, the use of structured training to follow any assessment of performance has to be regarded as being integral to the job. The need for training should not rely solely on something changing such as new approaches, techniques, methods of role. Upgrading performance in the present role should be reason enough for being involved in a training event. Organisations need also to recognise that their staff need to be trained. The decision to introduce new ways of working needs to include the reskilling of staff to implement them. An area where there is often a failure to take account of this is after a decision to invest in computer facilities. While it is normal for the capital purchase price to include initial training for the staff involved directly with the application, it is not usual for this to include staff involved on the margins or to allow for follow-up and refresher training. It is rare for the learning curve to be considered and adequate time allowances to be made in the staff's work load.

This is more important when approaches change. The change to the location of decision-making is an area we have experienced several times. The decentralisation of decision-making and the delegation of responsibilities to the lowest feasible level has become a feature of organisational development in recent years. This requires senior managers and those in the middle of the organisation to understand the implications of the change and the ways in which it will impact their existing roles. It also requires them to acquire a fresh set of skills which will enable them all to assume their new roles. Some parts of this change process can be assisted by the assessment of existing skill levels and the provision of training in areas that have been pre-specified and effectively acquired in this way.

## Definition and selection of training solutions

Training, we said earlier, is usually taken to mean courses. This definition is not adequate as it excludes many activities that can be included within our use of the term. A few examples are given below. The selection of training methods should be made against a set of criteria whose overriding purpose is to ensure the best satisfaction of the learning objective. See Table 8.1.

## Implementation of training

A formally organised training event is frequently spoilt by factors that have nothing to do with the content of the programme. Most complaints (and hence most evaluation questionnaires) focus on aspects such as domestic arrangements, style of presenter, standard of accommodation etc. It is important not to get these wrong; but no one really notices if they are right. There are checklists for organisers to use to help make these arrangements. The style and skills of the presenter are more difficult to control, especially if someone from outside is coming almost as a guest. Sometimes this is an inescapable risk and all that can be done is to learn from bad experiences and not use that presenter again. The pay-off can be, though, a comparison and re-evaluation of the existing internal trainer's skills – prophets can be valued in their own land.

Internal courses and events often attract sharper criticism than external ones. Finding ways of handling these comments is part of any internal trainer's learning, and identifying which are important is one of their skills. We have found though that training events which are organised as part of the managers' everyday jobs tend to be received more favourably. This is possible because, being closer to the actual job, participants can see the benefits more quickly – providing there are some. Irrelevant training, this close to reality, cannot be excused – most people can see waffle for what it is when it is very near to something they know about. Things that can be fudged on formal programmes cannot be escaped at this level. Our advice, therefore, to anyone planning on-the-job training, such as seminars or planned experiences, is to think carefully about what it is the event is intended to achieve, and what should be put in and what left out. There is not much point in padding an event out to make it last a day if there is only enough material available for half a day. Busy managers will not tolerate their time being wasted.

The most important aspect to take into account when planning internal training is the environment in which it is to happen. What is a learning environment? This is another piece of jargon that often gets thrown about

*Table 8.1* The selection of training methods

| Training method | Criteria for selection and use |
|---|---|
| Course (a structured programme, usually comprising timed sessions, led by a presenter or trainer. Tends to be pedagogic) | Objective set in relation to need<br>Content aimed at achieving objectives<br>Relevance to job |
| Seminar (presentation and discussion of an idea or theory) | As above |
| Demonstration (a structured session aimed at showing the trainees how to do or use something) | Complexity of new method or equipment<br>Availability and skills of demonstrator<br>Opportunity for trainees to practise and use learning<br>Cost of or danger of equipment being misused |
| Workshop (aimed at equipping the trainees with skills) | Need for skill acquisition and achievement of basic level of competence (more than knowledge of technique)<br>Amount of time available for practice during training |
| Conference (should be the opportunity for the participants to debate with each other, usually used to refer to highly organised sessions consisting of presented papers and sometimes small groups and seminars) | Importance and newness of content<br>Standing of presenters<br>Social and/or 'political' reasons for attendance<br>Need to update knowledge<br>Need to make/renew contact with peers<br>Cost and time needed to attend |
| Planned experience (a series of events or activities which are pre-arranged and planned with specific objectives to be achieved, eg guided reading, project work specifically assigned tasks) | Opportunities within the job or section<br>Skill of manager to arrange and maintain level of activity<br>Skills of manager to aid learning and individual's readiness to learn |

without anyone saying what they intend it to mean. We define it as involving, at a basic level:

- being able to propose an idea without attracting ridicule;
- being able to express doubt without it being taken as criticism;
- not having to witness co-presenters arguing;
- not having to listen to the presenter and a participant arguing;
- being allowed to make one's own mind up about the suitability of an idea;
- not having to struggle to see, read or hear the material being presented;
- receiving basic material on time and promised supporting material quickly afterwards;
- being able to trust the presenters and rely on the truth of what they are saying;
- being able to trust the other participants and know they will not repeat things said in confidence during the programme;
- being physically comfortable – warm enough, well seated, air to breathe, drinks and adequate food, clean rooms etc;
- being able to see where the programme is leading;
- knowing the timetable given will be maintained and any variation notified well in advance;
- being treated as an independent adult;
- being recognised as having an equal degree of vested interest as every-one else, including the presenters, in the programme.

There are other features of a learning environment which concern the organisation's culture and its component management style. These affect the application of learning as much as its acquisition. Another book could be produced on this topic alone.

## Evaluation of training

Proper evaluation of training is expensive. Various ways are available that enable different levels of evaluation to be carried out rigorously, but often training is not evaluated. Yes, the 'happiness' sheets are used and a conscientious trainer acts on the comments made when revising programmes. These benefit those who follow rather than those who have been. Most questionnaires that are used to evaluate at this level tend to concentrate on the tangible aspects of the programme.

It is not easy to assess whether the learning acquired on externally provided courses has been applied and helped to improve performance. Even when follow-up meetings are arranged to review action plans, it is nearly impossible to get all the participants together again. Internally provided events can be more easily evaluated and changes in performance assessed. However, the internal trainer and trainer/manager have relationships with the participants which tend to contaminate feedback comments and evaluations. Also, internal trainers are involved and have a degree of ownership in the event. This makes it difficult for them to stand back in order to carry out a dispassionate assessment of the worth of the event, and the value added to individual and organisational performance.

Proper evaluation of training can be carried out in a way that goes beyond the levels given above, namely:

the event's success in its own right;

the event's achievement of its behavioural objectives;

the event's satisfaction of the real training needs of the participants;

the event's contribution to the training and development function within the organisation;

training and development's contribution to the achievement of the organisation's objectives and overall effectiveness.

To enable evaluation to take place at these levels, some indicators of performance need to be developed. The National Health Service Training Authority, in its attempts to evaluate overall effectiveness, has published some indicators of training activity. These have focused, primarily, on activity rather than the outcome. Volume of training is no indicator of whether any learning has occurred during those activities. Most evaluations involve using levels of expenditure to make an assessment of worth. But, again, the cost of an event alone does not guarantee that its contents will satisfy the learning needs. Some of the most effective lessons, that result in profound changes and improvement in performance, can cost nothing.

Anyone wishing to explore evaluation more thoroughly is referred to Cascio (1987), who has developed some formulae by which to measure the cost and utility of training outcomes. Rather than go into that degree of depth here, we urge you, as a sponsor of training, to consider in advance what it is you want the activity to achieve and to decide how you will recognise success or failure. This can be done in the same way as that outlined above for the assessment of 'good' and 'bad' managerial performance. If this is done in advance and recorded for post-training evaluation, some degree of sophistication can be introduced to the evaluation. However, we do not really see the point of spending a lot of time working out whether something was worth doing, if this is going to take away effort from continuing development further. It is important to know what worked, what did not and to provide some answers to the question 'why' for both. Other aspects of assessment and performance improvement are often more important. The amount of time and energy to be spent is for each manager and organisation to decide for themselves.

## DEVELOPMENT

'Good, better, best
Never let it rest
Til your good is better
And your better best'

Every day can present a variety of learning opportunities. It depends on individuals recognising this and acting on the learning contained in their experience. It is said that someone can have seven years' experience or one experience that lasts seven years.

Two types of change are possible: first order change, doing more or less of the same thing; or second order change, doing things differently. Development is more concerned with the latter. Sometimes it can be difficult to describe what is to be achieved or required in terms of specific behaviours. First order change can be seen to be concerned with training, ie. the improvement of existing skills or the acquisition of those that are known to be required to improve the performance of the present job. In this case the use of competency statements is very useful as they provide a sense of direction and some indications of achievement.

However, in the case of second order change, which is generally what is needed when organisations face unprecedented change, unprogrammed and innovative development is required. In these circumstances it is nearly impossible for the skills required of managers to be rigorously defined using standard techniques such as job analysis. Managers are required to change and develop their performance rapidly, embarking on a steep learning curve, not knowing quite what will be expected of them next.

Development, therefore, can be intangible and very difficult to describe. Sometimes it is also hard for individuals to recognise that they have learnt and changed. We used the term development for activities that are concerned with realising potential and achieving growth. They can be opportunistic and future-oriented, targeted at achievement for both the individual and organisation involved, but not necessarily focused on specific objectives. Instead, they would be aimed at the more general goals. Trying to give examples of such activities can produce endless lists, which could fuel hot debate. Consequently we invite you to consider which of the following statements could be described as containing developmental opportunities:

*Statement*

|  | | Is developmental | Is not |
| --- | --- | --- | --- |
| 1. | What would you recommend? | | |
| 2. | Tell me only what you think I need to know about your operations and tell me why I should know about it. | | |
| 3. | I am not going to make your decisions for you, but I will discuss any areas in which you think you are having difficulty, whenever you wish. | | |
| 4. | This is a special project for you to work on that will give you experience in a new area. When you have finished a plan for accomplishing it bring it in to show me what you are going to do. | | |
| 5. | Please attend the next planning meeting instead of me. You know what we want to achieve and have full authority to commit us to whatever course of action you feel is appropriate. | | |

6. The decision you made to cancel the project was not made soon enough. Let's go through it together to see when it should have been halted so that our losses would have been minimised.

7. I have to make a policy on this matter. Please think about it and give me your recommendation.

8. I am meeting the staff representatives about that matter I mentioned to you last week. What do you think I should tell them?

9. This morning the head of finance told me that your section and the staff in the finance department are working well together. Keep up the good work.

10. I have decided not to implement the programme you suggested. Can you think why?

11. I have just read this new book on management. I would like you to read it too and then discuss it with me. We may find some ideas we can use to improve our operations.

12. It has just been announced that we are opening a new branch and so there will be a vacancy for a manager. I think this will be a real challenge for you and think you will be able to do a good job. I don't want to lose you, but I don't want to hold you back. I think you should think about applying.

13. Would you please review your staff's strengths and development needs and present your conclusions and plans for satisfying them to our next divisional meeting.

14. I would like to review your operations. Please list your duties and responsibilities so we can discuss them at next week's meeting.

15. I am preparing next year's operational plan. I would like to meet you to discuss our progress to date and any ideas you have for inclusion. Include any areas in which you would like to gain experience.

16. I am not satisfied you have simplified your procedures and systems enough. Please think again.

17. We have been asked to send someone to speak about our work to the next area meeting. If you will do it I think it will give you a chance to think broadly about all our operations, as well as just your function.

18. This is the latest outline of my job. Look at it and let me know which areas you wouldn't be able to do if you had to take over.

19. We have a spare place for a representative on the local chamber of commerce. I would like you to fill it. It will give you the opportunity to meet people from other organisations.

20. Which parts of your job do you not like doing? Why?

Most of those statements will be familiar to you. No doubt you have heard them or something like them during the course of your working life. All of them can contain developmental opportunities – depending on how they are put to the person concerned and used. Some of them could be extremely threatening if they were so presented. As with so many aspects of assessment, feedback, training and development the crux of their successful application is the style of the individual manager and the culture of the organisation.

Even accepting the large amount of influence the latter can have on the way a particular manager is able to work, there is still much that can be done internally to create a learning environment, in the full meaning of the term, for the staff within a particular section. Obviously, there are limits to what can be achieved, for no one part of an organisation can exist in isolation. But we all know of sections whose staff are the ones to get promotion and to which everyone wants to move. We also know of those that are regarded as dead ends. It must also be pointed out that a manager's achievements are often the results of their staff's work. The reasons for these reputations are as much to do with the manager's style and ways of working as with the work areas in which the staff are engaged.

## Need for development

Is continuous development always a good thing? It would be easy for us to indulge on a binge of growth and forget the quote 'growth without purpose is the ideology of the cancer cell'. Sometimes consolidation of learning is a vital phase of the whole process. Kolb's learning cycle (see page 198) provides a useful guide to all the stages of learning. There is a tendency for busyness rather than true activity. The wish to be seen as being committed to training and development can lead from one event to another without taking the time to go through the stages and reflect on what has been learnt. We repeat the cycle below, with a modification:

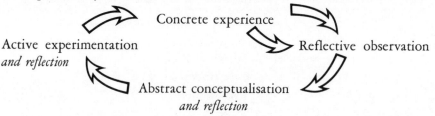

Concrete experience

Active experimentation *and reflection*

Reflective observation

Abstract conceptualisation *and reflection*

Sometimes no action can be very 'learningful' – do we take enough time to stand back from the day-to-day frenzy and think about what it is we are doing. True reflection demands concentration and effort.

- How often do you ask yourself if you are doing things right or doing the right things?

- Do you go back over events and consider how they could be done differently?

- Can you say what theories you have developed to explain your way of working?

- Can you outline your philosophies to your staff?

- Do you know what principles underpin your approaches?

- Do you think about your own perceptions of people and situations and consider whether they could be seen in a different way. (This 'reframing' can provide solutions to previously intractable problems.)

- What different ways have you tried? Which of them worked? Why did they, but could they have been done better? If they did not work, why not?

- What could have been done differently to ensure that they did? How could they be done if there is another chance?

All of these questions demonstrate areas for development, but none of them require activity, other than that required to stimulate the brain cells into action. We are in a world now where the only promise that can be made to staff, with any degree of certainty, is that something will change. Any organisation that hopes to remain totally stable is creating circumstances for disaster. The power of environmental and societal influences on all organisations are now so great that the only way of surviving into the future is by adopting mechanisms and learning how to adapt and respond appropriately. We do not expect this to be an amoeba approach. Obviously, an organisation should try to maintain some control or, at least, influence over its environment. An appropriate response may be that of resistance. However, to do this successfully the organisation's managers need to have some understanding of what it is they are doing. This will also require them to learn. Garratt (1987), in describing a learning organisation, gives a formula for helping the process. He says that $L > C$, namely that learning should exceed the rate of change. If it lags behind, the organisation, and its managers will fail to keep up with competitors and environmental pressures. Ultimately, this will lead to some form of failure.

Therefore, unless the need to develop manager's and their staff's personal, collective and organisational competencies is recognised, everyone's outlook for the future could be somewhat bleak.

## How to create developmental opportunities

If development opportunities are so intangible yet so necessary, what can a manager, committed to taking such an approach, do practically to make sure the opportunities are created and that learning can take place? The questionnaire above should give you some ideas. The following are also offered as suggestions.

- Be committed to learning, personally:
  - review your own performance through reflection and self-criticism.

- Ask for feedback about your own performance from colleagues, bosses and subordinates:

— learn from the way they give you feedback, including both positive and negative experiences.

- Give feedback to staff, watch how it is received and recognise ways in which it can be improved:

  — ask others how they give feedback to their staff, if at all;
  — ask staff how they felt about the feedback given and the way in which you gave it.

- Do not do everything yourself:

  — ask yourself if someone could do the job better than you;
  — does the task in question provide an opportunity for someone else to learn and be stretched?

- Talk constantly about your vision and what you are hoping to achieve for the section, department or organisation and the staff in it:

  — involve your staff in developing the vision and ways of realising it, making it theirs as well as yours;
  — involve them in reviewing progress towards the vision.

- Be honest about strengths and weaknesses:

  — yours, theirs, the section's, the organisation's;
  — give praise and celebrate successes.

- Learn from mistakes:

  — use techniques such as critical incident analysis to aid this and do not just rely on introspection or depression;
  — recognise that the only people that do not make mistakes are those who do nothing.

- Take risks and gambles:

  — sometimes it is worth following a course of action for the learning it contains;
  — sometimes it is worth taking a risk with people – you will never know unless you and they try.

- Be hopeful and believe in people:

  — development and learning is an investment, 'it costs a bit to make a bit';
  — most people repay the trust placed in them.

- Recognise development opportunities and point them out:

  — including the ones missed.

## How to plan and still be opportunistic

This could be seen as a contradiction in terms. Throughout we have stressed the need for assessment and for any follow-up action to be based on pre-determined criteria, related to the job, planned and systematically focused at specific objectives needed for the improvement in performance. Yet now we are saying that the best learning takes place on the job as a result of maximising opportunities that occur during the course of normal activity and change. How can intangible futuristic investments be planned systemati-cally? Obviously they cannot. What can be planned, however, are the desired outcomes.

It is possible for managers to identify broadly what is to be achieved. Perhaps this is aspirational and visionary. There is nothing wrong with this – most plans contain some elements that are not precisely defined at the beginning. Most important in taking this approach, is the ability to communicate the vision to the individuals concerned, other staff, colleagues and the boss.

The easy trap to fall into would be to say that since the best learning is opportunistic, there is no point in planning any part of the process at all. This is a recipe for failure. Even though opportunities have to be grasped as they fly by, they also need to be manufactured. This requires pre-thought and planning, and perhaps even some manipulation of events. Some opportunities must be planned and devised, if only to ensure that they happen in a way that achieves the desired end result.

## How to monitor that development is going in the 'right' direction

The approach recommended above for the implementation and monitoring of training is only marginally relevant to developmental action, as we have defined it here. There is a great danger of developmental being seen as faddish. The more experienced manager, especially, may suffer from a feeling of *déjà vu*. So many different approaches have been used in training and development, it may seem that they are ends in themselves without being focused towards the achievement of something tangible and beneficial to those involved and their jobs.

Many of these approaches have also become discredited through poor implementation and lack of follow-up. Do T-Groups (Training Groups), action circles, experiential, participative and self-managed learning strike cords in your memory? We now have open and distance learning, development centres, planned programmes of development and learning contracts. The techniques all have their place in time, just as any other management tool. Anyone initiating development activities should take account of the participants' previous contact with activities that have been concerned with aiding their development. The current approaches can then be used to build on, rather than contradict or ignore, previous experience. The desired outcome should also be made very clear so it can be seen by all involved that the technique is the means not the end.

Measures or indicators of achievement are also difficult to construct. Like any enactment of goals one must look to indications of manifestation and evidence of progress. Sometimes these can be clearly recognised achievements. At other times they are suggestions of steps along the road. Consequently, the 'monitor' needs to seek and be aware of suggestions as much as tangible evidence of progress. If circumstances are difficult it is easier to find evidence of failure rather than success. But, without being foolhardy, we do suggest that managers, in being developmental, should err on the side of optimism by looking for the evidence of success. Remember as we have already said, 'nothing succeeds better than success'.

## How to evaluate

If monitoring is difficult, how does one start to evaluate development? The methods cited by Cascio (1987) to find the utility of the activity can be used, if you really want to, or are required to spend your time in that way. Alternatively, you can use rules of thumb to guess. The critical, if rhetorical, question is 'what is the cost of not developing staff?'

Evaluation contains two elements – was the activity worth doing and did it achieve its objectives? The concept of added value is very useful here. In accountancy parlance, this is the process by which the value of the raw inputs is increased as a result of the organisation's actions. It is therefore more than the sum of its parts.

In training and development, we can calculate the input costs, quite precisely in amounts of time and hidden and actual costs, and even include opportunity costs. Unless we have measurable standards and targets of desired performance, the valuation of the outcome is difficult to assess. Is this not where we started?

## The manager's role as coach, mentor and role model

The very worst managers are those who follow the philosophy, 'Do as I say, not as I do'.

To obtain the commitment of staff to development and learning, the appropriate environment has to be created and maintained. To achieve this managers have to understand and believe, totally, that their responsibility is to guide, direct and enable their staff to do their jobs. A manager can only succeed through the efforts of others. If subordinate performance and development is inadequate it is as much a reflection on the manager as it is on the staff as individuals.

Therefore, it is a fundamental part of the manager's job to engage in activity that will result in the creation of development opportunities. These, like any resource, have to be deployed and maximised to their best effect for the benefit of all interested parties. This way of working cannot be play-acted, it has to be genuinely operated to be believed. It is the individual choice and a matter of personal style that each manager can reflect upon. From so many of the managers we have known who have followed a developmental way of managing their staff and operations, we have found that they, in addition to individual members of staff and their collective performance, have reaped benefits that by far outweighed the risks and degree of initial investment that was required to put this way of working into practice.

## SUMMARY

In this chapter, we have attempted to demonstrate the following:

- Feedback and follow-up action are essential and integral parts of the overall assessment process. We live in a world of quick-fix solutions and can see some danger signs that assessment is being used as an end rather than as a larger process for the management of staff. If staff are merely assessed and nothing is done to help them learn and improve their performance as a result of that assessment, they are not going to be very willing to expose themselves in that way in the future. There is a limit to the number of times that someone is prepared to complete a psychometric test, or give a presentation or prepare a portfolio of achievements if no feedback, guidance or action is received in return.

- Good development is not necessarily dependent on the amount of money available to send people on courses. Nor does it depend on working for an organisation which is committed to helping its staff learn. There is a lot that individual managers can do to foster a learning environment and help staff within their section to grow.

- While we may have somewhat undervalued the place of proper evaluation, we feel that all the principles that apply to the assessment of a manager's performance also apply to the processes being used to carry out that task. Pre-set objectives need to be established, techniques chosen to satisfy them, assessment made of their success against agreed criteria, and the assessment be used to modify the use of the technique and evaluate overall success. It's simple when you know how . . .

# 9

# The role of assessment in organisational development

Organisational development (OD), as an approach, has gone through several stages of its own development. Traditionally, the approach was mainly concerned with interpersonal relationships and the effect they had on the effective working of teams and groups within organisations. Bennis (1969), the 'father' of OD, defined it as being an educational strategy which concentrates on the people variable within organisations.

OD provides for a comprehensive approach to the management of organisational innovation and change, and has within its purview values, attitudes, interpersonal relations and organisational climate, as well as the structural and procedural aspects of change. Since the late 1960s, our understanding of organisations has deepened and with it OD has become more refined. It now covers a wider range of interests, and draws on skills and theories other than the original contributions made by behavioural scientists. While the role of the individual and the individual members of work groups remain a central concern – after all organisations cannot exist without people – other factors that have an impact are now taken into account.

OD is now generally regarded as being concerned with helping the members of an organisation to improve its total ability to manage and develop itself, so it is able to respond appropriately to the environmental pressures it faces. Development implies that the organisation needs to learn how to adapt and change its culture so it can continue to survive and achieve its core purpose.

If this definition is accepted, the approach is broader and use concepts additional to behavioural science. It draws from most of the disciplines concerned with people – how they behave, organise themselves, develop cultures, learn and communicate, establish systems to work together and manage themselves to achieve common tasks, and deal with conflict. For example, survival requires that the environment is scanned, therefore people in the organisation need some skills in strategic planning and marketing. Organisational survival also requires the effective utilisation of all resources which includes the management of financial and physical resources, in addition to the deployment of the human ones.

In this context assessment of the performance of the individual members of the group and its overall effectiveness provides a valid contribution to the techniques of the OD practitioner. If an organisation's members are to develop and learn how to adapt and change, they need to acquire skills additional to, or other than, those they already possess. We have shown above that an effective way of learning new skills and ways of working is the staged process of identification and development of skills needed, by the individuals for the job and for the organisation as a whole based on pre-specified criteria and assessment of existing performance.

## OD INTERVENTIONS – COMMON APPROACHES

Skills assessment will not be found in most textbooks on OD. The most comprehensive and useful is by Huczynski (1987). He provides clear explanations of most of the techniques available to the OD practitioner. Usually a consultant (internal and/or external) is used as the interested, knowledgeable outsider employed to aid individuals and the organisation in gaining greater insight into their processes and to facilitate development. Each consultant will have favoured techniques and will tend to focus on particular aspects of group/organisational dynamics.

The most frequently used approaches have recently been aimed at the improvement of team working. Techniques for this purpose include role analysis, negotiation and clarification and goal-setting, the examination of interpersonal relationships and the analysis of power. Tools such as repertory grids, the exchange of psychometric and other test results, sensitivity training, and the giving and receiving of feedback are among those most frequently used. Another approach is concerned with organisational health and employs techniques such as organisational health surveys, participative programmes aimed at gaining commitment to organisational goals, process observation and feedback to senior managers from other members of the organisation.

More task-oriented approaches can be taken, which focus more on overall organisational performance rather than solely on the human aspects of the organisation's culture. These include the use of techniques such as productivity improvement programmes (eg quality circles), process observation and feedback, management by objectives, and team briefing groups. Attention to the social as well as the technical aspects of the job and the organisation are normally taken into account in any resultant job redesign initiatives and training interventions based on the diagnosis of the organisation's needs.

A typical case could follow:

problem perceived (eg drop in production quality);

problem analysed to separate cause from symptoms (eg structured interviews with individuals involved in all stages of production process, group discussions, brain storming, systems analysis);

action plans formulated based on analysis phase and aimed at establishing ownership of problem and its solution (eg quality circles, task forces, project/task assignments);

action implemented and monitored by those 'who know, care and can';

action, solution and problem definition reviewed and success evaluated by owners of problem and other stakeholders.

## Common criticisms of OD

The criticisms levelled at OD, with some justification, concern the fact that the approach tends to be difficult to evaluate – that the improvements could have happened without the intervention. Interventions tend to be expensive in time and actual expenditure, especially if external consultants are employed.

The action plans resulting from the intervention can also be expensive to implement, yet the cost of not doing so can be even greater in terms of raised and dashed expectations of the participants. There have been incidents, in our experience, that show that engaging in OD activity can actually damage organisational performance. This can happen when the attention of those involved is diverted from the main problems facing the organisation by concentrating on (perhaps less important) group dynamics. Damage may also occur when hoped-for improvements and changes cannot be implemented. Before embarking on such a process, the possibility of these outcomes occurring should be assessed.

Another criticism often raised is that the interventions are not often directly related to the central task of the organisation. These in turn can be faulted for losing sight of the human and social concerns. The concentration on the technology of the task can detract from the social aspects of the work. The relationship between the social and technical needs, as shown by the work of the Tavistock Institute (Trist and Bamforth, 1951), has long been recognised, but sadly is known to be ignored during organisational change.

Alternatively, some of the approaches can be labelled as being airy-fairy and very intangible. Some people are not able to identify process issues easily and are genuinely confused by interpersonal dynamics. For them it can be hard to see how giving other members of the team personal feedback can improve production and sales figures. Therefore, in the design of any OD intervention, consideration needs to be given to the demonstration of its intended outcomes.

## A practical approach

Skills assessment seems to be an unlikely candidate for inclusion in the OD practitioner's tool-bag. It is usually oriented towards the job and, in many applications, can be seen as being concerned with the immediate needs of current performance. In fact it is known to have been used to good effect to aid the improvement of overall organisational performance. A local government service department became 'sold' on the assessment centre technique after using it for selection. An intended and valued spin-off from the selection process used was the identification of the newly appointed manager's training needs. Subsequently, the technique was used to identify the needs of managers at that level across the department. This was done in relation to and in the context of its overall needs and to assist in implementing the changes it needed to effect its continued survival.

It is not easy to say that planning development action as a result of the assessment of current performance levels alone contributed to organisational development, nor that any improvement has been long term, but it can be argued convincingly that the thinking and skill development embodied in the technique has made a positive contribution to this department and several other projects.

We know of other occasions when competency specification and assessment have been used as part of OD interventions. This approach was quoted by Powers and Cane during a conference organised by the Association of Management Education and Development in 1989 and Boyatzis (1982) discusses its wider implications. A model we use is very simple and demonstrates how the various stages interlink to form a developmental cycle:

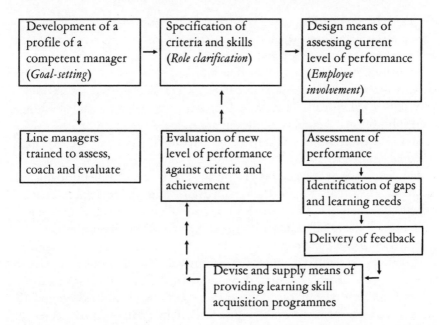

This model can be used to 'process' individual skill assessment. Individual managers are the subjects of the programme and are assessed by others. However, its benefits can be extended considerably by being highly participative. The value of involvement includes the sense of ownership that results, the increased acceptability of the process and feedback provided, and the overall commitment to developing the needed skills.

The strength of the model in OD terms is that it can be used as a total intervention aimed at achieving some tangible improvements in the management of the whole organisation, the performance and skills of individuals and groups through the involvement of managers at different levels, and from different parts of the organisation.

## MANAGERS' INVOLVEMENT

The role of an individual in an organisation can be equated to that of the keystone in a bridge. Alone and separate, the stone is a unique entity – valuable perhaps in its own right – but in a pile of stones, inert. It is only when the stone is located in its rightful place that its full contribution is realised. This is also so with people. Organisations are so complex and diverse that one person alone can not guarantee success. Those reliant on a charismatic leader or figurehead do not last very long. We can quote examples of organisational fractures which may be attributed to this over-reliance: Next and George Davis; Sinclair and Clive . . .

An organisation that allows the development of its people to go on in isolation from its core purpose is in danger of creating a group comprised of very skilled individuals. They may all be working very hard and skilfully at their jobs, but to paraphrase Drucker, are they doing the right jobs? Belbin (1981) also describes the failure of the Apollo teams comprised of high-powered individuals.

The first stage in the process given above is the development of a profile of a competent manager for the organisation. This can be achieved using a variety of techniques. Repertory grid or critical incident analysis can be used as indicated above. But in the context of an OD intervention, it is the cumulation of the perspectives of individual managers at different levels in the organisation that contributes to total growth. The definition can be top-down, bottom-up or a mixture, depending on the particular organisation's culture and desired outcome. Whichever is chosen is a reflection of the organisation and/or what it is trying to achieve by taking such an approach.

In the terminology of OD, this approach can be labelled as being cultural analysis, role clarification and conflict resolution (see Example 9.1).

The involvement of line managers in the design of the means of assessment can also be developmental for the organisation. It can enable the recognition of which tasks are critical to the success of the organisation and identify the skills that are needed for their effective performance. It can also identify which other areas of work will become critical in the immediate future. The questioning associated with this process can help the relative importance of the different areas of work to be compared, contrasted and determined. During the development of the centre for the pathology managers, referred to above in Example 6.12, staff from representative sections were involved in the design of the activities. This again spread ownership and helped to contribute to acceptability. It was widely known to the participants that the centre was being designed in a way that ensured that it was relevant to them in their work.

Involving line managers in the observation and assessment of others in the organisation can have wider impact than the improvement of their individual skills. In a local authority we were working with managers from two departments. These departments were required to operate jointly on service provision but there was a tradition of hostility between them. Managers from one were asked to work as observers with other managers at a similar level from the other department on a career development centre. This joint project helped them to gain greater understanding of their separate contexts

*Example 9.1*

In one local authority department the use of a development centre was a deliberate contribution to the OD intervention being made.

Following the appointment of a new chief officer, the department was radically restructured and a new management team formed. The team employed the services of an internal consultant to aid their development and clarification of the department's primary purpose, and their goals. The middle managers were later involved in events and fed back their perceptions of the organisation to their managers. Action plans were developed and implementation programmes established. These included team-building activities in other parts of the department using techniques such as an organisational health survey. Meanwhile, the senior management team continued work on its own development. (The first stages of the intervention are described in Blanksby (1987).) Two years into the restructuring and to enable further improvements to be made, it was recognised that it would be necessary to enhance the overall skill level of the department's managers.

As a result, the senior management team devoted two half days to the development of the profile of a good middle manager in their organisation. The first half day was spent brainstorming; the second was used to check the profile and clarify understanding of the terms being used. The middle managers were then asked to perform the same task in small groups. To aid the cumulation of the profiles, each group was given the headings from the Framework (Figure 7.1 on page 182) under which the core skills were to be classified. The profiles were then compared and the senior managers considered the differences and decided which should be included in the final profile.

The final profile was reported back to the middle managers. The criteria for the development centre were based on its contents. The strength of this approach was that everyone involved in the centre had contributed to the identification and agreement of the core competencies. The standards required of a competent manager were explicit and shared. A debate had been opened and involved all the senior and middle managers in the organisation. At times it had been heated, but it had enabled differences to be resolved and previously unclear requirements to be clarified.

The centre for the middle managers was run later and involved the senior managers in the role of assessors and coaches. The design followed the principles of assessment centre design, as described above. The main differences were in the degree of participation in the definition of criteria and the grounding of the activities in the context of the organisation. As it was intended to be developmental, there was also an increased use of self and peer assessment. The emphasis during the feedback was placed on the need for follow up action based on the criteria.

and the different problems faced by managers in each of the departments. This achieved a reduction in parochialism and improved working relations through increasing the knowledge and understanding of each other. An unexpected spin-off was changes to oper-ational practices that had been seen to be ineffective.

The skills of observation, assessment and feedback have been shown to impact on to other areas of work, especially recruitment and selection practices. One manager was heard to say that being involved in assessment centres had changed the whole way in which she looked at other people. Our use of per-sonnel specifications has grown from the use of development centres and the analytical, structured thinking encountered in the process has helped to identify performance indicators in areas other than behaviour.

Similarly, the differentiation of a good performer from a poor performer against a set of clear, pre-determined, agreed criteria can help managers face up to performance problems that have previously been intractable. We all know of people who 'get away with it' without being clear what 'it' is or how to prove it. We also know people who are successful, but we cannot quite say what 'it' is they do that makes them special.

The thinking required for the successful implementation of assessment techniques requires the difference between a good and a poor performer to be made explicit. Once this has been done for one purpose, there is no reason why the methodology cannot be used for another. (But we need to remember that the information obtained for one purpose should not be used for another.)

The skills used for observation are also transferable. One of the difficulties in dealing with substandard performance is the acquisition of useful evidence. Once a manager has learnt what to look for and how to observe it, these skills can be used to good effect elsewhere.

The skills of providing useful feedback and devising ways of improving performance can change a punitive approach to one which is far more developmental and constructive for all concerned. This method of giving feedback is very different from that often used in appraisal as it is based on behaviour displayed in controlled circumstances in a very limited time-band.

Most appraisal feedback concerns behaviour that has been displayed over a long period, usually 12 months. This can make it very difficult to provide examples of behaviour or to suggest other ways which may have been more effective for the specific situation under consideration. Lessons can be drawn here from sports coaching. Performance improvements are achieved through the repeated practice of patterns of behaviour in tightly controlled circumstances. While this is not always possible in management, there are situations that occur often enough for behaviour to be learnt in this fashion. Dealing with the morning's post is directly related to dealing with an in-tray activity, meetings can be seen as repeats of group activities and so on. Once a manager has learned the skills of giving good quality feedback as part of assessment, these can be used to help to coach the learner manager in every-day tasks.

Acting as a coach and mentor can lead you as a manager to develop close relationships with staff. Can you remember the people who shared major skills, exchanged knowledge and transmitted their values and styles? The role of medical consultants as tutors provides a classic example of how new-comers are conditioned into the ethics and values of a profession. The relation-ship can have two-way benefits. A sympathetic coach can also pick up a lot from those being coached. New techniques being taught as part of formal learning programmes can be fed back into senior levels of management. More importantly, valuable information regarding the world of the lower levels of management can be gleaned. Sometimes it is hard to recall what it is like down there. The phrase 'mushroom management' springs to mind. Those holding the manure shovel do not necessarily appreciate the sub-stance's heat and darkness.

Using performance assessment as a technique can require a manager to consider aspects of behaviour in different ways. It can also allow managers to witness alternative ways of achieving objectives not previously considered as possible or acceptable. It also focuses attention, quite clearly, on to what is and is not important.

Most of the time, it is the end that counts, not the means of getting there. Sometimes, though, while the means can be more important, they are not always given due recognition.

---

*Example 9.2*

An example can be found in group decision-making. If working relationships are difficult, the task contentious, but the final decision not important, the skills of steering the group to a decision acceptable to the group's members may be more valuable than those of making a decision alone.

A typical case could be whether the Christmas lunch should be at the Indian, Italian, Chinese or MacDonald's restaurant. The decision in many ways is inconsequential, but getting to it is highly important as it can have a long-term impact on group cohesion. More often than not, it is the decision that is remembered, not the process used to reach it.

The use of assessment technology requires the skills needed for effective performance to be made explicit. This permits different, but closely related skills to be identified and differentiated. Therefore, it can be seen from the above example that in those particular circumstances group processing skills are more important than decision-making.

The involvement in the evaluation of performance with other managers also helps to clarify, with them, the difference between effective and ineffective behaviour. In this way organisational norms can be revised and developed. Additionally, they become more explicit in managers' thinking. It helps a manager to communicate to others more clearly what is required, set standards and identify when and where performance is varying from what is expected in everyday working.

If a manager acquires the skills of assessment through being involved in a structured process, the learning can spin off into other areas of assessment, for example into recruitment, appraisal and other aspects of performance management.

The process outlined above is dynamic. Opportunities are created to review the standards and competencies on a regular basis. Good appraisal schemes require a manager and subordinate to review the latter's performance, but how often does an organisation openly review the criteria against which individuals are appraised? The above model almost forces this kind of review to take place.

## GROUP SKILLS IMPROVEMENT

Defining competencies requires managers to work together on a difficult task. Agreeing first on what is required of managers in their organisation is thought and debate-provoking. It necessitates that managers:

- think about what they expect;
- clarify their thinking so it can be communicated to others;
- explain complex concepts;
- listen to others' explanations of their concepts;
- find ways of agreeing critical competencies;
- find ways of resolving differences so that a profile of skills can be drawn up;

- explain the profile to others;

- accept collective responsibility for the profile.

For managers who are not used to working with others, and many are isolated, this task can be challenging and provide learning in its own right. It can bring together managers from parts of the organisation who normally would have no contact with each other, and in some circumstances bring in different levels of the organisation. In a series of assessment centres we designed, there was a high concern to ensure that different perspectives were taken into account, especially those from minority groups. Because the members of these groups were represented mainly in the lower levels of the hierarchy, the individuals asked to participate in the design were able to work with senior managers and vice versa. This contact gave other benefits to the individuals and the organisation. In addition to gaining more knowledge and understanding of the different positions, working relationships were established that would not otherwise have been forged.

Various techniques can be used to help the group to produce the profile and work effectively. We have used brainstorming and repertory grids to help elicit and clarify concepts and have experimented with the use of the Delphi technique to gain agreement to a profile. This is a process which makes use of experts who are consulted and their different opinions combined and then validated by re-consulting. However, this technique does not necessarily contribute to the development of group work skills. It is more concerned with gaining an overall consensus from 'experts' rather than developing relationships. Reference to its use can be found in Huczynski (1987).

The experience of being assessed can create a bond between participants across the organisation. In addition to sharing the experience, managers can gain an insight into others' perspectives through the activities, especially when they are grounded in the context of the organisation. For example, working on a problem-solving task can bring an accountant and an operational manager together in a totally novel way.

If, as part of the implementation of development plans, learning sets are established, managers are able to work together on each other's development and learning needs. Revans's (1980) approach to action learning may seem dated now, but the concept still holds good. In some ways, it is particularly appropriate to the development model given above. The basis premise of action learning, ie managers finding ways of dealing with previously intractable problems together, reflecting on the experience, conceptualising the learning and experimenting with other behaviours, seems to be totally congruent with the principles we are promoting here.

Working on learning with managers from other parts of the organisation, or even other organisations and at different levels of the hierarchy, can be a meaningful experience in its own right. This can be enhanced if the learning is focused towards the acquisition of specific skills and is supported through the involvement of coaches and mentors.

In this type of learning environment it is possible to address the process skills and increase the participating managers' awareness of cross-organisational communication needs. Most organisations function on the surface by using formal communication methods. Most have flaws that could prove to be dysfunctional. In practice, however, the informal communication systems ensure that the organisation works – for better or worse. We do not wish to denigrate the importance of informal communications, but if an organisation is trying to develop its processes it needs to know what they are and understand how they operate. Then it is possible to decide which parts need to be retained, which need improvement and which need to be changed. The drawing together of managers from different parts of the organisation to be assessors and participants in an assessment process can both create and strengthen the informal communication networks.

## MANAGEMENT IMPROVEMENT

Earlier, management development was defined as the improvement of the skills of the organisation's managers and being concerned with increasing the effectiveness of the practices and processes used to run the organisation, plan and adapt to meet its future, and implement those plans by undergoing the changes needed to achieve them. Any change will impact on how the organisation operates and, if the overt learning is part of the process of change, the underlying culture is affected.

---

*Example 9.3*

A group of managers are deemed to be in need of some improvement to their communication skills. They attend an intensive course and decide to implement one of the ideas they have learnt about. The change in their behaviour inevitably results in a change to the organisation's communication practices. This in turn means that eventually the workforce is better informed and they ultimately perceive their employer in a better light.

---

Assessment of current skill levels could have played an integral part in the above example. The need to improve communication skills could have been identified as a result of assessing skills on this dimension during an assessment centre.

Other collective needs can be identified in a less direct way. During a series of career development centres run for a housing department, it became apparent that the participants' perception of the organisation in its environment was very weak. While this dimension had been seen as important but not critical to effective performance of individual managers, it had been included as it was felt that staff at that level should be aware of the context in which they were operating. However, as the feedback reports were cumulated to assess the general needs, it became evident that the managers were unable to see their own areas in relation to the whole. This weakness was seen to have long-term implications, so it was decided that it needed to be covered in all development plans and included in any follow-up action.

The overall assessment of the pathology managers development centre, discussed in Chapter 6, revealed a deeper need. All the women who took part did unexpectedly well on all but one criterion – group skills. The planning of the centres had been done to ensure that the women (who were in a minority) were distributed across them all and as the assessment for each revealed a similar picture, it was concluded that two factors were inhibiting their performance. The first was their own ability to assert themselves, as individuals, in group situations; the second was the dynamics of the group which prevented them from doing so. It was decided that the development action would take account of these conclusions. So the approach determined was designed to address both factors. First, a single sex development group was set up for the women to work on assertiveness and dealing with sexism, while second, mixed development groups were set up so that the women would be able to try out their newly acquired skills in a 'safe', supported situation. They would then become more confident to translate the new behaviours into the everyday working environment.

The release, to the laboratory, of the women's other unknown talents was seen as being a major benefit. The increase to their confidence, as well as their greater contribution, was seen by the line manager as having a major advantage for the department's culture and its future. Recruitment was beginning to become difficult. Medically related laboratories were expanding in the area and were paying higher salaries than those paid by the NHS. The skills needed were also in short supply. However, more women were entering the profession. The pathology laboratory manager had had some niggling worries, not just about initial recruitment, but also longer-term retention.

We have said that the introduction of systematic assessment can improve the management practices of the organisation. Each stage requires new learning and imposes a discipline on how people are assessed and how that assessment takes place. The technique also requires a structured process of planning, implementation, review and evaluation to be followed. This structure, linked to a technique that can be implemented in a fairly short time-scale, can contain valuable lessons for other longer processes used by the managers to perform other aspects of their job.

Its use in selection, for example, can mean that new recruits can join the organisation with tailored initial training plans. These can be drawn up as a result of the assessments during their selection for appointment. This, in turn, can create a demand among existing managers – there is nothing like a bit of jealousy to spur others into action. This demand can be particularly beneficial in organisations where managers have resisted development and training. In one organisation we know, it was found that the evening training meetings arranged for the newly-appointed trainee supervisors were being swamped by the longer-serving supervisors who wanted to see what they were missing.

## ORGANISATIONAL IMPROVEMENT

The use of some assessment techniques can involve subordinate and operational staff. They can participate in role-plays or they can make a contribution to the assessment of managers' performance. This can have several benefits.

- The subordinates will have a different perception of behaviour to that of peer or more senior managers.

- They will have been properly involved and listened to in the course of a serious management operation. This can affect their level of motivation and influence that of their peers.

- The assessee will gain a strong impression of how the organisation values its staff's views by knowing that they have been actively sought and used.

- The organisation should be able to hear what sort of managerial behaviour is important to its staff.

The latter can, if heed is taken, result in changes to managerial behaviour and practice. Very simple changes can have a dramatic effect on the way the organisation works.

*Example 9.4*

A works gang were involved in a problem-solving exercise. During the tea-break discussions, the topic of form filling came up. It transpired that a new form had recently been sent out. The wording of part of the form had been written in a way that had been seen as insulting the workforce's intelligence. Additionally, its introduction had been badly handled. The workers had reacted by finding ways of falsifying the returns as imaginatively and as unrecognisably as possible. No one in the office had noticed, at the time of the discussion, that they were getting duff information. It is unlikely that this problem would have become known so quickly, in a non-confrontational way to a group of senior managers who were in a position to do something about it.

The use of behavioural, explicit criteria for assessment opens up the organisational standards of performance. First, they need to be defined. This process alone makes more people aware of them and what levels of performance are being required. It clarifies which measures will and will not be used to appraise their performance. The values the organisation espouses become explicit and subject to scrutiny. The very debate about these criteria and means of assessment can be developmental in its own right. Questioning the organisation's standards of performance and beginning to determine which are helpful and which are not can prompt and facilitate change.

This process can give subordinate staff some power. Their involvement during the assessment, especially the feedback stages and the planning of the developmental follow-up gives them some rights. A member of staff or a group is able to challenge the assessment. If they feel it to be unreasonable on the basis that the criteria is unreasonable, they too will have information on which to base their questioning. Similarly, if they feel the criteria are unrealistic or the assessments were unfair, they will have access to people who should be able to take note. The assessors have a responsibility to feed this sort of reaction back to the manager who sponsored the assessment process in the first place.

The commitment to development for the individual also gives power to subordinate staff. For if the plan is not enacted, they will have a 'contract' of some form which gives them a base from which to make legitimate demands. They also have access to the assessors (if they were not the line managers) in their role of coach and mentor. This gives another channel of communication into the higher levels of an organisation's management.

The use of assessment techniques can aid the understanding of changing roles. This is one of the main purposes behind the development centre in the mental health hospital, looked at in Chapter 6. The design of the centre helped the senior managers to think through what they were looking for from their staff. The centre itself helped to communicate the new role to the managers being assessed, while the action plans were aimed at developing the newly required skills.

Very positive experiences of role communication have been seen during selection centres. Several times, originally enthusiastic candidates for jobs have been known to withdraw their application, recognising for themselves that the job was not for them or they were not yet ready to work at the required level. On every occasion this has happened the candidates have said that they were happy about the decision, and that it was the centre that had helped them make it.

A similar approach is known to have been used by Powers and Cane in America. This was reported during an Association of Management Education and Development (AMED) conference in 1988. An organisation undergoing rapid, radical change used competency assessment to help its managers decide whether they wanted to remain at their current levels and help steer the changes through or whether they wanted to accept the severance deal being offered. Those who wanted to stay then went on to devise a development plan to help them assume the new responsibilities and acquire the new skills. Those who decided to go, went, knowing what they had rejected. Obviously the assessment also helped the organisation to be clear about the working levels of each of its managers. So it knew who it was losing and who it was retaining.

## SUMMARY

- The approach we are promoting for the assessment of skills and managerial effectiveness has direct parallels with any systematic planning process. It is structured, yet flexible, it is dynamic and participative, it has precise time-phases and requires evaluation and review.

- It may seem idealistic, yet the use of assessment techniques in this way, especially assessment centres, has shown that if good practice is used and the strictures of the approach followed, the spin-offs we claim are achievable. The examples we have used have been drawn from our own experience. Admittedly, some of the improvements may have been short-lived but this lack of longevity can reasonably be attributed to other causes. The main claim is that the benefit of the approach was evident and the people who had been involved as assessees and assessors recognised what had been gained. The technique is known to have high face validity and this has been borne out by our experience.

- Most people who participate in this approach feel that it has been a worthwhile experience and that they gained from it. Not many techniques can make such a bold claim. Our major worry is that a technique that contains so much potential for good is diminished in value. Growth in popularity encourages shortcutting. There is some evidence that our worry is justified, but we are heartened that many other exponents of the technique, for example Woodruff (1990), have similar concerns and express the same cautions as those given above.

- Assessing the performance of others is not difficult. It merely requires skills and discipline. The former can be acquired if so desired. The latter should exist in the world of work anyway. So many good techniques have been spoilt by sloppy practice, needlessly. As the world of work changes, people's expectations of it alter. The need for good, forward-looking and constructive assessment of the skills required for the present and future, becomes more important. This book is intended to help practising managers learn how to do it for themselves. Please give us some feedback on how it has helped to improve and develop your assessment of others.

# General Reading

Armstrong M (1989) *A Handbook of Personnel Management Practice* Kogan Page, London.

Bennett R (1981) *Managing Personnel and Performance: An Alternative Approach* Business Books, London.

Blanksby M (1988) *Staff Training: A Librarian's Handbook* Association of Assistant Librarians, London.

Buckley R and Caple J (1989) *The Theory and Practice of Training* Kogan Page, London.

Cashmore E E and Mullen B (1983) *Approaching Social Theory* Heinemann, London.

Cook M (1988) *Personnel Selection and Productivity* Wiley, Chichester.

Deaux K and Wrightson L S (1988) *Social Psychology* Brooks-Cole, Pacific Grove, CA.

Fletcher S (1991) *NVQ's, Standards and Competence: A Practical Guide for Employers, Managers and Trainers* Kogan Page, London.

Harrison R (1988) *Training and Development* IPM, London.

Honey P and Mumford A (1982) *The Manual of Learning Styles* P Honey, Maidenhead.

Kakabadse A, Ludlow R and Vinnicombe S (1987) *Working in Organisations* Gower, Aldershot.

Kenney J and Reid M (1986) *Training Interventions* IPM, London.

McKenzie Davey D (1989) *How To Be a Good Judge of Character* Kogan Page, London.

Megginson D and Boydell T (1979) *A Manager's Guide to Coaching* BACIE, London.

Smith M, Gregg M and Andrews D (1989) *Selection and Assessment* Pitman, London.

Stewart A and Stewart V (1982) *Managing the Poor Performer* Gower, Aldershot.

Torrington D and Hall L (1987) *Personnel Management: A New Approach* Prentice Hall International, Hemel Hempstead.

# Bibliography

Abelson R P (1981) 'Psychological status of the script concept *American Psychologist'* 39.

Alban-Metcalfe B (1989) *The Use of Assessment Centres in the NHS* Report published by the NHS Training Agency.

Arbitration and Conciliation Advisory Service (1977) *Disciplinary practice and procedures in employment.*

Bartram D (1991) 'Addressing the abuse of psychological tests' *Personnel Management* April 34–39.

Belbin R M (1981) *Management Teams: Why They Succeed or Fail* Heinemann, London.

Bennis W (1969) *Organisational Development, its Nature, Origins and Prospects* Addison-Wesley, Wokingham.

Blanksby M (1987) 'Changing a bureaucracy into an open organisation' *Journal of European Industrial Training* 11 (6).

Boam R and Sparrow P eds (1992) *Focusing on Human Resources: A Competency-Based Approach* McGraw Hill, London.

Boyatzis R E (1982) *The Competent Manager* Wiley, Chichester.

Boydell T H (1990) *Guide to the Identification of Training Needs* BACIE, London.

—— (1990) *Joy Analysis* BACIE, London.

Cascio W F (1987) *Applied Psychology in Personnel Management* Prentice Hall, Hemel Hempstead.

Clutterbuck D (1985) *New Patterns of Working* Gower, Aldershot.

Cockerill A (1989) 'The kind of competence for rapid change' *Personnel Management* September 52–56.

Dale M and Iles P A (1992) *Assessing Management Skills* Kogan Page, London.

Drucker P (1955) *The Practice of Management* Heinemann, London.

Fayol H (1949) *General and Industrial Management* Pitman, London.

Flanagan J C (1954) 'The critical incident technique' *Psychological Bulletin* Vol 51.

Fletcher C (1991) 'Candidates' reactions to assessment centres and their outcomes: a longitudinal study' *Journal of Occupational Psychology* 64, 2, 117–128.

Garratt B (1987) *The Learning Organisation* Fontana, London.

Glaze A (1989) 'Cadbury's dictionary of competence' *Personnel Management* July 44–48.

Gratton L (1989) 'Work of the manager' in P Herriot (ed) *Assessment and Selection in Organisations* John Wiley and Sons, Chichester.

Hackman J R and Oldham G R (1975) 'Development of the job diagnostic survey' *Journal of Applied Psychology* 60.

Handy C (1978) *The Gods of Management* Pan Books, London.

—— (1987) *The Making of Managers* NEDO, MSC and BIM, London.

Harrison R (1972) 'Understanding your organisation's character' *Harvard Business Review* 50 (3).

—— (1988) *Training and Development* IPM, London.

Herriot P (1989) *Recruitment in the 1990s* IPM, London.

Herzberg F (1968) 'One more time: how do you motivate employees' *Havard Business Review*.

Higgs M (1988) *Management Development Strategy in the Financial Sector* McMillan, London.

Hough L (1984) 'Development and evaluation of the "accomplishment record" method of selecting and promoting professionals' *Journal of Applied Psychology* 69, 1, pp 135–146.

Huczynski A (1987) *Encyclopedia of Organisational Change Methods* Gower, Aldershot.

Iles P A (1989) 'Using assessment and development centres to facilitate equal opportunity in selection and career development' *Equal Opportunities International* 8.5 1–26 (monograph).

Iles P A (1990) 'Managing change in the UK financial services sector through strategic HRD' *Paper to IODA International Congress, Caracas, Venezuela*, November 1990.

Iles P A and Robertson I T (1989) 'The impact of personnel selection procedures on candidates' in P Herriot (ed) *Assessment and Selection in Organisations* John Wiley and Sons, Chichester.

Iles P A, Robertson I T and Rout U (1989) 'Assessment based development centres' *Journal of Managerial Psychology* 4, 3, 11–16.

Iles P A, Mabey C and Robertson I T (1990) HRM practices and employee commitment: possibilities, pitfalls and paradoxes *British Journal of Management* 1, 147–157.

Iles P A and Auluck R K (1991) 'The experience of black workers' in M Davidson and J Earnshaw (eds) *Vulnerable Workers: Psychological and Legal Issues* John Wiley and Sons, Chichester.

Jacobs R (1989) 'Getting the measure of management competence' *Personnel Management* June.

Jackson L (1989) 'Turning airport managers into high fliers' *Personnel Management* October 80–85.

Janis I L (1972) *Victims of Groupthink* Houghton-Mifflin, Boston MA.

Janz T (1982) 'Initial comparisons of behaviour description interviews versus unstructured interviews' *Journal of Applied Psychology* 67, 577–580.

Jones A (1988) 'A case study in utility analysis' *Guidance and Assessment Review* 4, 3, 3–6.

Kelly G A (1980) *The Psychology of Personal Constructs Vol 1: Theory of Personality* W W Norton, New York.

Kolb D A (1974) *Organisation Psychology: An Experiential Approach* Prentice Hall, Hemel Hempstead.

Latham G, Saari L M, Pursell E D and Campion M A (1980) 'The situational interview' *Journal of Applied Psychology* 65, 422–427.

Lindblom L E (1979) 'Still muddling, not yet through' *Public Administration Review* (39).

Lurie J and Watts C (1991) *Using Assessment Centre in the Process of*

*Organisational Change* Paper presented to British Psychological Society Occupational Psychology Conference, Cardiff, January 1991.

McClelland D C (1965) 'Towards a theory of motive acquisition' *American Psychologist* (20).

Mabey C and Iles P A (1991) 'HRM from the other side of the fence' *Personnel Management* February.

Mager R (1986) *Preparing Instructional Objectives* Pitman Learning Inc, London.

Mager R and Piper P (1984) *Analysing Performance Problems* Pitman Learning, London.

Manpower Services Commission (Training Agency) (1989) 'Development of assessable standards for national certification: Assessment of competence' *Guidance Note 5* Training Agency.

Mintzberg M (1973) *The Nature of Managerial Work* Harper and Row, New York.

Moses J L (1975) 'Task Force on development of assessment centre standards', endorsed by Third International Congress on the assessment centre method, Quebec, May 1975.

Pearn M and Kandola R C (1988) *Job Analysis* IPM, London.

Peters T and Waterman R (1982) *In Search of Excellence* Harper and Row, New York.

Powers E and Cane S (1989) AMED conference on the competency approach to management development and assessment. Association of Management Education and Development.

Revans R (1980) *Action Learning* Blond and Briggs, London.

Robertson I T and Iles P A (1988) 'Approaches to managerial selection' in C Cooper and I T Robertson (eds) *International Review of Industrial and Organisational Psychology* John Wiley and Sons, Chichester.

Robertson I T, Gratton L and Rout U (1990) 'The validity of situational interviews' *Journal of Organisational Behaviour.*

Robertson I T, Iles P A, Gratton L and Sharpley D (1991) 'The psychological impact of selection procedures on candidates' *Human Relations* in press.

Rodgers A (1951) 'The seven point plans' *National Institute of Industrial Psychology*.

Schein E H (1984) 'Coming to a new awareness of organisational culture' *Sloan Management Review* Winter 1984.

Schroder H M (1989) *Managerial Competence: The Key to Excellence* Kendall/ Hunt, Iowa.

Shackleton V (1992) 'Using a competency approach in a business change setting' in Boam R and Sparrow P (1992) *Focusing on Human Resources: A Competency-Based Approach* McGraw Hill, London.

Shackleton V and Newell S (1991) 'Management selection: a comparative survey of methods used in top British and French companies' *Journal of Occupational Psychology* 64, 1, 23–37.

Smith J M and Robertson I T (1986) *The Theory and Practice of Systematic Staff Selection* McMillan, London.

Smith M, Gregg M and Andrews D (1989) *Selection and Assessment: A New Appraisal* Pitman, London.

Stewart R (1967) *Managers and Their Jobs* Pan MacMillan, London.

Stewart R (1976) *Contrasts in Management: A Study of Different Types of Managers' Jobs, Their Demands and Choices* McGraw Hill, Maidenhead.

Tannenbaum R and Schmidt W H (1973) How to choose a leadership pattern *Havard Business Review*.

Trist E L and Bamforth K (1951) 'Some social and psychological consequences of the longwall method of coal getting' *Human Relations* (4).

Tuchman B W (1965) Developmental sequence in small groups *Psychological Bulletin* 63 (6).

Walsh J P, Weinberg R M and Fairfield M L (1987) 'The effect of gender on assessment centre evaluations' *Journal of Occupational Psychology* 60, 4, 305– 309.

Weekley J A and Grier J A (1987) 'Reliability and validity of the situational interview for a sales position' *Journal of Applied Psychology* 72, 484–487.

Woodruffe C (1990) *Assessment Centres: Identifying and Developing Competences* IPM, London.

Wordsworth W (1807) *Intimations of Immortality From Recollections of Early Childhood.*

# Index